Social Quality Theory

Social Quality Theory

A New Perspective on Social Development

Edited by
Ka Lin and Peter Herrmann

berghahn
NEW YORK · OXFORD
www.berghahnbooks.com

Published by
Berghahn Books
www.berghahnbooks.com

The chapters in this volume were originally published as articles in the
European Journal of Social Quality Volume 3, Numbers 1 & 2; Volume 5,
Numbers 1 & 2; Volume 6, Number 2;
and the *International Journal of Social Quality*
Volume 1, Number 1; Volume 2, Number 1.

Library of Congress Cataloging-in-Publication Data
Social quality theory : a new perspective on social development / edited by Ka Lin and Peter
Herrmann.
    pages cm
Includes index.
 ISBN 978-1-78238-897-5 (pbk. : alk. paper) -- ISBN 978-1-78238-898-2 (ebook)
1. Social policy. I. Lin, Ka. II. Herrmann, Peter, 1955-
HN18.3.S596 2015
306--dc23
                                                                    2015017243

British Library Cataloguing in Publication Data
A catalogue record for this book is available from the British Library.

Printed on acid-free paper

ISBN 978-1-78238-897-5 (paperback)
ISBN 978-1-78238-898-2 (ebook)

SOCIAL QUALITY THEORY
A New Perspective on
Social Development

Edited by Ka Lin and Peter Herrmann

Contents

List of Figures

Figures

Tables

Introduction

Ka Lin and Peter Herrmann

In the development of modern social sciences, various theories influencing the debate of global development came from European researchers. One of these theories is the social quality theory, which emerged almost two decades ago from Europe but later extended to Asia and Australia, and thus beyond the original boundaries of the 1990s (van der Maesen and Walker 2012). This theory assesses the progress of human societies and makes proposals that are relevant for policy development. With other theories such as human security and social exclusion theories, social quality theory not only aims at the ideal of a "good society" but also provides an analytical perspective for understanding the condition of such societies (Phillips 2006; Therborn 2001). Although critical about many aspects of the European tradition, social quality thinking continues to find itself in the footsteps of progressivism and solidaristic thinking, rephrased in modern terms with a focus on socio-economic security, social inclusion, social cohesion and social empowerment. Although the content, orientation and features of this theory come from a European tradition, the theory can be used to contribute to wider debates in the international social sciences.

In order to underscore the European features of this theory, we should refer to three key factors. First, we must consult the broad heritage of social thinking about the relations between individual and society and between state and market (Beck et al. 1997; Bourdieu 1984). This tradition provides a fertile ground of information and ideas that allows an understanding of the nature of social relations along collectivist thinking. This stream of thinking is reinforced by social policy studies, especially from the mid-twentieth century onward, and often results in a variety of progressive social reforms (Kaufmann 2013; Townsend 1975). Accordingly, we see the impact of a stream of collective thoughts on social development and social quality thinking.

The second factor to be noticed is the strength of the theoretical foundation. Discussing social policy from a social quality perspective has been understood as a meta-theory, facilitating the studies of social and public policies. This feature is particularly visible when comparing European theories with the American approach of social research. The latter favors empirical studies that back up positivist perception, while the former is especially strong in theoretical thinking or theoretically grounded understandings with reference to philosophical considerations. Moreover, such empirical studies and positivist perceptions are also present in a wide view on the nature of society. This allows for the foundation of a wider societal perspective and institutional analysis.

The third key factor behind the dynamics of the theory's elaboration is the development of welfare state systems. Since the postwar period, the idea of progressivism (as presented, for instance, by "social engineering" approaches) functioned in Europe as a powerful and dynamic force for social development. Later, European states set the laudable goal of establishing "welfare states." This practice presented a challenge for intellectual considerations about how to assess social progress (Titmuss 1974). The debate of the "crisis of the welfare state" (see Pierson 1991) and efforts of looking for policy alternatives further required social researchers to renew their studies of European societies. In all of these perspectives, social quality theory is nourished by engagement in these debates (Walker 2011).

Since the mid-2000s, social quality theory has developed beyond the European world. The engagement of Asian and Australian scholars has made significant steps in broadcasting this theory on a global scope. This expansion provides new inputs for the theory, going beyond the concern of European problems and presenting a qualitative leap in research perspectives (Herrmann 2009; Lin et al. 2009). While the major themes of debates at the early stage had been about contrasting quality of life theories and social quality theory, researchers have more recently emphasized the interaction between the different theories and their complementarities (Gasper et al. 2008; van der Maesen 2012). Previous emphasis on conceptualizing welfare societies for European developments shifted toward a discussion of global issues on development, social policy and governance. Reference to Asian experiences and other parts of the world is of crucial importance, enriching the issues and questions of this theory.

Thus, after more than fifteen years of development, social quality theory has entered a new stage. This is a challenge but also an opportunity to upgrade the theory with new issues, new demands and new problems, all contributing to finding new solutions. These solutions can cope with new circumstances of social change happening not only in Europe but also in other regions worldwide. Such global expansion can generate and stimulate theoretical thinking about society in completely new ways, rethinking not only development studies but general social theories as well. This rethinking is particularly important in respect to methodology and how the theory can more effectively answer issues of everyday life in contemporary societies. The present volume is edited against this background, allowing a review of the past and an assessment of current work in order to foster further developments.

The Origin of the Theory's Development

Social quality theory emerged from policy debates during the mid-1990s among member states of the European Union. Its first manifestation can be found among a 1997 conference held in Amsterdam, when the Amsterdam declaration was produced and subsequently signed by numerous academics, law experts and leading representatives of political administrations (Beck et al. 1997). The signatories of the declaration underlined a need to develop a new perspective on social policy and developmental strategies for EU member states, the fundamental assumption being Europe's need for the vision of a "welfare society." Active citizenship was emphasized as being essential (Ivan 1999; Yeandle 1999), and the need to develop a coherent approach was discussed. These discussions resulted in the establishment of the European Foundation of Social Quality, an organizational framework aimed at promoting research on social quality and disseminating ideas among European researchers, activists and politicians.[1]

To be sure, such demands were rooted in the European context of the time. The discussion on social policy reform in Europe created a need for a general view of society, as the debate had not been limited to the field of social policy in a narrow way. The signatories of the declaration came from various professional areas such as economics, law and politics, indicating a consensus among these scholars the need for social quality discussion. This consensus emerged from recognizing challenges to the European welfare states from a manifold of perspectives, requiring the analysis of the whole system (van der Maesen and Walker 2003). The atmosphere stimulating the debate of the time can be captured in a brief outline of the following concerns.

The first concern was about the development of welfare states. Influenced by the international debate in the 1990s, swapping over the (neo)liberal ideas from North America and Latin America, the idea of privatization prevailed in Europe. According to the interpretation of "new right" policies of Reaganomics and Thatcherism in the 1980s (see George and Wilding 1994), and of the privatization experiences in Brazil and Chile in the 1990s (Bertranou and Rofman 2002; Draibe and Riesco 2009), the need for restructuration of the social fabric was also suggested in Europe. This perspective's development, however, led to an emphasis on competitiveness, which generated a debate on the orientation of future development for European welfare states. In many European countries, the ideal of privatization once worked as a guiding principle of welfare state reform, and in the public spheres, measures to reduce public expenditures, or the "reduction of the burden of social expenditure," became the norm.

Though many policy analysts of the right favored the proposed reform strategies of privatization, some social scientists and social policy analysts, nevertheless, raised their voices against privatization policies. In the early 1990s, the ideal of "social Europe" and its associated idea of a "European social model" were proclaimed as potential alternatives. For instance, in the mid-1990s, a set of workshops was organized with support of the European Commission (such as the "Cost 13" series) to discuss these ideas in the wider context of European integration. Against this background, the future of European states was discussed, and strategies of social policy reform were seen as essential components. A consensus among many scholars toward ongoing privatization emerged, emphasizing the European particularities of different social and cultural conditions, as these European member states should (and would) never go the same way as the United States (Ebbinghaus 1999; Scharpf 2002). They engaged in social policy discussion against the Washington Consensus, and these debates defined the basic context for addressing policy ideas about future developments.

The debates also concerned the relation between economic policy and social policy. In the early 1990s, many European states suffered from increasing unemployment rates and reduced rates of economic growth under the pressure of global competition, thus highlighting the impacts of globalization. This pressure supported liberal-oriented reform for increasing economic vitality. In the discussion of globalization, on the other hand, many social policy scholars emphasized that social policy should not be "annexed" or "adjunct" to economic policy nor subordinated under economic thinking (Abrahamson 1999). Rather, they argued in favor of a balance between the production (of market and economy) and reproduction (of human resource management and daily life). Thus, against the emphasis of the economic rationale of growth, many scholars also valued the significance of people's everyday lives and livelihoods as part of policy analysis. With this, orientation on promoting collective actions was emphasized against individualist orientation of mainstream policy-making. This emphasis linked to the popular notion of the theory of solidarity, as it had been already promoted by writers like Paul Spicker in the 1980s (1984; 1988). This collective idea should be nurtured by policy measures that encouraged people's participation, reinforcing social empowerment. In this way, the question of empowerment also links to the social quality factors of social cohesion and social inclusion, and so the fundamental elements of the social quality theory were highlighted.

To expose the theoretical foundation of social quality theory further, we must also clarify the concepts of the "social" and "quality." In this theory, the definition of the social is understood as the nature of human beings, standing against the individualist interpretation of the nature of society (Walker and Naegele 2009). Presented by van der Maesen and Walker (2012), this definition identifies the social as "the interaction between people (constituted as actors) and their constructed and natural environment" and that "the constitutive interdependency between processes of self-realisation and processes governing the formation of collective identities is a condition for the social and its progress or decline." Thus, in social quality theory, this definition supports a societal point of view of social systems, which implies a fundamental rejection of the individualist approach toward society.[2]

The notion of "quality of society" serves as a conceptual instrument against the intention of using economic growth as a standard for assessing the extent of social development. According to the proposed view, the important point for social development should be not only to emphasize the condition of economic growth and employment but also to tackle all aspects of social life and societal issues as essential. This argument implicitly refers to early discussion on the relation between the economic and social systems presented by Karl Polanyi, who urged the development of new ways of understanding this relation in the context of new social developments.

Based on these points of understanding, we can further discuss the central issues of social quality through the selection of a few topics.

The Central Issues of Discussion

The Individual and the Social

There are two lines of social thinking about the nature of society: one supported by liberal views on society, emphasizing the autonomy of individuals and regarding society as an agglomeration of individuals with citizen rights, and the other focused on the collective notion, referring to conservative and socialist ideas that underscore society as an association of individuals living in mutual interdependence. In the latter case, the ideal of solidarity is emphasized, and social empowerment and citizens' active engagement is highlighted (Spicker 1988; George and Wilding 1994). Social quality theory starts its theory from this tension, focusing on the centrality of "the social." However, to emphasize the notion of the social does not mean to deny the importance of individual freedom and autonomy by giving power only to abstract collectives; instead, this idea suggests a relational perspective—that is, as a matter of a dialectical, or productive, tension between biographical and societal development. With this understanding, social quality theory takes solidarity as a central normative factor, social cohesion as a conditional factor and social recognition as a constitutional factor, and sees their interplay as the most crucial issue. This means that the debate on the tension of "individual versus social" plays a major role in social quality debates (Therborn 2001).

Social Europe and Welfare Society

From a practical perspective, social quality theory promotes the idea of a "social Europe." By insisting on the collective nature of individuals, the image for further development is encouraged by this idea as a response to the debate of a European social model that EU institutions had promoted during the 1990s. Following this topic, social quality studies present an idea of a "welfare society" for building up a social Europe, which had been of special importance during the first half of the 1990s when the European economy was in a manifold crisis. This proposal of a welfare society can also refer to the East Asian experience, as Japan and China, for example, presented the ideal in the late 1980s (see Lin 1999). However, the context of this proposal should be understood by considering very different backgrounds in Europe, where the idea was presented in the context of looking for the solutions of welfare reform. The differences between these political ideas are also apparent if we look at the content of the welfare society in East Asia (Rose and Shiratori 1986), which was proposed with the intent of shifting policy away from the productivist line and toward an improvement of people's livelihood and welfare. In the context of social quality thinking, the issue of welfare society is constructed through active citizens in a democratic setting, by which the European ideas of social participation and social empowerment become major ways to achieve the goals.

Social Indicator Issues

In respect to measuring social progress, social quality studies must take social indicators as necessary instruments for reflecting social quality conditions and, more crucially, as means for monitoring social progress (Abbott et al. 2011). Some early works have constructed a complex system of social quality indicators to describe the conditions of society (Gordon 2005); however, the emphasis on the difference between quality of life and social quality has, to some extent, set up some barriers to this development. The vigilant highlighting of the difference between these theories prevents social quality research from strongly developing this theory. Nevertheless, this orientation changed after the mid-2000s when Asian scholars engaged in the social quality discussion (van der Maesen and Walker 2012). This does not mean that indicators can be employed as measurement instruments in a strict science, but to develop a complex and integrated assessment with reference to indicators, profiles and judgment is the kernel of any assessment.

Welfare Service, Social Policy and Elderly Care

In its early origin, social quality research has a close relation to social policy and welfare services (Herrmann et al. 2007). Issues of redistribution and inclusive social policy are direct policy measures to improve social quality, and community work and social organization were also connected to issues of social participation and empowerment in the context of social quality analysis (Oishi 2007). In this way, the general theoretical discussion about social quality is welded with practical issues of policy-making and service provision, which can be extended from welfare issues toward general well-being. Such development allows us to concentrate our discussion on macro-level issues, such as the future of the welfare state and social expenditure, to the middle-range issues of social services, such as work-family balance, migrant and human rights, and life satisfaction and happiness (Lin 2014). With these applications, social quality research pushes the debate of social development beyond the economic rationale and the GDP-related measurement (Herrmann 2012) to a wider sense of social progress for people's well-being.

Social Exclusion

The issue of social exclusion has been at various points relevant to social quality thinking (Room 2000). Social inclusion and its counterpart, social exclusion, are in their very essence mutually related, although some scholars may argue that phenomena of social exclusion should not be understood as simply the lack of social inclusion (Walker and Mollenkopf 2007), and the close relationship between these two cannot be overestimated. A lot of research has been undertaken on related questions, typically concerning the unemployed, the elderly and minority groups, which have high risks of social exclusion (Lin et al. 2013). This orientation of research demonstrates how citizenship rights can be protected in different kinds of societies and how excluded groups obtain social services, thus contributing to increased social quality. In Europe, the EU endorsed this orientation when the task of combating social exclusion was highlighted, primarily since the late 1990s (Berghman 1995).

Sustainability

The context of discussing sustainability in the perspective of social quality has changed several times. In its early stage, this discussion was relevant to the compressing issue of "the crisis of welfare states," raising an ideal of "welfare society" for the sustainability of the European states (Berghman 1997; Beck et al. 1997). This has not least been an issue of the financial pressure on welfare states and of the problems of shortsighted economic orientations, which limit growth, competitiveness and employment (Huber and Stephens 2001). This context changed in the twenty-first century when discussion shifted toward the sustainability of human society with reference to environmental issues (Giddings et al. 2002). Engagement with questions of human security and development has been hugely relevant in this context, as disclosed by a number of papers on sustainability and environmental issues, as well as on human security and global governance (Thomas 2001). Environmental issues will play a crucial role in policy debates of the global governance, as announced at the Rio Declaration (Panjabi 1997), so the major challenge is searching for a close link to debates on the political economy of social questions.

Urban Development and Local Administration

Being concerned with everyday life, it is logical that the discourse of social quality theory moved from the level of a general theory toward more practical issues in various dimensions, including its application to issues of urban development and local administration. Studies on local administration and urban development contributed to establishing collaborative work at the city levels of Hangzhou (People's Republic of China) and The Hague (the Netherlands). This collaboration creates a new line of thinking about the application of social quality theory in respect to local practice (Li et al. 2012), involving issues of local policy innovation, urban development and social administration. These efforts led researchers to new ways of thinking beyond welfare states as the policy focus. The results can be presented in a very positive light by comparing the conditions for social quality in different cities, communities and political practices. In this way, social quality theory opens access for contributing to the goal of urban development in relation to topics of local development, employment services, migration issues and social exclusion (Saunders 2003). This corresponds with the need to develop a new understanding of "responsibility"—that is, the responsibilities of individuals and corporate actors, civil society, states and systems of regional cooperation, and the interwoven character of issues relevant for developing perspectives. Issues of economy, culture and lifestyle, sustainability, and the like can only be properly understood if approached by looking at their interconnectedness.

The Aim of This Collection

This volume contains a selection of works previously published as articles in the *European Journal of Social Quality* and the *International Journal of Social Quality*,[3] supported by the European Foundation of Social Quality and now the International Association of Social Quality, respectively. The collection reflects more than a decade of collaboration among researchers who gathered for critical dialogue. These journals, which are the most important platforms for academic discussion about social quality research, were the outcome of cooperation with Berghahn Books—a collaboration characterized by the spirit of mutual understanding and support during the editorial process that proved to be extremely valuable for the theory's development. The limit of our selection from these journals allows for a concise overview of the development. In this way of organizing the book, the repetition of some aspects of the "architecture of social quality," as well as the theory's general assumption and perceptions, could not be avoided. However, careful reading will also show differences in the interpretation of certain facets of social reality with varying emphases on particular issues and thus distinctive stances promoted by individual researchers.

Among the published works in these journals, the standards of our selection are outlined by the following considerations. First, these chapters can help understand the social quality approach by reviewing its origin and relevant backgrounds, although some works also refer to the more recent stage of development with new focus and emphasis. Despite the retrospective orientation, those studies can still help scholars to foresee future development. Second, the selected contributions mostly focus on the theoretical aspects of the theory, that is, on its assumptions, perceptions and methodology, as well as some questions of developing relevant issues. For these reasons, the chapters do not engage in the theory's policy studies but rather in the theoretical dimension. Third, we intend to demonstrate the theory's early work as well as its later development, thus including both the old and the new issues and ideas in response to ongoing societal processes.

Accordingly, the presentation of the chapters is very much oriented on capturing the basic nature of social quality theory. The book consists of two parts, the first focusing primarily on theoretical discussions. While the second part consists mostly of research on individual countries, the selection's intention focuses not on the values of the region-specific case studies but rather on their theoretical implications. For example, in Taylor-Gooby's chapter, the significance for social quality research is not the policy study of the United Kingdom's national health care system but rather the study's explorative discussion on the relation between social trust and health policy. Accordingly, each chapter deals with specific issues of research and provides some information about the relevant theory for the development of social quality theory. At the same time, they still show that for social quality thinking, the national context plays an important role not solely as an institutional issue but also as a complex socio-historical background.

The Contributions in This Volume

The framework of social quality analysis and its rationale is clearly defined by the volume's first two chapters. We begin with a definition of "social quality," as proposed by Anne Fairweather and others, that looks at issues of labor skills, collective goods, services, institutions and infrastructure and matters outside of working life. This first chapter aims to uncover the logic of different social quality quadrants that reflect the "social quality architecture," which demonstrates a clear rationale for each social quality domain through its conceptual inquiry. We then move to the next stage in the history of theory's early development with a report on the outcomes of research conducted by the European Network on Indicators of Social Quality. In this chapter, Laurent van der Maesen and Alan Walker present a rich set of variables of the four social quality quadrants with four tables, which provide a clear vision of the items that should be key to the social quality analysis.

With the infrastructure and intentions of the theory established, the next two chapters then concern the question of how to use social quality theory to analyze social realities within particular socio-cultural contexts. Walker's piece on welfare system sustainability first addresses a theoretical exploration of social quality theory before moving on to its application to European social policy. In the first respect, Walker explores the meaning of the constitutional, conditional and normative factors of the social quality analysis, and in the perspective of the second dimension, he discusses issues of welfare sustainability with reference to East Asia. In this way, Walker investigates the concept of sustainability from the perspective of social quality with the implied social, cultural and economic reasons. The next chapter, on the theory's applicability to Asian societies, emphasizes four approaches of social quality studies in order to reflect four kinds of conditional factors. Ka Lin refers to this social quality theory's European origin and evaluates its meaning of policy analysis. He suggests reviewing social quality as a meta-theory by uprooting the particular European contexts in order to ensure its power as a general theory that can be applied to the analysis of social realities within different societies. In this way, the investigation mediates the need for a general theory and for the cultural analysis of social quality studies.

The following two selections concern the policy aspect and theoretical aspect of social quality studies, respectively. First, Peter Herrmann's chapter illustrates the policy-oriented analysis by applying the theory as a point of reference and discusses the Stiglitz Commission report, which claims an orientation of going "Beyond GDP." However, Herrmann presents a relational appraisal that allows for an understanding of social relationships as the basis of policy-making, against the challenge of economic globalization that deteriorates the degree of social justice, solidarity and human dignity. In this perspective, the investigation emphasizes the need for an integrated approach to analyze trends of economic performance and social progress instead of eclectically combining measurements of different areas. Des Gasper's chapter, on the other hand, engages in a theoretical discussion of the social quality theory, comparing the discourses of quality of life, human security and human development. The author develops this comparison by analyzing their focus, score and guiding values, as well as by their purposes and standpoints of difference. These discussions disclose the theoretical grounds of social quality thinking through comparison.

The remaining five chapters are dedicated to country-specific issues of social quality analysis. However, in serving the volume's overall goal of presenting the theoretical perspective of research work, these contributions were selected not because of their focus on the selected countries but rather because they enrich the scope of social quality studies in the general sense, which can thus develop new areas of social quality analysis. For this reason, each chapter highlights a unique feature of social quality studies. Through these studies, we can strengthen social quality research from the theoretical level to more concrete aspects of social systems. Accordingly, these five contributions deal with particular issues that are not addressed by the previous chapters of theoretical construction. The intention is also to develop the policy-oriented implications of social quality studies.

Sue Hacking's chapter on Britain and Göran and Sonia Therborn's chapter on Sweden both use the social quality framework to analyze each region's social systems but feature distinctive applications. Hacking adopts the conventional framework of social quality analysis for the case of the United Kingdom, offering readers a most convenient (or "the standard") way of analyzing the sovereign state's social quality. Meanwhile, Therborns' work describes Sweden's social quality conditions by emphasizing particular themes as key factors for the evaluation, including poverty, housing, health care and socio-economic security. In addition, altruism and tolerance, social contracts, networks and identities are evaluated as matters of social cohesion, with citizenship rights, services and social networks as social inclusion, and openness of institutions, public space and personal relationships as social empowerment. These issues represent essential aspects of social quality analysis in the four domains.

The next two chapters reveal new issues of social quality studies from Japan and Russia. As these two countries are not part of the EU, where the theory was generated, they provide enlightening perspectives on the previous emphasis of social quality studies. Interestingly, we observe that Yoshinori Hiroi's work on social quality conditions in Japan emphasizes productive policies and argues that social policy is also a strong driving force for economic development. The author maintains welfare, environment and economy as three sorts of development factors, which interact and mutually support each other. With this outlook, Hiroi reviews the evolution of public and social policies in Japan and highlights policy implications of the Japanese discourse on social development. In other words, we find a development-oriented approach toward social quality. On the other hand, Vyacheslav Bobkov, Olesya Veredyuk and Ulvi Aliyev refer to the instability of employment in Russia, exposing social risk and precarity as the major barriers for the country's development. The chapter presents three kinds of social systems—state-monopoly capitalism, state-monopoly socialism and people-humanistic socialism—and argues that the social quality conditions in these models differ greatly. Currently, in Russia consumption, income and employment become the key factors in social quality assessment, making social quality a labor market issue.

The final chapter comes from Peter Taylor-Gooby and addresses health care system reform in the United Kingdom, referring to issues of the New Public Management. The discussion of health care closely links to social trust, as great emphasis is put on political pressure of the welfare system. However, through the discussion on health care reform, the author proposes a view of rational choice as an engine of social quality, which connects macro-level observation with individual motivation of the micro-level. Thus, opinion surveys are important instruments to assess solidarity and trust as relevant issues when it comes to the provision of public services and social quality.

Challenges for Further Theoretical Development

There will be many difficulties for the discussion social quality in the future. The first challenge in developing social quality thinking further pertains to its scientific value. We must find effective ways to genuinely link the theory with empirical evidence in order to test the theory's feasibility for explaining social realities. In the past, a lack of observational data was a barrier to moving forward with this work, as many social quality studies stayed on the normative levels or worked with general assumptions (van der Maesen 2000). At the current stage, some important steps of development have been made with empirical data coming from social quality teams of six Asian societies (Lin 2013; Munro 2013; Sub and Shi 2013). Studies based on these data demonstrate the particular features of social quality assessment to study social realities different from quality of life studies. The relation between social quality and quality of life requires further study, both in terms of their differences and similarities (Lin 2014).

The second challenge concerns the need for quantitative studies of social quality. So far, social quality researchers have reached a basic agreement on which indicators to use, though individual cases may differ and some studies may use more indicators than others. This consensus was developed with reference to early work (van der Maesen 2012) and applied to the analysis by late empirical data (Lin 2013). However, how to define the boundaries of each dimension, as well as the division of these indicators into certain domains, still needs further exploration, as some indicators may be relevant for different dimensions at the same time. For instance, education indicators can be used in respect to socio-economic security, social inclusion and social empowerment. In addition, we still need technical measures to reveal the different factors' correlation in order to clearly define the domains. More attention to constitutional and normative factors is necessary because only in the interplay of indicators, profiles and criteria for assessment can essential progress be made, distinctively assessing social quality. Moreover, we can still adopt new mathematical and statistical methods to address the calculation of survey data, allowing an emphasis of the close relation among social quality's four dimensions. Still, to assess trends and mark characteristic issues, we need further investigations of social quality indicators so that they are suitable for providing measurements, not in the strict sense but for predicting the future trends of development.

The third issue relates to extending social quality into new thematic areas. Earlier we criticized methodological individualism as a major shortfall of mainstream social science, but in the present context, we capture a genuine connotation between individualist policy orientations and social cohesion. The proposed orientation for enhancing social quality is to adopt the social orientation as matter of relationality. Indeed, social quality theory understands human actions as part of a complex socio-relational system for individual actions based on collective values (Berghman 1997). Thus, we need to highlight the meaning of cultural codes in determining social actions and, therefore, to explore constitutive factors within the settings of different cultures. Strengthening the cross-national comparative perspective will also foster further development of social quality thinking (Lin 2011) and help relevant research to go beyond the original European context. In light of practical implications, we should study different developmental patterns through social quality analysis in order to understand different policy solutions.

A fourth major difficulty is how to assess social change. Social development can happen in both incremental and revolutionary ways, and policy measures can be geared to one or the other way of social transformation. Further discussion is required for how social quality thinking can be used in the context of revolutionary change, not only allowing a reflection of the consequences of such change but also providing analytical tools to develop ex ante relevant policies. This has been an important issue for Russia and eastern European countries (Herrmann et al. 2014), where rapid social change has been accompanied with social dumping, affecting many aspects of people's living standards in extremely harsh ways—but the exact overall impact of these changes will only be visible after several years. We need to investigate whether the social quality theory can be useful for assessing social progress by telling us more about social trends, not simply reflecting on the given situation at a specific moment in time. This question is also important when it comes to Latin America and Africa, where we have seen major changes in democracy within short periods of time, without having yet sufficiently considered thinking about social quality.

Finally, we must expand the scope of social quality research by way of systematically comparing this theory with various other relevant social approaches that are currently prevalent in social (development) research. Since social quality studies refer to social inclusion and social cohesion, an essential task is to discuss theories of social stratification, class relation, social capital, marginalization, social exclusion and the like (e.g., Bobkov et al. 2013). Moreover, comparative studies of indicator systems with underlined perceptions from quality of life studies, the human development index and environmental indicators and indicators of political systems (e.g., the corruption index) can be expected to bring about many unpredicted findings (Noll 2002). We also need to think about how to develop the theory itself by way of its remodeling, reshaping and reconstructing. In order to do so, we must adopt new issues of those in the global scientific community devoted to these discussions and dealing with issues such as good governance and social innovation, which are currently high on the EU agenda. Migration is still another important issue for both Europe and Asia, the place of immigration for the former and emigration for the latter. The discussion is often led by employing the human security theory, but we must also apply the social quality approach to meet the need we are facing by these processes.

Taking this all together, there is much space for further theoretical development on social quality issues. In order to meet this demand, we need to recognize the theory's special features, differences from other theories, key issues and focus (Vogel 1997). And not least, it is important to establish the capacity to apply the theory to the analysis of social problems. We must develop a clear awareness of the approach's reach, that is, define those questions this theory is able to answer and those to which it is unable to provide satisfying insights. This also means that we need to remove some barriers for its further development. Some of the barriers are imposed by self-constraint or even bias, and others come from the debate of the orientation on a rigid counter-positioning of approaches. This does not mean to overlook the fundamental differences from other theories such as the quality of life approach with different ontological and epistemological points of reference. However, one can keep an open mind in order to work for concepts that are able to provide a comprehensive analysis of present global problems and allow developing answers that are able to work toward a generic social sustainable development.

Notes

1. See www.socialquality.org.
2. Basically, this means the rejection of methodological individualism, which had been so far more or less accepted as uncontested foundation of social science.
3. The *International Journal* is the successor of the *European Journal*, which was published until 2006.

References

Abbott, P., C. Wallace and R. Sapsford. 2011. "Surviving the Transformation: Social Quality in Central Asia and the Caucasus." *Journal of Happiness Studies* 12: 199–223.

Abrahamson, P. 1999. "The Welfare Modeling Business." *Social Policy and Administration* 33(4): 394–415.

Beck, W., L. van der Maesen and A. Walker, eds. 1997. *The Social Quality of Europe.* The Hague: Kluwer International.

Berghman, J. 1995. "Social Exclusion in Europe: Policy Context and Analytical Framework." In *Beyond the Threshold: The Measurement and Analysis of Social Exclusion*, ed. G. Room. Bristol: Policy Press.

Berghman, J. 1997. "Social Protection and Social Quality in Europe." In *The Social Quality of Europe*, Beck et al.

Bertranou, F. M. and R. Rofman. 2002. "Providing Social Security in a Context of Change: Experience and Challenges in Latin America." *International Social Security Review* 55: 67–82.

Bobkov, V., O. Veredyuk and U. Aliyev. 2013. "Risks of Society Stability and Precarity of Employment: A Look at Russia." *International Journal of Social Quality* 3(1): 21–43.

Bourdieu, P. 1984. *Distinction: A Social Critique of the Judgement of Taste.* Cambridge, MA: Harvard University Press.

Draibe, S. and M. Riesco. 2009. "Social Policy and Development in Latin America: The Long View." *Social Policy and Administration* 43(4): 328–346.

Ebbinghaus, B. 1999. "Does a European Social Model Exist and Can It Survive?" pp. 1–26 in *The Role of Employer Associations and Labour Unions in the EMU: Institutional Requirements for European Economic Policies*, ed. G. Huemer, M. Mesch and F. Traxler. Aldershot: Ashgate Press.

Gasper, D., L. van der Maesen, T.D. Truong and A. Walker. 2008. *Human Security and Social Quality: Contrasts and Complementarities.* Working Paper no. 462. The Hague: Institute of Social Studies.

George, V. and P. Wilding. 1994. *Welfare and Ideology.* New York: Harvester Wheatsheaf.

Giddings, B., B. Hopwood and G. O'Brien. 2002. "Environment, Economy and Society: Fitting Them Together into Sustainable Development." *Sustainable Development* 10(4): 187–196.

Gordon, D. 2005. "Indicators of Social Quality." *European Journal of Social Quality* 5(1/2): 4–6.

Herrmann, P. 2009. *Social Quality – Looking for a Global Policy Approach: A Contribution to the Analysis of the Development of Welfare States.* Bremen: Europäischer Hochschulverlag.

Herrmann, P. 2012. "Economic Performance, Social Progress and Social Quality." *International Journal of Social Quality* 2(1): 41–55.

Herrmann, P., V. Bobkov and J. Csoba. 2014. *Labour Market and Precarity of Employment: Theoretical Reflections and Empirical Data from Hungary and Russia.* Vienna: Wiener Verlag für Sozialforschung.

Herrmann, P., A. Brandstätter and C. O'Connell. 2007. *Defining Social Services in Europe between the Particular and the General.* Baden-Baden: Nomos.

Huber, E. and J.D. Stephens. 2001. *Development and Crisis of the Welfare State: Parties and Policies in Global Markets.* Chicago: University of Chicago Press.

Ivan, S. 1999. "Some Conceptual and Operational Considerations on the Social Quality of Europe." *European Journal of Social Quality* 1(1/2).

Kaufmann, F.X. 2013. *Thinking about Social Policy: The German Tradition.* Berlin: Springer-Verlag.

Li, Yong, Y. Sun and K. Lin. 2012. "Social Innovation, Local Governance and Social Quality: The Case of Intersectoral Collaboration in Hangzhou City." *International Journal of Social Quality* 2(1): 56–73.

Lin, K. 1999. *Confucian Welfare Cluster: A Cultural Interpretation of Social Welfare.* Tampere: University of Tampere.

Lin, K. 2011. "The Prototype of Social Quality Theory and Its Applicability to Asian Societies." *International Journal of Social Quality* 21(1): 57–70.

Lin, K. 2013. "A Methodological Exploration of Social Quality Research: A Comparative Evaluation of the Quality of Life and Social Quality Approaches." *International Sociology* 28(3): 316–334.

Lin, K. 2014. "Social Quality and Happiness: An Analysis of the Survey Data from Three Chinese Cities." *Applied Research in Quality of Life* 9(3): 1–18.

Lin, K., L. van der Maesen and P. Ward. 2009. "Social Quality Theory in Perspective." *Development and Society* 38(2): 201–208.

Lin, K., Y. Xu, T.H. Huang and J.H. Zhang. 2013. "Social Exclusion and Its Causes in East Asian Societies: Evidences from SQSQ Survey Data." *Social Indicators Research* 112(3): 641–660.

van der Maesen, L. 2000. "Social Quality: A New Vision for Europe." *European Journal of Social Quality* 2(2): 139.

van der Maesen, L. 2012. *Welfare Arrangements, Sustainable Urban Development, and New Forms of Governance: The Current Demonstration Project of the City of the Hague as Example.* Working Paper no. 8. The Hague: European Foundation on Social Quality.

van der Maesen, L. and A. Walker. 2003. "Indicators of Social Quality: Outcomes of the European Scientific Network." *European Journal of Social Quality* 5(1/2): 8–24.

van der Maesen, L. and A. Walker. 2012. "Social Quality and Sustainability." pp. 250–274 in *Social Quality: From Theory to Indicators*, eds. L. van der Maesen and A. Walker. Basingstoke: Palgrave Macmillan.

Munro, N. 2013. "The Socio-Political Bases of Willingness to Join Environmental NGOs in China: A Study in Social Cohesion." *International Journal of Social Quality* 3(1): 57–81.

Noll, H.H. 2002. "Social Indicators and Quality of Life Research: Background, Achievements and Current Trends." pp. 151–181 in *Advances in Sociological Knowledge: Over Half a Century*, ed. N. Genov. Paris: International Social Science Council.

Oishi, A. 2007. "Indicators of Social Quality in Japan." pp. 85–110 in *The Second Asian Conference on Social Quality and Sustainable Welfare Societies*. Taipei: National Taiwan University.

Panjabi, R.K. 1997. *The Earth Summit at Rio: Politics, Economics and the Environment*. Boston: Northeastern University Press.

Pierson, C. 1991. *Beyond the Welfare State? The New Political Economy of Welfare*. University Park: Pennsylvania State University.

Phillips, D. 2006. *Quality of Life: Concept, Policy and Practice*. London: Routledge.

Room, G. 2000. "Social Exclusion, Solidarity and the Challenge of Globalization." *International Journal of Social Welfare* 9(2): 103–119.

Rose, R. and R. Shiratori. 1986. *Social Welfare: East and West*. Oxford: Oxford University Press.

Saunders, P. 2003. "Can Social Exclusion Provide a New Framework for Measuring Poverty?" SPRC Discussion Paper no. 127. Sydney: Social Policy Research Centre.

Scharpf, F.W. 2002. "The European Social Model." *Journal of Common Market Studies* 40(4): 645–670.

Spicker, P. 1984. *Stigma and Social Welfare*. London: Croom Helm.

Spicker, P. 1988. *Principles of Social Welfare: An Introduction to Thinking about the Welfare State*. London: Routledge.

Sub, K.W. and S.J. Shi. 2013. "Emergence of New Welfare states in East Asia? Domestic Social Changes and the Impact of Welfare Internationalism in South Korea and Taiwan (1945–2012)." *International Journal of Social Quality* 3(2): 106–124.

Therborn, G. 2001. "On the Politics and Policy of Social Quality." pp.19–30 in *Social Quality: A Vision for Europe*, eds. W. Beck, L. van der Maesen, F. Thomése and A. Walker. The Hague: Kluwer Law International.

Thomas, C. 2001. "Global Governance, Development and Human Security: Exploring the Links." *Third World Quarterly* 22(2): 159–175.

Titmuss, R.M. 1974. *Social Policy: An Introduction*. Ed. B. Abel-Smith and K. Titmuss. London: Allen & Unwin.

Townsend, P. 1975. *Sociology and Social Policy*. London: Allen Lane.

Vogel, J. 1997. "The Future Direction of Social Indicator Research." *Social Indicators Research* 42: 103–116.

Walker, A. 2011. "Social Quality and Welfare System Sustainability." *International Journal of Social Quality* 1(1): 5–18.

Walker, A. and H. Mollenkopf. 2007. *Quality of Life in Old Age: International and Multi-Disciplinary Perspectives*. New York: Springer.

Walker, A. and G. Naegele. 2009. *Social Policy in Ageing Societies: Britain and Germany Compared*. Basingstoke: Palgrave Macmillan.

Yeandle, S. 1999. "Social Quality in Everyday Life: Changing European Experiences of Employment, Family and Community." *European Journal of Social Quality* 1(1/2).

CHAPTER 1

Reconceptualization of Social Quality

Anne Fairweather, Borut Rončević, Maj Rydbjerg, Marie Valentová and Mojca Zajc

―――――――――◄○►――――――――◄○►――――――――◄○►―――――――――

Social Quality

Social quality was first conceptualized and developed in the book *The Social Quality of Europe* (Beck et al. 1997). This book, through a series of articles, develops the background to the concept and then produces a theoretical framework of social quality. Finally it critically assesses the possibilities for and problems with the concept. In this chapter, we will first look at the concept of social quality itself and then go on to examine the four components of social quality: socio-economic security, social inclusion, social cohesion and empowerment. In each section on individual components, the general conceptualization of this component is discussed, followed by a discussion of how it fits into the social quality quadrant. A number of issues are then identified and will require further research.

Conceptualization and Use of Social Quality

"Social quality" as a term was conceptualized in order to "emphasise the importance of social quality and the necessity for it to be regarded as a political priority as the process of European unification gathers pace" (Beck et al. 1997: 1). It is also a response to the "economic policy versus social policy" debate, arguing that there should be a synergy between the two rather than a prioritization of economic policy over social policy.

The concept is expected to find proper usage once fully developed: "social quality is intended both as a standard by which the citizens of Europe can assess the effectiveness of national and European policies and as a yardstick for policy makers" (Beck et al. 1997: 3) It is therefore intended to lead to the production of indicators that measure the level of social quality in a defined space, thus creating "an authentic bench-mark in order to draw conclusions about good and bad social policies and by which to assess the impact of economic policies" (Beck et al. 1997: 267).

Social quality is first explored through the synthesizing approaches of employment; social protection; economic, social and political integration; and social exclusion. From these perspectives Room (1997) concludes that social quality has been approached in three main ways, which are not mutually consistent:

- *Social Quality as Labor Skills*: the need to develop human resources through training so that the European Union can compete on the global market as a high wage, high skills economy.
- *Social Quality as Collective Goods, Services, Institutions and Infrastructures*: the assumption that quality of life, both for individuals and communities, cannot be delivered by the market alone. This concept extends to the need for social, economic and political inclusion.
- *Social Quality outside Working Life*: as a contribution to the debate that defines European citizens in wider terms than just workers, thus developing European citizenship further. "A narrower notion of citizenship and of social policy itself tends to reinforce social exclusion, at least of those outside the labour market" (Room 1997: 259).

Beck et al. (1997) then try to define social quality as a concept in itself, aside from the debates surrounding the EU. This is done through the use of the quadrant in Figure 1.1.

This figure illustrates how the four components of socio-economic security, social inclusion, social cohesion and empowerment are used to define the concept of social quality. While they have to be understood in the context of the whole quadrant, the task of our conceptualization is to make the meaning of individual components more focused in order to be able to define the frontiers between each of them. None of these components are defined in *The Social Quality of Europe* in a way that could make them

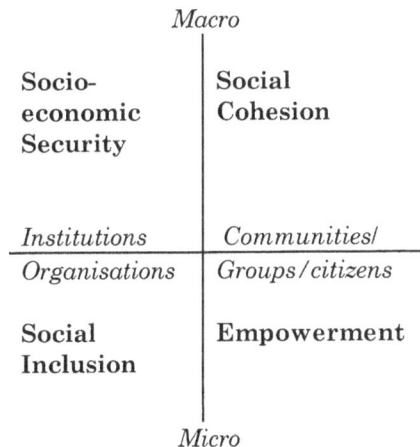

Figure 1.1. The Social Quality Quadrant

operational. Therefore, the components are defined at length in their respective sections later in the chapter.

The components are placed on two axes. The vertical axis represents the micro-macro continuum. The horizontal axis represents the divide between institutions and organizations on the one side and communities, groups and citizens on the other. The problem with these two axes is that there is much scope for overlap between the macro and institutions/organization ends of the axes and the micro and communities/groups/citizens ends of the axes. As a result we have decided to introduce a formal and informal aspect to the horizontal axis (as discussed by Svetlik 1998).

We have defined the micro level as the individual level and the macro level as any group beyond the individual. On the horizontal axis, institutions/organizations are defined as formal institutions (i.e., the state and the market). On the other end of the continuum, communities/groups/citizens are defined as informal groupings of citizens but not as individuals. The difference between formal and informal is one between organizations and rules on the formal side and actions and attitudes on the informal side of the axis.

The quadrant can be understood in a static and dynamic way. We have chosen to use the components as static concepts because of the problems that are encountered when trying to measure a continuous process. Furthermore, we have not discussed the causal relationships between the components at any length due to the complexity of these relationships. This results in a significant problem when it comes to measuring the concept of social quality itself. It therefore becomes very difficult to positively use results gained from measuring the four components individually. This ongoing problem with the social quality quadrant is yet to be resolved.

Development of Social Quality Indicators

The quadrant with the axes defined as above allows for the use of predominantly objective indicators on the left-hand side of the quadrant and predominantly subjective indicators on the right-hand side of the quadrant. Additionally, the socio-economic security component of the quadrant lends itself to indicators relating to outputs, whereas the social inclusion component lends itself to indicators measuring outcomes. It may be reasonably simple to link cause and effect on the left-hand side of the quadrant, but it is much harder to link them on the right-hand side of the quadrant.

Several problems relating to the concept of the quadrant itself are encountered when analyzing the model in depth and making it operational:

- It is unclear whether more of each one of the components therefore means greater social quality overall. There are reasons to believe that in some instances more of one component could decrease the need and utility of another component. An example of such reasoning is the communitarian discussion around the high provision of socio-economic provision by the state and the related decrease in social cohesion.[1]
- In the interest of using this model for comparability, any benchmarks that are created through this model need to be sensitive to the heterogeneous nature of social policy in Europe (Baars 1997: 305).

- It is ambiguous whether social quality only refers to the quality of social policy in Europe or whether a wider definition embraces the level of participatory democracy in Europe and the role of the EU in the world (see the Amsterdam Declaration on the Social Quality of Europe). This confusion partly results from the multidisciplinary approach of *The Social Quality of Europe,* which embraces articles from the fields of economics, political science, law, social policy and sociology.

For this chapter we will use the quadrant as presented to us in *The Social Quality of Europe* with the definitions of the axes as discussed above. This is in order to evaluate the quadrant itself and investigate what happens when you try to put it into practice. However, it was decided to define social quality more narrowly than some definitions in *The Social Quality of Europe.* While the need to counteract the democratic deficit in the EU and the role of the European Union in the world are undoubtedly important issues, it is very hard to make the concept operational if it is allowed to embrace such a breadth of issues. We therefore define social quality as follows:

> Social quality is a concept with which to measure the impact of social policy from the state, the market and civil society, on individuals and groups. The four components of social quality are socio-economic security, social inclusion, social cohesion and empowerment. Through measuring these components it is possible to measure the impact of social policy on daily life and therefore arrive at a measure of social quality that can be used as an alternative to economic indicators.

Socio-economic Security

Conceptualization of Socio-economic Security

The concept of economic security is strongly linked to the notion of paid employment. When paid employment became the predominant form of earning a living, the presence of a wage-earning individual in the family ensured economic security (i.e., the income of the family). Economic security, a regular income, was available only when a person had a job in the labor market.

Social security instruments began to evolve as a response to the existence of many cases when this was not possible. Socio-economic security in the form of social insurance prevents the loss of income in instances such as sickness, injury, old age and unemployment. Such programs arose during the later nineteenth and twentieth centuries, to ensure minimum decent standards of living for all citizens and to a lesser or greater degree to redress imbalances of wealth and opportunity.

No matter the underlying rationale for introducing social security measures in the Industrial Age, today there are several functions attributed to social security provision in general[2]:

- provision for needs;
- remedying disadvantage;
- the changing of behavior (recent trends in welfare to workfare);

- the development of potential (its focus at the individual level being the development of individuals' capacities, whereas on the collective level it is about encouragement of solidarity and integration) (Spicker 1993: 104).

Today, social security rights are well established. They are a part of United Nations Universal Declaration of Human Rights (1948), which declares among others the right to social security, work, rest, education and a standard of living adequate for healthy well-being. However, some are now calling for the abolition of social security, arguing that "social security emerged in response to the social problems created by industrialisation and ... the advent of post-industrial society has rendered social security obsolete" (Midgley 1999: 91). However, the moral underpinnings of social security are connected to a general societal consensus that the whole of society is to a lesser or greater extent responsible for its members who are unable to provide for their own reasonable standard of living. Also, even though we are now in the post-industrial era, the predominant form of earning a living still remains working for payment, (i.e., employment), therefore putting the assumptions about the obsoleteness of social security on somewhat shaky grounds.

Although many articles and books deal with the issue of social security, not many of the authors define precisely what they understand by this term. Spicker (1993: 109) claims that social security is distinct from other forms of social services in the sense that "it provides not goods but money with which people can purchase goods." Van Ginneken (1999: 51) also defines social security as "the provision of *benefits* to households and individuals through public or collective arrangements to protect against low or declining living standard arising from a number of basic rights and needs." Van Ginneken's definition allows for the inclusion of different providers of social security, not just the state but also civil society and the market, when he specifically recognizes the role of collective as well as public arrangements. Still, his definition stays focused on money transfers. It is also unclear whether this conception leaves room for tax relief.

The question of whether only money transfers constitute social security or if there is a case for also including social services is essential in the issue of definition of basic needs. If, following Maslow's (1968) classical definition, the human needs of the lowest rank are physiological needs and the needs of security and safety, one could argue that these could be sufficiently addressed by measures to protect income. However, Allardt's definition of having needs embraces not only income but also housing conditions, employment, health and education (Maslow 1968: 202). If basic needs were defined as all of these, the definition of social security would come closer to embracing social services and not only income protection measures. Such a definition is also accepted in the International Labour Organization (ILO 1984: 2–3):

> The expression has acquired a wider interpretation in some countries than in others, but basically it can be taken to mean the protection which society provides for its members, through a series of public measures, against the economic and social distress that otherwise would be caused by the stoppage or substantial reduction of earnings resulting from sickness, maternity, employment injury, unemployment, invalidity, old age and death; the provision of medical care; and the provision of subsidies for families with children.

The ILO goes even further, saying that "social security cash benefits and social services can be regarded as two sides of one coin" (1984: 7).

Socio-economic Security and the Social Quality Quadrant

In discussing the concept of socio-economic security, it is important to link it to the social quality quadrant. Beck et al. (1997: 286) define social security as referring to "the way essential needs of citizens with respect to their daily existence are addressed at macro level by different systems and structures responsible for welfare provision." The position of the socio-economic security component in the upper left part of the quadrant is an important limiting factor in the determination of the providers of social welfare. We have defined the left part of the horizontal axis as those formal institutions relating to the state and the market. Therefore, it has been impossible to include the indicators relating to informal organizations of civil society. This omission, while it is a grave shortcoming of the whole component, has been necessary in order to keep the structure of the whole social quality concept.

Furthermore, Beck et al. (1997) name the concept social security, while they are talking about the way essential needs of citizens are met. Because the essential needs of citizens are usually met with income resulting from their activities in the labor market, a more appropriate name for this concept is socio-economic security.

This kind of conceptualization leaves room for inquiry into the systemic provision for the needs of the citizens. Beck et al. (1997), when graphically presenting the component of socio-economic security, have put it in the formal/macro sphere, therefore leaving no room for the inclusion of the family as a provider of welfare. This is a large omission, as the family has been and still is an important agent in the provision of socio-economic security. Additionally, such a position of socio-economic security leaves little room for the inquiry into transfers over time, when one individual is taking care of themselves. Also, viewing the concept of socio-economic security as a systemic provision for needs by the state and the market says little about the actual use of it—an issue discussed later in the section on social inclusion.

This is not the only relation between the four concepts embraced within the social quality framework. It can be argued that social cohesion (as conceptualized in this chapter), especially its solidarity proxy, reflects informal provision of solidarity while socio-economic security is concerned with formal issues. Last but not least, it could be argued that the political empowerment of groups that are users of social security can improve the level of socio-economic security provision. Also, psychological empowerment of the individual in the form of acquiring knowledge and skills in the informal sphere is an important asset that can be sold in the labor market. The components of social quality are therefore intrinsically linked, and the distinctions between them are more of an analytical nature than of a reflection of real life. The social quality concept also implies that more of each component (i.e., socio-economic security, social inclusion, social cohesion and empowerment) will result in more social quality. Perhaps it is safer to say that a high level of socio-economic security is above all a necessary though not a sole prerequisite for social quality:

Socio-economic security in context of this chapter therefore refers to income, employment, provision of benefits and services to individuals through public or collective arrangements—either on basis of need, previous contribution or remuneration for special services—with the aim of protection of living standard, arising from a number of basic rights and needs, including the right to equal opportunities.

While this definition draws heavily on the definition of social security by Van Ginneken, three changes have been made:

- In order to accommodate the inclusion of economic security, employment has been added.
- While Van Ginneken talks about the provision of social security to households and individuals, the position of socio-economic security within the social quality quadrant does not allow for the inclusion of the family/household as a provider.
- The right to equal opportunities has been added.

Social Inclusion

Conceptualization of Social Inclusion

Social inclusion and its inverse social exclusion have come to play a major role in the policy debate over disadvantaged people in Europe. The concepts of social exclusion and social inclusion are thus widely used, although their definition and hence the relation between them remain subject to a wide range of opinions.

On a general level, both concepts are concerned with individuals' integration, or lack of, into the wider society. However, whereas social exclusion literature is relatively comprehensive and therefore offers an insight into what is to be understood by the term social exclusion, the concept of social inclusion remains vague. In general, social inclusion can be seen either as a term that simply denotes the absence of exclusion or as a concept that describes the quality or degree of inclusion into a particular group or into society as a whole. Regardless of the choice of definition, it seems impossible to conceptualize social inclusion without referring to social exclusion. The following discussion of the conceptualization of social inclusion will therefore explore the meaning of social exclusion as a route to define social inclusion.

As mentioned before, considerable variations exist in the definitions and analysis of social exclusion. However, social exclusion broadly involves the disconnection from the labor market and from social and political participation. More narrowly, Trbanc points out that the term social exclusion is used to label "the processes and situations of the exclusion of individuals and groups from the opportunities, benefits and rights commonly available in contemporary societies" (1996: 99).

Recent developments in the conceptualization of social exclusion originate from the European poverty debate.[3] In this debate, the concept was introduced as a multidimensional and dynamic approach to deprivation in contrast to poverty, which was seen as solely focusing on a lack of financial resources. In this line of thought, questions of poverty and inequality are encompassed within the concept of social exclusion; hence, social exclusion is a more comprehensive concept that embraces many more dimensions.[4] According to Room (1995) the main distinction between social exclusion and poverty is that, while social exclusion focuses on relational issues such as low social participation, lack of social protection, lack of social integration and lack of power, poverty is concerned with distributional issues in relation to the distribution of resources in society.

Furthermore, social exclusion stresses the relationship between the individual and society, in the sense that the main focal point is the exclusion of individuals from taking part in various societal spheres. In this vein, the EU debate has evolved around the denial or non-realization of the social rights of citizens, which are seen as a consequence of the breakdown of the major societal system that should guarantee full citizenship and subsequently social rights (Berghman 1995).[5] Hence, social exclusion is seen mainly as a result of restrictions in terms of access to resources and institutions, which are important for realizing the social rights of individuals. Moreover, social exclusion involves disadvantage and exclusion from more than one societal sphere. Therefore, according to Trbanc, "one can talk of situations of exclusion in its broad sense when there is an overlapping of exclusions on different dimensions (civic, economic, social, interpersonal) or in spheres within the dimensions" (1996: 99).

The EU discourse on social exclusion borrows from the French solidarity paradigm, in the sense that social exclusion is seen as resulting from the breakup of the social bond that links the individual to society. Social exclusion should thus be combated through policies that facilitate integration (Cousins 1998).[6] However, as pointed out by Silver (1995), there are competing understandings of social exclusion, based on different theoretical perspectives, political ideologies and national discourses. Besides the approach drawing on the French tradition, Silver identifies two other exclusion paradigms: a specialization paradigm and a monopoly paradigm. The first arises from a liberal tradition and therefore sees social exclusion as reflecting voluntary choice, contractual relations between individuals and, most important, as discrimination, market failures and non-enforced rights. The second paradigm sees social exclusion as a result of group monopolies. The reasoning behind the approach is based on a Marxist tradition that sees inherent conflicts in society as the result of different groups controlling different resources, and so they guard against outsiders by creating barriers and restricting access to these resources, goods and services.

The three paradigms have different understandings of the meaning of being integrated in society. Under the solidarity paradigm, to be integrated into society is taken to mean being a part of the society as a whole (sharing norms, participating in the different spheres, etc.). However, the growth of multiculturalism and the fact that societies are becoming more specialized and thus more complex arguably contest the logic of this paradigm. The specialization paradigm sees inclusion as the result of formal contractual relations, and equal opportunities guaranteed by the state as the instrument to secure integration. The first shortcoming of this paradigm is that it neglects the informal dimension of society—in other words, the family and the community. Furthermore, it only focuses on rights and not on the implementation and impact of these rights. Finally, inclusion in the monopoly paradigm is when individuals are part of a social group.

Needless to say, social exclusion is therefore a very broad concept that draws upon diverse traditions in different contexts. Accordingly, it is difficult to make social exclusion an operational concept. However, the European Observatory on National Policies to Combat Social Exclusion has been instrumental in creating a definition, which is operational in relation to empirical studies. The Observatory (1992) states that individuals suffer from social exclusion when:

- they suffer general disadvantages in terms of education, training, employment, housing, financial resources and so on;
- their chances of gaining access to the major social institutions that distribute these life chances are substantially lower than the rest of the population;
- these disadvantages persist over time.

Furthermore, according to Trbanc, social exclusion exists at different levels: the relation between individuals as citizens and the state on the one hand and the relation between individuals as private persons and the community (groups, networks) on the other. To these two levels one can add the relation between individuals as workers and consumers and the market. The nature of the first and the last relation is formal because the relationship between the citizens and the state is based on a set of rights (civic, political and social) guaranteed by the state. The relation between individuals and the market is regulated either through contractual relations (employer/employee) or through a medium such as money. The nature of the second relation is informal since it is based on identification, a feeling of belonging and shared values.

In conclusion, social exclusion encompasses the following features. First, it is a relational concept, as it focuses on the relationship between the individual and society, whatever the understanding of the nature of the relation, which varies according to different traditions (cf. the three exclusion paradigms). Second, it is multidimensional, as it is concerned with the exclusion from a range of spheres in society. Third, exclusion exists in relation to different actors in society that can be both formal and informal. Finally, it encompasses both a static and a dynamic dimension.

In this context, how can social inclusion be conceptualized? One approach would be, as mentioned before, simply to understand social inclusion as the absence or opposite of social exclusion. Social inclusion would thus be taken to mean *not* being denied access to or the opportunity to take part in the different societal spheres. However, this conceptualization of social inclusion will not provide us with any knowledge about the quality or the extent to which individuals are included. Arguably these questions are very important for determining social quality and different degrees and kinds of inclusion need to be distinguished.

The three exclusion paradigms outlined above offer three distinct understandings of integration. However, none of them seem to have exhausted the meaning of integration or fully pinned down what it means to be included. Mouzelis (1995) identifies three different types of inclusion, which may be helpful in regard to the conceptualization of inclusion.[7] The first is termed a parceled inclusion, which refers to a situation where individuals have access to, and participate in, different spheres but without being a part of the whole; therefore the chances of influencing society are small. Second, monological inclusion means that individuals are subordinated to the dominant norms, and this corresponds to a situation of total assimilation. Finally, differentiated inclusion reflects mutual respect and openness, and ultimately the possibility of influencing society, which is responsive to the existence of diverse groups and therefore different needs. Mouzelis's focus is thus the nature of the relationship between the individual and society. The nature of this relationship varies in relation to first, the extent to which the society is responsive and able to accommodate the particular needs of the individual and second, the extent to which individuals can influence the different societal systems. The reason for bringing Mouzelis into this debate is that we can use the possibility of influence and the degree of the state's responsiveness toward citizens as indicators for the quality of social inclusion.[8] Finally, before deciding on our definition of social inclusion, we will discuss the component in relation to the social quality quadrant.

Social Inclusion and the Social Quality Quadrant

Beck et al. (1997) relate social inclusion to the principles of equality and equity, though in line with the vast majority of the work on social inclusion, they primarily define social inclusion negatively as the absence of exclusion. However, the principles of equality and equity are equally important for our conceptualization of social inclusion, since both concepts are related to the idea of equal opportunities, which are essential when dealing with the inclusion of marginalized groups such as people with disabilities.[9]

The placing of social inclusion in the lower left corner of the social quality quadrant provides us with two important pieces of information about the concept. First, on the micro-macro axis, social inclusion is positioned at the micro-level. As such, social inclusion is concerned with the individual's inclusion into different spheres in society. Second, social inclusion is related to the formal dimension since it is positioned at the formal side of the formal-informal axis. Consequently, the question of the individual as a private person's access to the community (sharing norms, being a part of social networks, a feeling of belonging, etc.) is not included in our approach to social inclusion. In other words, the focal point of social inclusion is the relationship of individuals to the formal institutions. This is to avoid any conceptual overlaps with social cohesion, which is dealt with in the section about social cohesion.

Definition of Social Inclusion in the Context of Social Quality

The fact that our conceptualization of social inclusion is concerned with the individuals (as citizens, consumers and workers) in relation to formal institutions/systems does not imply that we only focus on formal rights. We are primarily concerned with the individuals' access to different organizations, institutions and systems (as defined in the section on socio-economic security) that contributes to the overall socio-economic security of these individuals. More specifically, access to social security, social services health, education, housing, meaningful social activities and the spatial sphere (i.e., removal of architectural barriers) are put to the fore. However, since we do not only focus on formal rights, access is measured here as actual inclusion. The problem with this approach is that the possibilities/opportunities that individuals voluntarily do not use will be weighted negatively.

Moreover, social inclusion should not merely be seen as the inverse of social exclusion. Rather, it should be understood as something that goes beyond the absence of exclusion in qualitative terms, to encompass different kinds of inclusion into the formal institutions. As such, social inclusion conceals both a qualitative and a quantitative dimension. The qualitative dimension focuses on different kinds of inclusion, which broadly should be understood as to what extent the systems are open to or tolerate the specifics or particularities of individuals and the question of the individuals' possibilities for influencing social systems. Needless to say, the reasoning behind this is that the more flexible the systems are toward the particularities of the individuals, the more the individuals can influence the systems and the more inclusive the systems are.

The quantitative dimension refers to the fact that social inclusion is a relative concept in the sense that different degrees of inclusion exist. Degrees should be understood as establishing how many social systems the individuals are included in. The assumption is of course that the more systems the individual has access to the better. This raises the issue of whether inclusion in some spheres makes inclusion in others unnecessary or even impossible.

Furthermore, social inclusion encompasses both a static dimension (i.e., the situation of inclusion in different spheres) and a dynamic dimension (i.e., the process of inclusion itself.) However, we have chosen to focus only on the static dimension, for reasons discussed in the introductory section:

> Social inclusion is taken to mean access to the resources, benefits, opportunities and rights that are important for realizing the standard of living commonly accepted as the norm in a society and the possibility of influencing the systems and institutions that provide this.

Social Cohesion

Conceptualization of Social Cohesion

In the past, the concept of social cohesion was often used synonymously with that of social integration. We believe that today this cannot be done. However, certain aspects of the social integration concept are relevant when conceptualizing social cohesion. Landecker (1951) distinguishes between four types of integration: cultural (internal consistency of culture in the form of absence of alternatives), normative (integration in the relation between standards and persons), communicative (the extent to which communicative integration permeates a group) and functional (the degree of mutual interdependence among elements of a whole). However, there are serious problems with different types of integration. As far as cultural integration is concerned, in today's highly pluralist and diversified society, it would be extremely difficult to claim the absence of various alternative values or subcultures as a precondition for an integrated or cohesive society. This would come close to the concept of a homogeneous society[10] (see also the critique of monologic inclusion of Mouzelis in the previous section on social inclusion). Additionally, no one has yet offered a valid answer to the question "what degree of social cohesion—'sense of community' or '*Gemeinsinn*'—is necessary to co-exist in plural and highly differentiated society?" (Hirschmann 1994). Until the answer to this and some related questions is given, we cannot include the concept of cultural integration in our conceptualization of social cohesion. The concept of normative integration is quite relevant but problematic since—once being made operational—it shares common flaws with the classic discussions on social deviance and is therefore very difficult to make operational in an unbiased manner.[11] The heuristic potential of functional integration is also questionable since in today's societies it would generally be difficult to talk about functionally independent units. How would we then plausibly make operational the extent to which modern societies are complex, in the sense that they are highly diversified and functionally interdependent? The most interesting and promising concept from all of those, therefore, is communicative integration since it refers to certain aspects that we find important in our conceptualization of social cohesion.

The concept of social cohesion originates in natural sciences. However, it is now a frequently used sociological concept. The fact that it is used regularly does not imply that it has been properly defined. As long as we remain in the realm of natural sciences, the meaning of this concept is quite clear: it describes a phenomenon whereby two or more entities are pulled, bound or glued together. When we transplant this concept into social sciences, its meaning becomes less evident. It is often used as a buzzword in both theoretical and empirical social analysis. We still use the term "cohesion" to describe a social entity that is "glued" together. However, not many conceptualize this term in a proper manner that would allow for a plausible operationalization in empirical research. When it appears, it usually does so together with other concepts that are at the center of analysis, such as civic engagement, social capital, networks, trust, cooperation and so on. We will not be able to avoid these concepts in dealing with social cohesion since they describe different aspects of the same general phenomenon. However, one must carefully distinguish between them. Even though some authors use terms such as "social capital" (Bourdieu 1986) or "networks" as synonyms for the definitions of social cohesion, these terms are not necessarily synonymous.

Putnam clarifies the links between the concepts above as follows:

> the mechanisms through which civic engagement and social connectedness produce such results: better schools … and more effective government are multiple and complex. While these briefly recounted findings require further confirmation and perhaps qualification, the parallels across hundreds of empirical studies in a dozen disparate disciplines and sub-fields are striking. Social scientists in several fields have recently suggested a common framework for understanding these phenomena, a framework that rests on the concept of *social capital.* By analogy with notions of physical capital and human capital: tools and training that enhance individual productivity "social capital" refers to features of social organization such as networks, norms, and social trust that facilitate co-ordination and co-operation for mutual benefit. (1995: 67)

Social Cohesion and the Social Quality Quadrant

How do we understand these concepts? We do not conceptualize the concept of social cohesion as such but rather relate it to that of social quality. In order to achieve a certain level of social quality, one must "enjoy a certain level of social cohesion" (Beck et al. 1997: 284). However, the concept of social quality is insufficiently defined and does not provide us with the answer to important questions such as why social cohesion is relevant for social quality. The authors also do not define the concept of social cohesion in a clear manner: "Social cohesion (versus anomie) concerns the macro-level processes which create, defend or demolish social networks and the social infrastructures underpinning these networks" (Beck et al. 1997: 288) Above all, there is not an answer to the following question: What aspects of this concept are especially relevant for making this dimension of social quality operational?

Definition of Social Cohesion in the Context of Social Quality

What is it that concerns the processes the authors mention in their definition above? For our purpose, we can start to define the concept with the help of the social quality model. The position of social cohesion in the upper right quadrant is relevant since it provides us with information about two important characteristics of social cohesion. The first one is its position in the micro-macro axis. A specific quality of social cohesion is that it simply cannot exist at the micro level. Individuals cannot be described as cohesive toward the society or vice versa, even though their actions contribute to the level of cohesiveness at different levels in the micro-macro axis. We see social cohesion as a specific quality of social entities at the mezzo- and macro-level. Only different groups, networks and communities or the society as a whole can exhibit social cohesion. The second characteristic derives from its position in the formal-informal axis. Social cohesion and empowerment as well are distinct from the other two components of the quadrant in that they cannot be legally prescribed or enforced by a third party.

It can be claimed that in modern societies social capital is the "structural" aspect of the social cohesion phenomenon in the context of social quality. The availability of social capital at a certain level is the necessary precondition for social cohesion at the same level and, at the same time, its consequence. Hence, the presence of social capital in the form of various cooperative networks appears to be an important indicator of cohesive community or society. If cohesion describes a "glued" society, then social capital represents the "social glue." Putnam for instance argues that "voter turnout, newspaper readership, membership in choral societies and football clubs—these were the hallmarks of a successful region. In fact, historical analysis suggested that these networks of organised reciprocity and civic solidarity, far from being an epiphenomenon of socio-economic modernisation, were a precondition for it" (1995: 66).

However, the very existence of social capital, which can be made operational for the purpose of empirical research, is not a sufficient description of a cohesive society. Certain mechanisms for effective interpersonal and intergroup communication are the building bricks of social capital and therefore cohesive entities and society itself. These are:

- *common norms*, which we understand as voluntary compliance with established rules, be they formal or informal,
- *trust* toward other social actors, which enables
- *forms of cooperative behavior* that exhibit the orientation beyond the promotion of specific personal or group goals, which enables us to transcend simple zero-sum relationships.

As we can see, social cohesion originates in social relations. The quality of these relations therefore determines the level of social cohesion. This means that when we analyze a level at a particular point on the micro-macro axis, we only have to analyze it as the relations between entities at this level. As we move away from the micro end of the axis, it becomes more important to understand the level of social cohesion is conducted by collective not individual actors. We can assign less credibility to the theoretical strands that see the actions and attitudes of individuals as important determinants of social cohesion at the mezzo- and macro-level. If we focus on individual actors' actions, we should focus on their organizational role rather than their personal actions.

Here we must also say that it would not be plausible to directly measure social cohesion, so instead we will use social capital as a proxy variable. The approach we will adopt is therefore to measure the level of social cohesion by several tentative indices measuring the existence of the building bricks of social capital, that is, the level of voluntary compliance to common norms, trust and cooperative behavior at both the mezzo- and the macro-level. We also have to emphasize that social cohesion at a specific level is not necessarily good or bad. Furthermore, a low level of social capital and social cohesion at certain levels does not imply that it is lacking in society in general (Fukuyama 1995).

Empowerment

Conceptualization of Empowerment

This concept is widely used, but it can be claimed that there is no unified definition of empowerment. The definition (or definitions) of empowerment depends on the theoretical context in which it is discussed and used. Generally, we can say that the empowerment ideology is rooted in social action, where empowerment is associated with community interest and with attempts to increase the power and influence of oppressed groups (such as workers, women and minorities). Since the 1970s this ideology has been adopted to promote the rights of ethnic and sexual minorities, for training and education programs as well as in organizational development programs, and by the feminist movement. There has been also a growing recognition of the importance of the characteristics of, and actions by, the individuals.

In literature we can find three main theoretical approaches to empowerment, and this therefore brings three slightly different definitions of empowerment. The approach can be based on:

- the critical social theory and emancipatory theory, in which empowerment is associated with improving the living conditions of oppressed groups such as ethnic minorities, women and disabled people;
- organizational theories, in which empowerment is associated with the delegation of power and the subject's opportunity to take an action;
- the social psychological theory, in which empowerment originates within the individual and is concerned with the individual's perception of the environment.

This suggests that empowerment can be defined in different ways, but there are some common elements to all definitions:

- Empowerment aims at the improvement of individual and collective skills so that people have control over their living and working conditions and their well-being.
- Empowerment is the aim as well as the process of community organization.
- Empowerment refers to a constant process of enabling individuals and groups to take part in collective action (Erben et al. 1999).

Empowerment is an abstract concept positively associated with growth and development, referring to solutions rather than to problems. It can be understood as a static concept (to be or not be empowered and to what extent) or as a dynamic concept (to become empowered): power can be taken, given away and shared.

We can discuss empowerment as a process, which means how individuals, organizations and communities pursue maximum impact on their own lives and eventual choices. (The process of individual empowerment requires a critical introspection and then a change in the pattern of behavior. At the community level, empowerment is understood in terms of people uniting to achieve common goals.) Thus, Somerville (1998) argues that the question of "how to empower someone" can be better answered by distinguishing different categories in aspects of the empowerment process. Somerville classifies the empowerment process according to:

- Whether the source of empowerment is with those with the power or those who need to be empowered. When empowerment is initiated from above (through policy interventions), we can talk about top-down empowerment. When the initiative comes from below (from those without any power), we can speak about bottom-up empowerment.
- The change in the dependency relationship between the two parties, those with and those without power. According to Somerville, dependency can increase or decrease during the empowerment process.
- The institutional change. There are three types of institutional empowerment processes. The conservative empowerment process is when existing institutional structures tend to stay and expand on the same level during the empowerment process. Institutional structures can also break up and create new, separate power bases. This is a radical empowerment process. Finally, there is the reformist empowerment process, where institutional structures are reformed into structures within which power is more equally distributed.

- The beneficiaries. The beneficiaries can be, according to Somerville, the individuals, collectives or elites.

The static understanding of empowerment is closely related to the concept of power. Static empowerment does not answer the question of "how to empower" but is focused on whether individuals, communities and organizations are empowered and whether they have a defined power to impact their own lives and eventual choices. Speaking about power requires us to specify what we mean by the term. For a better understanding we can use Friedmann's (1998) distinction between three types of power relevant to empowerment discussions, that is, social, political and psychological power. Social power is concerned with access to information, knowledge and skills, participation in organizations, financial resources, defensible life space, surplus time, appropriate information and social networks based on reciprocity, instruments of work and livelihood. Political power concerns individuals' access to the process by which decisions, particularly those that affect their own future, are made. Political power is not only the power to vote but also the power of voice and of collective action. Psychological power is the individual sense of potency expressed by self-confident behavior.

It is clear that the understanding of empowerment varies according to the context in which this concept is used. There is no unified definition of empowerment. It means that for our project we must come up with our own understanding of empowerment based on the social quality quadrant and our target group. From the discussion above we can aggregate some key dimensions of empowerment that can be very useful for this context:

- The unit of empowerment is the individual, the organization or the community.
- The dynamics of empowerment are those of whom are to be empowered (in order to create a certain amount of social, political and/or psychological power) or those of whom will become empowered (the process of empowering, which has its origin in the top-down approach—from governmental interventions, for instance—or in the bottom-up approach—the citizenship level, developed from below).
- The type of empowerment (i.e., empowerment focused on social, political and/or psychological power.

Empowerment and the Social Quality Quadrant

According to Beck et al. (1997), empowerment (versus subordination) primarily concerns the micro-level, enabling people as citizens to develop their full potential. Thus, this component of social quality refers to the development of their competence as citizens in order to participate in processes that determine daily life. While we conceptualize empowerment in the context of the social quality quadrant, we must also be aware of some limiting factors, the main being that the quadrant needs to contain four relatively independent components.

In this context we will focus on the limitation above and its consequences for our definition of the empowerment concept. According to Beck et al. (1997), the position of the empowerment within the social quality quadrant is on the micro- (individual) level on the vertical axis and in the informal (everyday life) side of the horizontal axis. Because empowerment is situated on the micro-level within the quadrant, we must think about the unit of empowerment in terms of individuals, as private persons. If we were to include organizational or community empowerment in our conceptualization of empowerment, this would entail an overlap with the social cohesion component of the quadrant. As mentioned before, the unit of our interest will be the individual as a private person, not as a citizen practicing social and political rights. Individual citizens and their access to organizational formal structures are discussed in the section on social inclusion. Our focus on the individual also does not allow us to work with access to social networks, as participation in informal networks is discussed in the social cohesion component.

Individual empowerment can be understood as the resources produced on the individual level (bottom-up) and not provided by the system (top-down). Top-down empowerment in this case could overlap significantly with the socio-economic security component.

These points have defined the unit of empowerment for the purpose of this chapter. The next step of the conceptualization of empowerment should be to choose between a static or a dynamic conception of empowerment. However, this is a choice that has been solved in the discussion at the beginning of the chapter, and we will therefore follow our previous decision to work with just the static concept of empowerment. The next step is to specify the type of empowerment we should focus on. Defining static empowerment in the same terms as Friedmann (1998), we can use his concept of three powers and try to apply them within the social quality quadrant. The first type of power is political power. For us, the main problem with political power is the fact that it is related to individuals as citizens practicing their rights. To avoid overlap with the social inclusion component, it is better to leave political power out of the discussion about empowerment.

From Friedmann's definition of social power, we have to take out elements such as participation in social networks (which overlaps with social cohesion) and formal organizations (which overlaps with social inclusion), financial resources and defensible life space and instruments of work and livelihood (all three of which overlap with the component of socio-economic security, i.e., top-down formal sources of empowerment). This means that for our analysis, the relevant elements of Friedmann's conception of social power are knowledge and skills and appropriate information, all individual sources of empowerment. Friedmann's conception of psychological power is included in our definition of empowerment because it is based solely on individual resources.

Definition of Empowerment in the Context of Social Quality

Empowerment can be understood as a static concept, focused on individual internal resources (skills, knowledge, appropriate, self-confidence) that empower individuals to control their own living and working conditions and the impact on their well-being and life decisions.

Summary

The concept of social quality is a valuable concept, especially when trying to assess development in a more holistic light, as it legitimizes itself by breaking away from the predominant economic discourse. In the case of the European Union, the concept of social quality could be of particular use when trying to highlight the need for effective social as well as economic policies. However, it remains an extremely vague concept that needs a more concrete definition

In an effort to clarify the concept of social quality in order to use it for empirical research, the social quality quadrant has been developed as a framework for research. This has the positive aspect of giving some direction to what is to be understood by social quality, especially when developing indicators for a specific group. It also ensures that any research conducted has a broad perspective when incorporating the four components of socio-economic security, social inclusion, social cohesion and empowerment with the micro-macro and formal-informal axes. This is an obvious advantage over purely economic studies, though the broad scope of social quality results in a potentially large number of indicators, which in turn can make the actual research very complex to carry out.

Moreover, this framework limits as well as enables the possibilities for research. The problems identified in this chapter are indeed considerable. For example, the roles of civil society and the family in ensuring socio-economic security have been left out of our conceptualization due to the position of components in the formal half of the quadrant. We see this as a severe omission. Additionally, our definition of social inclusion is likewise limited to the formal sphere, thus leaving out the importance of individuals being included in the community. This aspect must therefore be covered in the components of empowerment and social cohesion.

Further problems relating to the conceptualization of social inclusion occur when relating it to state institutions because it is difficult to create indicators that do not overlap with the indicators for the systemic level. Though an important part of empowerment, political empowerment has been omitted from the empowerment component due to its position on the micro side of the vertical axis. Political power of the individual people has been reconceptualized as the extent to which the individuals can influence the systemic level and therefore placed in the social inclusion component.

With a visual representation of the different aspects of social quality, how research into each component of the social quality quadrant would eventually result in a measure of social quality itself remains a question for answering. For example, it is difficult to make value judgments about the value of a certain amount of social cohesion at a certain level. How this then relates to the level of social quality itself is impossible to tell.

Thus, the concept of social quality is underpinned by the assumption that more of each component will automatically lead to a higher social quality without clarifying the relation between the individual components. This is problematic because it is unclear whether or not one or more of the components enables the others (i.e., does socio-economic security enable social inclusion or are they mutually dependent). It can also be argued that the components do not have the same importance for social quality, but the quadrant does not offer any tools that could help to determine which are more important. Furthermore, it could be argued that more of one component could make the need or utility of another one smaller. Accordingly, we need to solve these issues through further exploration of the social quality theory.

Anne Fairweather has a BA(Hons) from the University of Leeds in Politics and European Parliamentary Studies and an MSc from the University of Bath in European Social Policy Analysis. She also studied at the University of Ghent (Belgium), Roskilde University (Denmark) and the University of Ljubljana (Slovenia) during these degrees. She went on to work on labor market and financial services policy in Brussels and London for a variety of employer organizations. Currently, she works on pensions policy for the National Employment Savings Trust (NEST), a workplace pension scheme set up for the automatic enrollment of workers into pension saving.

Borut Rončević, PhD, is professor of Sociology at the School of Advanced Social Studies in Nova Gorica, Slovenia. His research falls at the intersection of sociological theory, economic sociology and regional studies. More recently he has published on the topics of social and cultural factors of development, regional development and societal steering. He is currently researching social aspects of industrial symbiosis and has been a visiting scholar at a number of institutions in the United States, the United Kingdom, Ireland, Russia and Germany.

Maj Rydbjerg works as an officer in the European Parliament.

Marie Valentová holds a PhD in Sociology and since 2002 has worked as a researcher at the Luxembourg Institute of Socio-economic Research (LISER). She is also a visiting fellow at the Catholic University of Leuven (Belgium) and teaches at the International Master in Social Policy Analysis (IMPALLA). Her main research interests concern social policy analysis and evaluation, reconciliation of family and paid work, female labor market participation, gender issues, integration of immigrants and social cohesion. She acts as a member of the Experts' Forum of the European Institute for Gender Equality and independent expert in the Peer Review in Social Protection and Social Inclusion and Assessment in Social Inclusion program.

Mojca Zajc completed her MS degree in European Social Policy Analysis at the University of Ljubljana (Slovenia) in 2000.

Notes

1. Discussed further by Putnam (1993) and Coleman (1990) in relation social capital, and Wolfe (1998).
2. Among many other explanations, for example, bottom-up processes such as linking the emergence of the social security concept to the power and size of the working classes, as well as the availability of

financial means of the state to address these demands; or in the case of Bismarckian Germany, to cover for illegitimate deficiencies of the system.

3. The concept of social exclusion was first introduced in France in the 1970s. The concept referred to various categories of people unprotected by social insurance. In the 1980s the term was taken to mean a process of social disintegration in the sense of a breakdown in the relation between the individual and the society (Cousins 1998).

4. Trbanc argues that this distinction between social exclusion and poverty is misleading, as the distinction only remains clear for as long as poverty is understood and measured indirectly in terms of income. Trbanc points out that if poverty is defined and measured directly (i.e., the measuring of the dimensions of living conditions and consumption) in terms of relative deprivation, then the distinction becomes less obvious (1996: 101).

5. The EU conceptualization borrows from T.H. Marshall's theory about citizenship. According to Marshall (1965), the idea of citizenship developed first through the introduction of civic rights then through the extension to political and, in the twentieth century, social rights.

6. Trbanc disagrees with this interpretation. She states that the EU approach should be seen in the context of social policy, the creation of measures for the integration of excluded groups and the evaluation of existing policy measures (1996: 101). First, however, there is no inherent contradiction between the two, and second, the European debate has in our opinion to a significant degree been stimulated by a rhetoric concerned with the fear of disintegration of the social fabric and subsequently societal polarization and social exclusion.

7. Mouzelis (1995) uses the term integration; however, the way the term is used makes it, for our purposes, interchangeable with inclusion.

8. This should be broadly understood as encompassing exercising one's political citizenship and as a parallel to political empowerment.

9. Policies aiming at facilitating social inclusion are ultimately concerned with creating equal opportunities for individuals and groups in society.

10. Homogeneity of a social entity is, in our opinion, positively correlated with its cohesiveness. However, the concepts are not synonymous, and for analytical purposes and for further operationalization we would have to distinguish between them.

11. For example, how could we claim that various crime statistics validly indicate the level of normative integration in the light of bias that is present in these statistics? For instance, it has been suggested that white-collar crime is difficult to detect and that the police tend to be less strict about reporting the disruptive activities of middle- or upper-class children (Clinard 1974; Sutherland 1962).

References

Allardt, E. 2000. "An Attempt at Discussion about the Quality of Life and Mortality in Industrial Society." *MESPA Reader: Social Quality Indicators in the case of Marginal Groups – the Disabled.* MESPA: Ljubljana.

Amsterdam Declaration on the Social Quality of Europe. 1997. Amsterdam: The European Foundation on Social Quality.

Baars, J., K. Knipscheer, F. Thomése and A. Walker. 1997. "Conclusion: Towards Social Quality in Europe" in *The Social Quality of Europe*, Beck et al.

Beck, W., L. van der Maesen and A. Walker, eds. 1997. *The Social Quality of Europe.* The Hague: Kluwer Law International.

Berghman, J. 1995. "Social Exclusion in Europe: Policy Context and Analytical Framework" in *Beyond the Threshold: The Measurement and Analysis of Social Exclusion,* ed. G. Room. Bristol: Policy Press.

Bourdieu, P. 1986. "The Forms of Capital" pp. 241–258 in *Handbook of Theory and Research for the Sociology of Education,* ed. J.G. Richardson. New York: Greenwood Press.

Clinard, M.B. 1974. *Sociology of Deviant Behaviour.* New York: Holt, Rinehart and Winston.

Coleman, J.S. 1990. *Foundations of Social Theory.* Cambridge, MA: Harvard University Press.

Cousins, C. 1998. "Social Exclusion in Europe: Paradigms of Social Disadvantage in Germany, Spain, Sweden, and the United Kingdom." *Policy and Politics* 26(2).

Erben, R., P. Franxkowiak and E. Wenzel. 1999. "Building Social Capital in the 21st Century." *Health Promotion Journal of Australia* 9.

European Observatory on National Policies to Combat Social Exclusion. 1992. *Agencies, Institutions and Programmes: Their Interrelationships and Coordination in Efforts to Combat Social Exclusion.* Lille: European Economic Interest Group.

Friedmann, J. 1998. *Empowerment – The Politics of Alternative Development.* Oxford: Blackwell.

Fukuyama, F. 1995. *Trust: The Social Virtues and the Creation of Prosperity.* London: Penguin Books.

Hirschmann, A.O. 1994. "Wieviel Gemeinsinn Braucht die Liberale Gesellschaft." *Leviathan, Zeitschrift Fuer Sozialwissenschaft* 22(2).

ILO (International Labor Organisation). 1984. *An Introduction to Social Security.* Geneva: ILO.

Landecker, W.S. 1951. "Types of Integration and their Measurement." *American Journal of Sociology* 56.

Marshall, T.H. 1965. *Citizenship and Social Class.* Cambridge: Cambridge University Press.

Maslow, A.H. 1968. *Towards the Psychology of Being.* New York: Van Nostrand Reinhold.

Midgley, J. 1999. "Has Social Security Become Irrelevant?" *International Social Security Review* 52(2).

Mouzelis, N. 1995. *Strategies of Integration and Socio-Cultural Differentiation.* Copenhagen: CIO Studies No. 11.

Putnam, R.D. 1993. "The Prosperous Community: Social Capital and Public Life." *The American Prospect* 13: 35–42.

Putnam, R.D. 1995. "Bowling Alone: American's Declining Social Capital." *Journal of Democracy* 6(1): 65–78.

Room, G. 1995. "Poverty in Europe: Competing Paradigms of Analysis." *Policy and Politics*, 23(2).

Room, G. 1997. "Social Quality in Europe: Perspectives on Social Exclusion" in *The Social Quality of Europe*, Beck et al.

Silver, H. 1995. "Reconceptualizing Social Disadvantage: Three Paradigms of Social Exclusion" in *Social Exclusion: Rhetoric, Reality, Responses*, eds. G. Rodgers, C.G. Gore and J.B. Figueiredo. Geneva: International Institute of Labour Studies.

Somerville, P. 1998. "Empowerment through Residence." *Housing Studies* 13(2).

Spicker, P. 1993. *Poverty and Social Security – Concepts and Principles.* London: Routledge.

Sutherland, E.H. 1962. "Is 'White Collar Crime' Crime?" in *The Sociology of Crime and Delinquency*, eds. M.E. Wolfgang, L. Savitz and N. Johnston. New York: Holt, Rinehart and Winston.

Svetlik, I. 1998. "Some Conceptual and Operational Considerations on the Social Quality of Europe" in *MESPA Reader: Social Quality Indicators in the Case of Marginal Groups – the Disabled.* MESPA: Ljubljana.

Trbanc, M. 1996. "Social Exclusion: The Concept and Data Indicating Exclusion in Slovenia." *Družboslovne Razprave* 2(22/23).

UN Universal Declaration of Human Rights. 1948. New York: UN.

Van Ginneken, W. 1999. "Social Security for the Informal Sector – A New Challenge for the Developing Countries." *International Social Security Review* 52(1).

Wolfe, A. 1998. *Whose Keeper? Social Science and Moral Obligation.* Berkeley: University of California Press.

CHAPTER 2

Indicators of Social Quality
Outcomes of the European Scientific Network

Laurent van der Maesen and Alan Walker

────◄○►────────────◄○►────────────◄○►────

Social Quality and Quality of Life

In October 2001, the Network Indicators of Social Quality started the process of creating social quality indicators. This project of the European Foundation on Social Quality (now the International Association on Social Quality) was supported by the European Commission (DG Research) under the Fifth Framework Programme (van der Maesen et al. 2000). The Network consisted of representatives of universities from fourteen partner countries and two European NGOs. Over its forty-two-month life, the Network held four meetings. Three plenary meetings were organized with all assistants thanks to the financial support of the Netherlands Organisation for Scientific Research (NWO). Also, through the creation of unique national reference groups on social quality, the Network has engaged more than a hundred scientists and policy makers in its work. The project was completed in April 2005. The intriguing question was how to theoretically legitimize the choice of social quality indicators compared to the indicators constructed in the context of "quality of life" approaches, as developed for example by the Centre for Survey Research and Methodology (ZUMA) of the University of Mannheim (Noll 2000; Berger-Schmit et al. 2000) and the European Foundation for the Improvement of Living and Working Conditions (Eurofound) in Dublin (Fahey et al. 2002).

Contributors to the social quality approach argue that while respect for differences and the openness of the future can be seen as the main themes of the intellectual debate among the social theorists and philosophers, the mainstream of the behavioral sciences has turned its empirical interest to individual perspectives on "quality of life." This can be seen as a way to address the question what "the" quality of life might be from a scientific perspective, trying to avoid political and normative issues. This research has been conducted worldwide and has produced numerous descriptions of "quality of life," as can be gathered from the many thousands of publication titles (cf. the website of the Australian Centre on Quality of Life, of Deakin University). Impressive in quantitative output as the research paradigm appears to be, it shows, overwhelmingly, the many different individual responses to many different questions. These responses do not point in a common direction. More importantly, they presuppose different social and cultural contexts that cannot be methodologically explored in the same research program.

By merely reproducing the enormous diversity of individual perspectives, this paradigm is prevented from articulating a perspective on "social quality" as it takes the perspective of isolated individuals as the ultimate reality (Baars 2005). According to Peter Herrmann, lifestyles, living situations and life circumstances and well-being— essential themes in the quality of life approaches—are highly individualist concepts. This is true even if we acknowledge that they are concerned with the localization of the individual in a social context. The unanswered challenge is that the social is not only assumed but, in addition, indirectly defined as an external entity, not needing a clear definition nor actually being constituted as part of this process (Herrmann 2005). Therefore, both quality of life and social quality are promoted as positive concepts that have the potential to benefit society. While social quality provides a vision for the future, a normative statement about how the social quality of the people of Europe can and should be improved, the quality of life approach aims to measure changes in objective living standards and subjective well-being through a series of social indicators. However, the absence of a theoretical rationale for quality of life tends to undermine its usefulness in the policy world. Thus, the inclusion or exclusion of particular domains may be a matter of common sense or up to the individual researcher or policy maker (Phillips 2006). In other words, the content of any index constructed on the basis of quality of life is always likely to be open to question, and therefore, its role in the policy process may be, at best, contested and, at worst, manipulated to suit particular interests—a deficiency that the ZUMA group has tried top address in its comprehensive framework (Walker et al. 2004).

For the elaboration of social quality indicators, we have to explain some theoretical aspects of the social quality theory, with which to enable its application to policy-making processes. The legitimization of specific "social quality indicators" refers to the theory's applicability to interpret daily circumstances in Europe (its member states, regions and cities) as a consequence of these processes. We will then present some aspects of the methodology as outcomes of the Network's activities for addressing the connection between the theory and policies influencing daily circumstances. Based on this exercise, the Network was able to develop the first-stage indicators of social quality as explored empirically in fourteen countries.

Some Theoretical Questions

The theory of social quality is explained in two main studies up until now. The first work (Beck et al. 1997) paves the way for arguments with which to explain its rationale. The unequal relationship between economic policy and social policy, and the increasing tendency for the former to define the content and scope of the latter, was identified as the main source of the recent crises in European social policy. Another essential thesis of the first study is that a clear understanding of "the social" vanished from social science itself. Over time, the interpretation of the social and the individual developed into a direction that confronts the two as distinct areas, relating as mutually external "faits sociaux" (the Durkheimian approach) and "faits individuals" (the utilitarian approach). Moreover, individuals are seen as the actual core of life, confronted with a society that is a seemingly superior work of power.

The second social quality approach (Beck et al. 2001) tries to oppose such a position, claiming that the individual and the social can fundamentally be grasped as a constitutive entity. By taking such a relational view, we can understand the social—and its quality—as distinct from interactions. This study presents the theoretical design of the social quality approach with which to start the application of the theory in the empirical world. It delivered the starting points for the Network. An important aspect of the theory is that we can distinguish between four conditional factors of social quality (Beck et al. 2001). The challenge is to measure the nature of these factors in EU member states, regions and cities by means of social quality indicators.

The Network started to elaborate the theoretical understanding of these four conditional factors on the basis of both deductive and inductive forms of reasoning with the help of first order explorations in fourteen countries. Their connection enabled the creation of a consensus by the Network's participants about the definitions of the four conditional factors in relation to the theory's interpretation of "the social" (van der Maesen et al. 2005). The theory says that the processes of individuals' self-realization and the formation of collective identities will influence each other. Therefore, there exists between them a constitutive interdependency. This interdependency will happen in the context of two basic tensions, illustrated by the horizontal axis and the vertical axis. The horizontal axis refers to Jürgen Habermas's theory of communicative action (1989: 309), which claimed to go beyond Lockwood's theory about the distinction between system integration and social integration (Lockwood 1999). But the social quality theory does not understand the relationship between both poles of the axis as being antagonistic. Rather, it regards the horizontal axis as the field of interaction between unequal actors. In other words, this axis emphasizes the interaction between people and systems. The horizontal axis is confronted with processes referred to by the vertical axis. They correspond with the theory of Wilhelm Heinz about the tension between societal developments and biographical developments. According to Heinz, modern societies create contingencies for the life course, which force people into flexible responses in the sense of self-reflexive decision making and risk taking. Biographies do not follow predetermined life course patterns anymore (Weyman et al. 1996). We may illustrate both basic tensions below in Figure 2.1.

According to the theory of social quality, the social world is realized in the interaction (and interdependencies) between the self-realization of individual people as social beings and the formation of collective identities that occurs in the context of both basic tensions. We call this the constitution of "the social." Four basic conditions determine the opportunities open for these processes or social relations to develop: people must have the capability to interact (social

Societal development

systems
institutions
organisations

communities
families
networks
groups

Biographical development

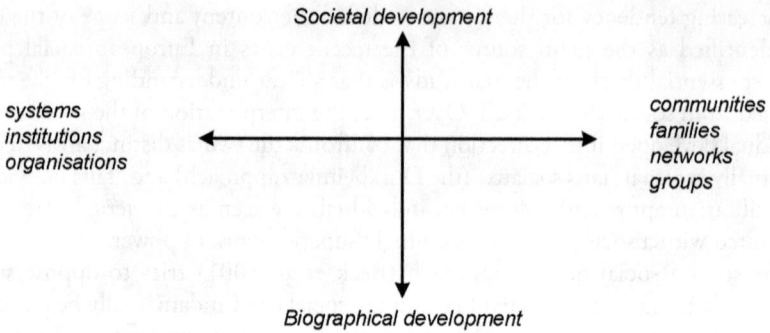

Figure 2.1. Two Basic Tensions as the Context for the Constitutive Interdependency

empowerment), the institutional and structural context must be accessible to them (social inclusion), they must have access to the necessary material and other resources that facilitate interaction (socio-economic security) and the necessary collective accepted values and norms, such as trust, that enable community building (social cohesion). In light of these considerations, social quality is defined as the extent to which people are able to participate in the social and economic life and development of their communities under conditions which enhance their well-being and individual potential. Thanks to this capacity they will contribute to society and the outcomes will influence the conditions for their self-realization. The quadrangle of the conditional factors takes the shape in Figure 2.2.

Based on the second study and collaboration by the participants of the Network to apply their knowledge about the circumstances at the national levels and the European level, they defined precisely the four conditional factors. This iterative process produced the following definitions of the essential aspects of each factor:

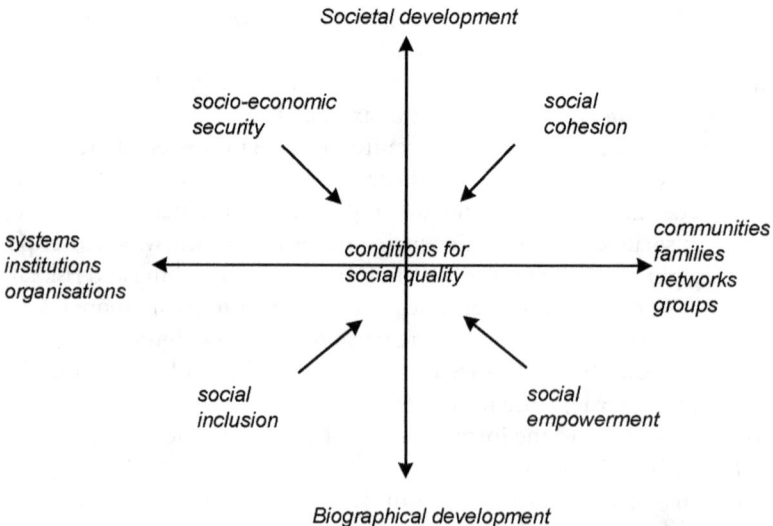

Societal development

socio-economic
security

social
cohesion

systems
institutions
organisations

conditions for
social quality

communities
families
networks
groups

social
inclusion

social
empowerment

Biographical development

Figure 2.2. The Quadrangle of the Conditional Factors for Social Quality

- Socio-economic security is the extent to which people have resources over time.
- Social cohesion is the extent to which social relations, based on identities, values and norms, are shared.
- Social inclusion is the extent to which people have access to and are integrated into the different institutions and social relations that constitute everyday life.
- Social empowerment is the extent to which the personal capabilities of individual people and their ability to act are enhanced by social relations.

Some Policy Issues

As has been said, the Network was focused specifically on the development of indicators by which to measure the four conditional factors determining social quality. The project was intended as an exploratory, path-clearing exercise, and thus its key scientific objectives were to design a preliminary index of social quality, to identify data gaps and requirements, to create the basis for a new yardstick with which to assess the impact of social and economic policies and to develop benchmarks for social quality. Other scientific objectives related to the processes involved in this work, engagement with wider research and policy communities and dissemination. The Network's policy objectives were as follows. It should, first, contribute to public policies—employment, aging, urban development, public health and so on—by exploring the four conditional factors in order to assess more effectively the impact of structural changes on the quality of citizens' daily circumstances. Second, the Network should contribute to such a consistent system of relevant public policy categories that will create a basis to address different policy areas from the same social quality perspective. Third, it will deliver new types of contributions, with help of the outcomes of the first and second objectives, to stimulate the interconnectedness of (1) the Lisbon Strategy, (2) the Social Agenda policies, (3) the development of the Constitution and (4) the enlargement of the EU. This would help to counteract the indefensible neo-functionalistic form of reasoning. Thereby, the Network will contribute to an alternative approach to the social policy classification in terms of three models or regimes that squeeze all member states into different categories. Additionally, the dynamism of European welfare states is downplayed by such broad comparisons, especially the rapid development of the southern and the eastern states and the degree of policy convergence within the European Union. Of course, these objectives are highly interrelated (Beck et al. 1997).

Some Methodological Questions

In addition, the Network had explicit theoretical and policy objectives concerning the creation of a more rational and theoretically grounded basis for policy at national and EU levels. Linking theory to processes of public policies in order to measure their outcomes, we need a specific methodology as an intermediary, as illustrated in Figure 2.3.

An interesting example of a different approach is presented by Tony Atkinson and his colleagues in their study about indicators of social inclusion. This group assumes,

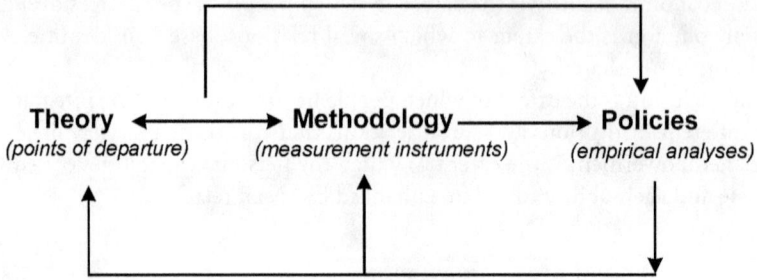

Figure 2.3. Relationship between Theory, Methodology and Policies

first, that thanks to ZUMA, a very clear account is provided of the relation between concepts of quality of life, social cohesion, social capital and social exclusion. They argue as follows:

> In seeking to establish analytical foundations, one can draw on academic research in statistics, sociology, social policy, geography, welfare economics, and political science. …We do not attempt to provide a thorough grounding for the terms "social exclusion" or "social inclusion"—even though the latter appears in our title. These terms are employed in a wide variety of different ways. While this part of their (political) appeal, it can undermine their value in an analytical context. … However, in line with our pragmatic objective of contributing to the policy-making process, we simply accept here the use of the terms as shorthand for a range of concerns considered to be important in setting the European social agenda. (Atkinson et al. 2002)

This group explicitly did not define the concept of social inclusion and proposed a pragmatic approach, aiming at the description of life situations. In other words, they did not reflect the connection between theory, methodology and policy research, and therefore their methodology did not aim at going beyond descriptive explorations. The absence of the definition of social inclusion prevents an understanding of "indicators of social inclusion" and the application of these indicators for analyzing policy outcomes. What is missing is a connection with a theory of social inclusion. Thus, it is unclear what social inclusion means in the field of policy making and what the outcomes of social inclusion policies can be in the daily circumstances of people. In fact, they did not accept the logical connections illustrated in Figure 2.3. Recent work of this group shows the shortcomings of this approach. They highlight the necessity of defining the political aims of social inclusion policies according to which they want to frame an elaborated empirical description. However, this requires a theory of social inclusion and a related methodology (Atkinson et al. 2005).

The measurement tools of the conditional factors are indicators. As has been said, the Network's challenge was to develop a robust set of these indicators. A condition was to clarify and to elaborate the social quality theory. This was done by applying deductive and inductive approaches that increased substantially the understanding of the nature of the four conditional factors (Beck et al. 2001). Thanks to four plenary sessions of the Network's participants and three plenary sessions of their assistants, all those engaged could reach an agreement on the final definition of the four conditional

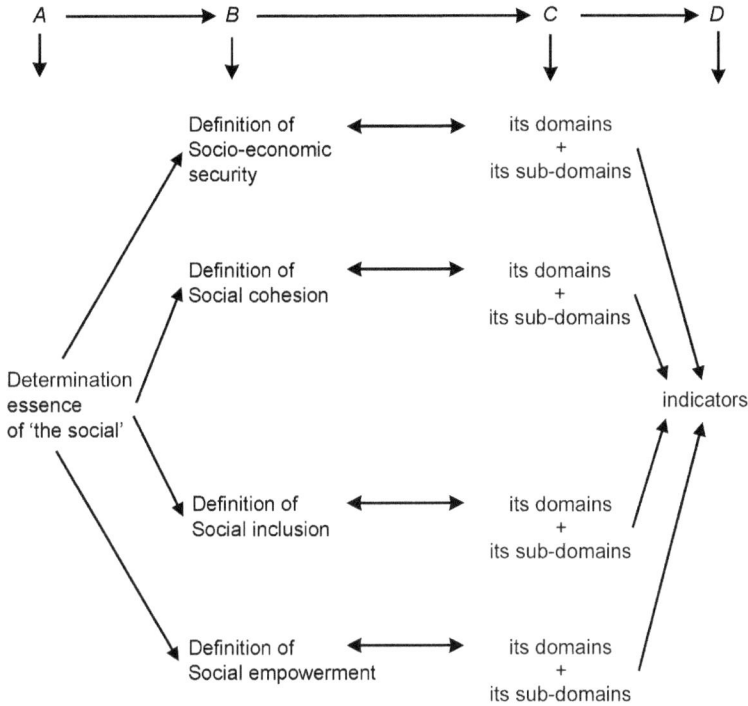

Figure 2.4. The Network's Analytical Schedule

factors and elaborated their domains and sub-domains. This delivered the consensus necessary for the development of indicators for all sub-domains that are relevant to understand of the nature of the conditional factor in question. The steps the Network followed are illustrated in Figure 2.4.

By following the steps from A to D, the basis has been created for a new approach to measuring the quality of the social context of everyday life and to assessing the impact thereon of social and economic developments and policies. The painstaking process involved in creating these indicators is described in the Final Report (van der Maesen et al. 2005). The list was not plucked from thin air, but rather each proposed indicator was chosen iteratively according to its relationship with the core theory of social quality. This is not to suggest that the indicators are unique to social quality. What is unique is the process of deriving them and, of course, the social quality framework itself.

First of all, it redefined and analyzed the four conditional factors separately in relationship to the ontologically based ideas about "the social": this regards the step from A to B. Second, the Network derived the domains from the new precise definitions of the conditional factors: it regards the step from B to C. This was a decisive one for the determination of the indicators of the four conditional factors. The outcomes are shown in Figure 2.5. Third, the Network determined the nature of the related sub-domains in order to formulate the indicators of these sub-domains and, therefore, of the conditional factors compromising these sub-domains: this

Socio-economic Security	**Social cohesion**
Financial resources	Trust
Housing and the environment	Other integrative norms and values
Health and care	Social networks
Work	Identity
Education	
Social Inclusion	**Social Empowerment**
Citizenship rights	Knowledge base
Labour market	Labour market
Services (public and private)	Openness and Supportiveness
Social networks	of Institutions
	Personal relations

Figure 2.5. Domains of Social Quality

regards the step from C to D. The final outcomes are presented in the following section.

Indicators of Social Quality

The Network was able to reach a consensus about the indicators of the sub-domains of social quality in the middle of 2003. The outcomes were discussed later by extensive e-mail communication. Finally, the Network could start the exploration of these indicators in fourteen countries in order to test their applicability and for the assessment of data availability. The question is, first, if the indicators really measure essential aspects of the sub-domains and, second, whether there are data in the member states with which to measure these aspects. In the Network's Final Report, both questions are addressed. In this section we will present the final list of the social indicators as developed by the Network (see Tables 2.1 to 2.4).

Conclusion

As well as the joint efforts toward the creation of indicators of social quality, each national partner in the Network undertook an analysis of the trends affecting social quality. Here we conclude by emphasizing the policy dimension of the Network's research and outlining the next steps.

Recent years have seen a huge expansion in the statistical data available to policy makers and the general public in Europe, including statistical digests from Eurostat, DG Employment's Social Situation report and the Quality of Life in Europe series from Eurofound. While this expansion of information indicates a positive step, as such information is part of the lifeblood of democracy, it has a paradoxical dimension. As vital as statistical data is to both policy making and political participation, it tends to reinforce

Table 2.1. Indicators of Socio-economic Security (Keizer et al. 2003)

Domains	Sub-domains	Indicators
Financial resources	Income sufficiency	Part of household income spent on health, clothing, food, and housing (in lower and median household incomes).
	Income security	How certain biographical events affect risk of poverty on household level.
		Proportion of total population living in households receiving entitlement transfers (means-tested, cash and in-kind transfers) that allow them to live above EU poverty level.
Housing and environment	Housing security	Proportion of people who have certainty of keeping their home.
		Proportion of hidden families (i.e., several families within the same household).
	Housing conditions	Number of square meters per household member.
		Proportion of population living in houses with lack of functioning basic amenities (water, sanitation and energy).
	Environmental conditions (social and natural)	People affected by criminal offenses per 10,000 inhabitants.
		Proportion living in households situated in neighborhoods with above average pollution rate (water, air and noise).
Health and care	Security of health provisions	Proportion of people covered by compulsory/voluntary health insurance (including qualitative exploration of what is and is is not covered by insurance system).
	Health services	Number of medical doctors per 10,000 inhabitants.
		Average distance to hospital, measured in minutes.
		Average response time of medical ambulance.
	Care services	Average number of hours spent on care differentiated by paid and unpaid.
Work	Employment security	Length of notice before employer can terminate or change terms and conditions of labor relation/contract.
		Proportion employed workforce with temporary job contract.
		Proportion of workforce that is illegal.
	Working conditions	Number of employees who reduced work time because of interruption (parental leave, medical assistance of relative, palliative leave) as proportion of employees entitled to these kinds of work time reductions.
		Number of accidents (fatal/non-fatal) at work per 100,000 employed persons (if possible: per sector)
		Number of hours a full-time employee typically works a week (actual working week).
Education	Security of education	Proportion of pupils leaving education without finishing compulsory education (early school leavers).
		Study fees as proportion of national mean net wage.
	Quality of education	Proportion of students who, within a year of leaving school with or without certificate, are able to find employment.

Table 2.2. Indicators of Social Cohesion (Berman et al. 2004)

Domains	Sub-domains	Indicators
Trust	Generalized	Extent to which "most people can be trusted."
	Specific	Trust in: government, elected representatives, political parties, armed forces, legal system, media, trade unions, police, religious institutions, civil service, economic transactions.
		Number of cases being referred to European Court of Justice.
		Importance of: family, friends, leisure, politics, respecting parents, parents' duty to children.
Other integrative norms and values	Altruism	Volunteering: number of hours per week.
		Blood donation.
	Tolerance	Views on immigration, pluralism and multiculturalism
		Tolerance of other people's self-identity, beliefs, behavior and lifestyle preferences.
	Social contract	Beliefs on causes of poverty: individual or structural.
		Willingness to pay more taxes if you were sure it would improve the situation of the poor.
		Intergenerational: willingness to pay 1 percent more taxes to improve the situation of elderly people in your country.
		Willingness to do something practical for people in community (e.g., picking up litter, shopping for elderly/disabled/sick people, assisting neighbors with filling out fax/municipal forms, cleaning the street/porch/doorway.
		Division of household tasks between men and women (do you have an understanding with spouse about division of household tasks, raising children and gaining household income?
Social networks	Networks	Membership (active or inactive) of political, voluntary, charitable organizations or sport clubs.
		Support received from family, neighbors and friends.
		Frequency of contact with friends and colleagues.
Identity	National/ European identity	Sense of national pride.
		Identification with national and European symbols.
	Regional/ community/local identity	Sense of regional/community/local identity.
	Interpersonal identity	Sense of belonging to family and kinship network.

Table 2.3. Indicators of Social Inclusion (Walker et al. 2003)

Domains	Sub-domains	Indicators
Citizenship rights	Constitutional/ political rights	Proportion of residents with citizenship. Proportion having right to vote in local elections and proportion exercising it.
	Social right	Proportion with right to public pension (i.e., pension organized or regulated by government). Women's pay as proportion of men's.
	Civil rights	Proportion with right to free legal advice. Proportion experiencing discrimination.
	Economic and political networks	Proportion of ethnic minority groups and women elected or appointed to parliament, boards of private companies and foundations.
Labor market	Access to paid employment	Long-term unemployment (12+ months). Involuntary part-time or temporary employment.
Services	Health services	Proportions with entitlement to and using public primary health care.
	Housing	Proportion homeless, sleeping rough. Average waiting time for social housing.
	Education	School and higher education participation rates.
	Social care	Proportion of people in need receiving care services. Average waiting time for care services (including child care).
	Financial services	Proportion denied credit differentiated by income groups. Access to financial assistance/advice in case of need.
	Transport	Proportion of population with access to public transport system. Density of public transport system and road density.
	Civic/cultural services	Number of public sport facilities per 10,000 inhabitants. Number of public and private civic and cultural facilities (e.g., cinema, theater, concerts) per 10,000 inhabitants.
Social networks	Neighborhood participation	Proportion in regular contact with neighbors.
	Friendships	Proportion in regular contact with friends.
	Family life	Proportion feeling lonely/isolated. Duration of contact with relatives (cohabiting and non-cohabiting). Informal (non-monetary) assistance received by different types of family.

Table 2.4. Indicators of Social Empowerment (Herrmann 2003)

Domains	Sub-domains	Indicators
Knowledge base	Application of knowledge	Extent to which social mobility is knowledge-based (formal qualifications).
	Availability of information	Percent of population literate and numerate.
		Availability of free media.
		Access to Internet.
	User friendliness of information	Provision of information in multiple languages on social services.
		Availability of free advocacy, advice and guidance centers.
Labor market	Control over employment contract	Percent of labor force that are members of a trades union (differentiated to public and private employees).
		Percent of labor force covered by collective agreement (differentiated by public and private employees).
	Prospects of job mobility	Percent of employed labor force receiving work-based training.
		Percent of labor force availing of publicly provided training (not only skills based). (Outline costs of such training if any.)
		Percent of labor force participating in any "back to work" scheme.
	Reconciliation of work and family life	Percent of organizations operating work/life balance policies
		Percent of employed labor force actually making use of work/life balance measures (see indicator above).
Openness and support of institutions	Of political system	Existence of processes of consultation and direct democracy (e.g., referenda).
	Of economic system	Number of instances of public involvement in major economic decision making (e.g., public hearings about company relocation, inward investment and plant closure).
	Of organizations	Percent of organizations/institutions with work councils.
Public space	Support for collective action	Percent of national and local public budget reserved for voluntary, not-for-profit citizenship initiatives.
		Marches/demonstrations banned in past 12 months as proportion of total marches/demonstrations (held and banned).
	Cultural enrichment	Proportion of local and national budget allocated to all cultural activities.
		Number of self-organized cultural groups and events.
		Proportion of people experiencing different forms of personal enrichment on regular basis.
Personal relationships	Services supporting physical/social independence	Percentage of national and local budgets devoted to disabled people (physically and mentally).
	Personal support services	Level of pre- and post-school child care.
	Support for social	Extent of inclusiveness of housing and environmental design (e.g., meeting places, lighting, interaction layout).

policy fragmentation, which makes it difficult for policy makers to tackle problems in a holistic way and for citizens to comprehend what is happening to society.

As previously noted, a key aim of social quality is to overcome the present fragmentation of policy, for example, at the EU level, between social policies, economic policies and employment policies. This is where the social quality concept comes in. By creating a coherent, theoretically grounded concept that embraces not only all policies but also all stages of the policy process, it is intended to furnish both policy makers and the general public with an analytical tool with which to understand society and to change it. For example, while the ranking of countries (out of ten) for the quality of their health services in the Eurofound report—from 8.1 for Austria to 3.7 for Slovenia—is informative, it is not apparent how it should be used in the policy process (Eurofound 2004). A similar ranking derived from the social quality concept would point directly to policy domains in socio-economic security, social inclusion and social empowerment and the connections between them.

This is precisely why the activities of the Network on Social Quality Indicators is such an important first step in realizing a practical measure of social quality. As outlined above, the Network has so far identified a draft list of ninety-five indicators linked to eighteen domains and forty-nine sub-domains. Obviously, this is too unwieldy in its present form, so the next stage of work on social quality indicators, therefore, will comprise the refinement and reduction of this list and its testing in a representative survey. Parallel methodological work will be conducted on the subjective dimensions of social quality and on the combination of these with the indicators of the conditional factors. These next steps are dependent on European research funding. Meanwhile, we welcome contributions to the refinement of the indicator list presented here.

Laurent van der Maesen is Director of the International Association on Social Quality (previously the European Foundation on Social Quality) dedicated to the study and development of the social quality theory and approach, and member of the *International Journal of Social Quality* editorial board. The IASQ participated in the The Hague Demonstration Project in Laak and an EU-China project on environmental citizenship participation. Van der Maesen coordinated the European Network on Indicators of Social Quality. Before, he worked as head of the department of health, social care and well-being at SISWO, a Dutch social science coordinating institute.

Alan Walker, CBE, is Professor of Social Policy and Social Gerontology at the University of Sheffield. He is currently Director of the New Dynamics of Ageing funded by five United Kingdom research councils, Mobilising the Potential of Active Ageing in Europe and Social Innovations for an Ageing Population funded by the European Union. Previously, he directed the European Research Area in Ageing. In the 1990s, with Wolfgang Beck and Laurent van der Maesen, he originated the concept of social quality and established the European Foundation on Social Quality.

References

Atkinson, T., B. Cantillon, E. Marliers and B. Nolan. 2002. *Social Indicators: The EU and Social Inclusion*. Oxford: Oxford University Press.

Atkinson, T., B. Cantillon, E. Marliers and B. Nolan. 2005. *Taking Forward the EU Social Inclusion Process: An Independent Report Commissioned by the Luxembourg Presidency of the Council of the European Union*. Luxembourg: Ministère de la Famille et de l'integration.

Baars, J. 2005. Research Proposal to the Netherlands Organisation for Scientific Research (NWO): The Social Constitution of Social Quality as Morality – A Social Philosophical Reflection. Utrecht and Amsterdam: University of Humanistics and EFSQ.

Beck, W., L. van der Maesen and A. Walker, eds. 1997. *The Social Quality of Europe*. The Hague: Kluwer International.

Beck, W., L. van der Maesen, F. Thomése and A. Walker, eds. 2001. *Social Quality: A Vision for Europe*. The Hague: Kluwer International.

Berger-Schmitt, R. and H.H. Noll. 2000. *Conceptual Framework and Structure of a European System of Social Indicators*. EuReporting Working Paper no.9. Mannheim: Centre for Survey Research and Methodology (ZUMA).

Berman, Y. and D. Phillips. 2004. *Social Quality and the Conditional Factor of Social Cohesion*, 3rd draft.

European Foundation for the Improvement of Living and Working Conditions (Eurofound). 2004. *Quality of Life in Europe*. Dublin: Eurofound.

Fahey, T., B. Nolan and C.T. Whelan. 2002. *A Proposal for the Future Activities on Living Conditions and Quality of Life*. Dublin: Eurofound.

Habermas, J. 1989. *Theory of Communicative Action, Vol. 2: Lifeworld and System: A Critique of Functionalist Reason*. Oxford: Blackwell.

Herrmann, P. 2003. *Social Quality and the Conditional Factor of Social Empowerment*, 3rd draft. Amsterdam: European Foundation on Social Quality (EFSQ).

Herrmann, P. 2005. "Social Quality: Opening Individual Well-Being for a Social Perspective." Presentation on the Annual Conference of the Social Policy Association, June 2005 in Bath. Cork: University of Cork.

Keizer, M. and L. van der Maesen. 2003. *Social Quality and the Conditional Factor of Socio-Economic Security*, 3rd draft. Working paper. Amsterdam: EFSQ.

Lockwood, D. 1999. "Civic Integration and Social Cohesion" in *Capitalism and Social Cohesion: Essays on Exclusion and Integration*, eds. I. Gough and G. Olofsson. London: Macmillan.

Maesen, L. van der, A. Walker and W. Beck. 2000. *Report: Indicators of Social Quality: Proposal to DG-Research of the European Commission*. Amsterdam: EFSQ.

Maesen, L. van der, A. Walker and M. Keizer. 2005. *European Network Indicators Social Quality: Final Report*. Amsterdam: EFSQ.

Noll, H.H. 2000. *The European System of Social Indicators: An Instrument for Social Monitoring and Reporting*. Mannheim: ZUMA.

Phillips, D. 2006. *Quality of Life: Concept, Policy and Practice*. London: Routledge.

Walker, A. and L. van der Maesen. 2004. "Social Quality and Quality of Life" pp. 13–31 in *Challenges for Quality of Life in the Contemporary World*, eds. W. Glatzer, S. von Below and M. Stoffregen. The Hague, London and Boston: Kluwer Academic Publishers.

Walker, A. and A. Wigfield. 2003. *Social Quality and the Conditional Factor of Social Inclusion*, 3rd draft. Amsterdam: EFSQ.

Weyman, A. and W.R. Heinz, eds. 1996. *Society and Biography: Interrelationships between Social Structure, Institutions and the Life Course*. Weinheimn: Deutscher Studien Verlag.

CHAPTER 3

Social Quality and Welfare System Sustainability

Alan Walker

Introduction

The dominant global discourse on welfare system sustainability has, for too long, been trapped in a very narrow economistic perspective that prioritizes costs over needs and outcomes. The main intention of this chapter is to contribute to an understanding of, and transformation in, the political economy of welfare system sustainability in both the East and the West. Employing the concept of social quality, it attempts to shift the focus of "sustainability" toward its social dimensions and encourage a more balanced approach than the present one. A necessary starting point is the concept of social quality itself: what it consists of and how it was derived. The idea is a European one in origin and is not yet very familiar in Asia and other regions. In Asian and other less developed countries, the concept of human security is used quite widely in social policy and development circles; therefore it is sensible to compare it with social quality. The main part of the chapter then concentrates on welfare system sustainability and, in particular, the present global discourse that is driven by narrow economism. This leads onto the consideration of a possible new approach to sustainability, based on the concept of social quality, which may be applied far beyond national welfare systems. Instead of emphasizing only economic growth and its trade-offs, a social quality perspective encourages a more balanced approach that encompasses the social and ecological dimensions as well as the economic one.

Social Quality

The concept of social quality was developed in the 1990s as a response to the increasingly overt conflict between the economic and social dimensions of the European Union (EU) that threatened to undermine the western European social model. The originators of the concept sought a new balance between economic and social development in Europe and the term "social quality" captured the sense of achievement on the part of many of the EU's welfare regimes but also the idea of a mission unfinished. Thus, social quality was originally proposed as a standard by which to measure the quality of citizens' daily lives. It differs substantially, however, from the more familiar idea of quality of life because its outcome conditions and their specific indicators are derived from a theoretical model of social relations (Walker and van der Maesen 2004).

The essence of the idea of social quality is the social nature of human beings. This is reflected in the definition:

> the extent to which people are able to participate in the social, economic and cultural life of their communities under conditions which enhance their well-being and individual potential. (Beck et al. 1997: 3)

Although the definition emphasizes individual well-being and potential, it means that these are derived from social engagement or participation. Thus, the focus is on the extent to which the quality of social relations promotes both participation in social development and individual human growth and development. In other words, there is no individual well-being and development without social relations. Starting from the assumption that people are essentially social beings, rather than atomized economic agents, it is argued that self-realization depends on social recognition. In other words, a person's self-realization is derived from their interaction with others in a world of collective identities (families, communities, companies, institutions). Thus, there is interdependency between processes of self-realization and those of collective identity formation. Of course, to participate in these processes, people must have the capacity for self-reflection and the collective identities they interact with must be open. It is here, in these interdependent processes, that the "social" is located. The field in which these interdependent processes take place is that represented by the interaction of two critical tensions, as illustrated by the two axes in Figure 3.1: the horizontal tension between the formal world of systems and the informal life-worlds of families, groups and communities; and the vertical tension between societal development and biographical development.

Three sets of factors play the key roles in the creation of social quality. It is, first of all, the factors as outcome of processes of self-realization, strongly influenced by the interplay of processes concerning the formation of a diversity of collective identities across two main tensions. These result in the constitution of competent social actors. Therefore, the first set of factors is called constitutional factors: personal (human) security, concerning the institutionalization of the rule of law; social recognition, concerning interpersonal respect between members of the community; social responsiveness, concerning the openness of groups, communities and systems; and personal (human) capacity, concerning the individual's physical and/or mental ability

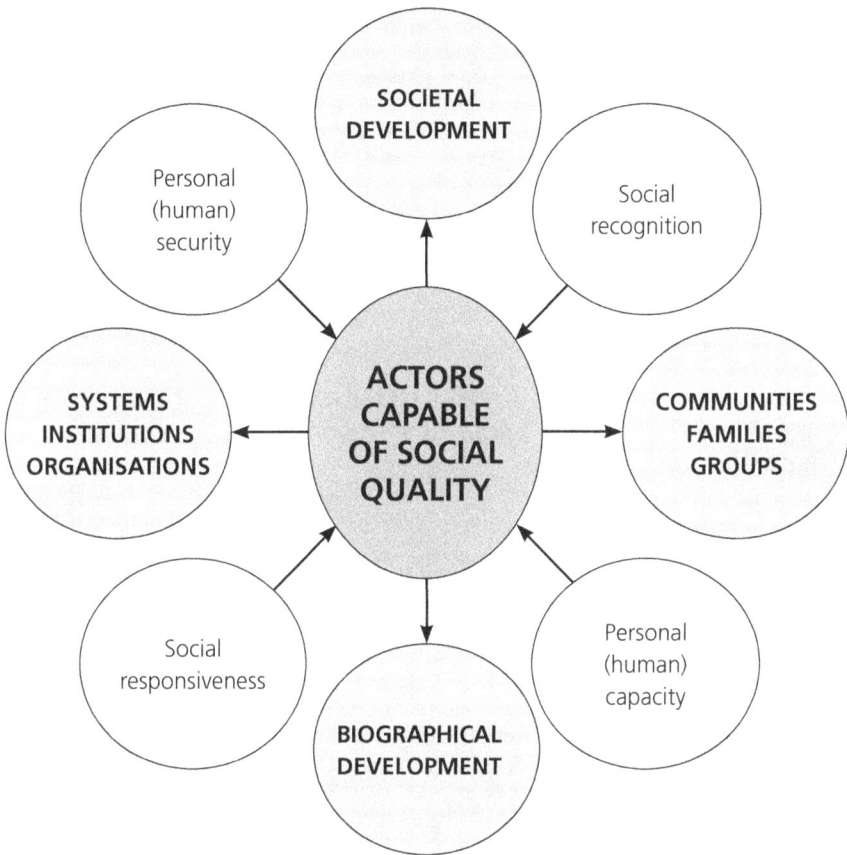

Figure 3.1. The Quadrangle of the Constitutional Factors

to engage socially. Each factor is mainly influenced by two aspects of the interaction between the two main tensions and is, therefore, especially situated in one part of the quadrangle of the constitutional factors shown in Figure 3.1 (Beck et al. 2001).

Once competent actors are constituted, the opportunities for and outcomes of social quality are determined, by four conditional factors (Figure 3.2): first, people have to access socio-economic security in order to protect them from poverty and other forms of material deprivation. In a European context, socio-economic security requires good quality paid employment and social protection to guarantee living standards and access to resources: income, education, health care, social services, environment, public health, personal safety and so on. It also relies on environmental or ecological security. Different societies and different stages of development will witness a variety of combinations of actors—state, market, family and civil society—in the production of welfare.

Second, people have to experience social inclusion in, or minimum levels of social exclusion from, key social and economic institutions such as the labor market. Social

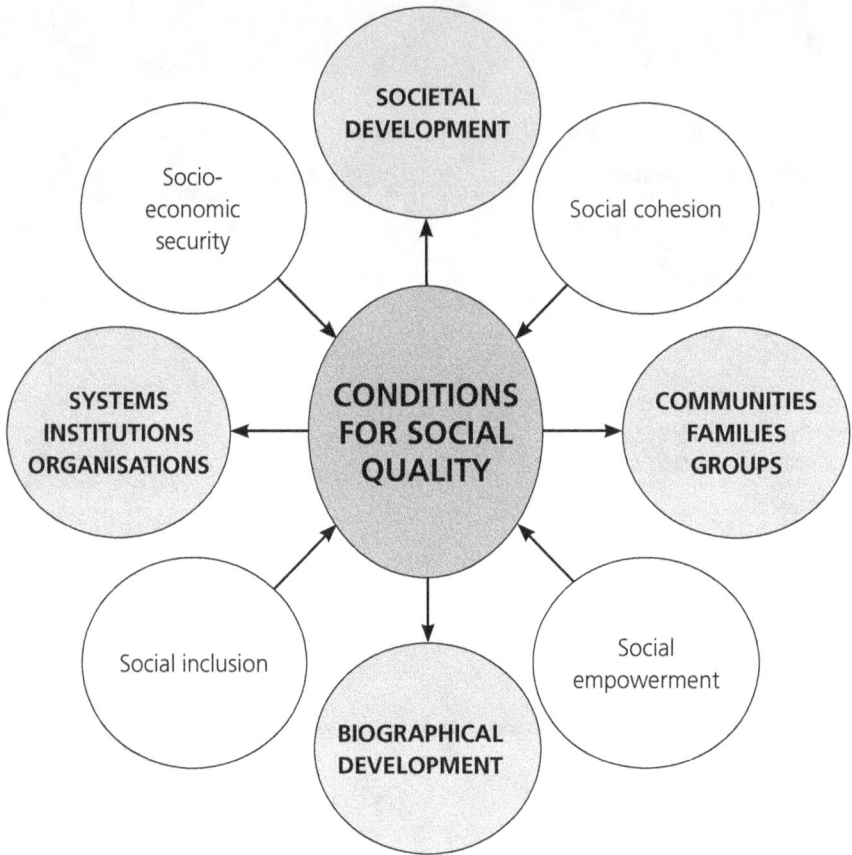

Figure 3.2. The Quadrangle of the Conditional Factors

inclusion concerns citizenship. This may be a wide and all-embracing national or regional citizenship, or it may be "exclusive," with large numbers of outcasts and quasi-citizens (denied citizenship completely or partially by means of discrimination).

Third, people should be able to live in communities and societies characterized by social cohesion. Social cohesion refers to the "social glue" that holds together communities and societies. It is vital for both social development and individual self-realization. The contemporary discussion of cohesion often centers on the narrow popular concept of social capital, but its legacy stretches back, via Durkheim, to solidarity, shared norms and values.

Fourth, people must be to some extent autonomous and socially empowered in order to be able to fully participate in the face of rapid socio-economic change. Social empowerment means enabling citizens to control their own lives and to take advantage of opportunities. It means increasing the range of human choice. Therefore, it goes far beyond participation in the political system to focus on the individual's potential capacities (knowledge, skills, experience and so on) and how far these can be realized.

It is "social" because this realization is via relationships. Each factor is an outcome of processes concerning the formation of a diversity of collective identities, strongly influenced by the interplay of processes of self-realization across two main tensions, and is, therefore, also situated in one part of the quadrangle of the conditional factors (Beck et al. 2001).

Third, a set of normative factors are used to make judgments about the appropriate or necessary degree of social quality, based on the linking of the constitutional and conditional factors at a specific place and a specific time. The normative factors are social justice, in relation to socio-economic security; solidarity, connected to social cohesion; equal value, as a criterion in relation to social inclusion; and human dignity, in relation to social empowerment. The connection of biographical development and the genesis of groups, families and communities—the interplay between actions toward self-realization and those leading to the formation of collective identities—inevitability influences the nature of both the constitutional factors and the conditional ones.

Thus, methodologically, it is feasible to examine the interplay between these processes in order to explain changes in them over time, in the same way that analytical dualism assumes that structures and agents are, at least temporarily, distinguishable (Archer 1995: 66). These dynamic interactions lead to the emergence of new relationships, social structures and, therefore, new expressions of the social. Thus, the two quadrangles (Figures 3.1 and 3.2) are not in practice separate but mutually interact to construct the dynamic nature of the social. For example, we may hypothesize a critical relationship between personal (human) capacity at the individual level and the possibilities presented by social empowerment at the social one.

An overview of the three sets of factors—the social quality architecture—shows the three dimensions and their connectivities (Figure 3.3). In terms of measurement, the European focus has been on the conditional factors, the hardware of social quality. This is not surprising because these represent the outcomes of the processes involved rather than measuring the processes per se. In line with welfare regime theory, we hypothesize that there are different "social quality regimes" depending on variations in the interactions between the constitutional and conditional factors, together with their normative context, and the various sources of quality in conditional factor outcomes in different societies (Esping-Andersen 1990, 1999; Lewis 1992).

Figure 3.3. The Social Quality Architecture

Constitutional Factors	Conditional Factors	Normative Factors
Personal (human) security	Socio-economic security	Social justice
Social recognition	Social inclusion	Equal value
Social responsiveness	Social cohesion	Solidarity
Personal (human) capacity	Social empowerment	Human dignity

Social Quality and Human Security

The concept of social quality did not spring up instantly: it was the product of a long tradition of socio-political and political economic thinking. Among the immediate impetuses was a lack of clear conceptual thinking about the goals of social policy and social development, such as reductions in social exclusion or increases in social cohesion. The introduction of new terminology such as "social capital" only added to the confusion: the absence of a coherent methodology by which to integrate the various goals of and key actors in social change; the increase in the long-term subordination of social policy to economic policy (a mirror image of the relationship between economic and social development); and the political assault on the European social welfare systems inspired by neo-liberalism.

While social quality does not pretend to be the only concept by which social progress may be measured, it is unique in the combination of these driving factors behind its evolution. It is also one of the few concepts, probably the only one, that offers a framework in which to understand as well as measure the quality of society. It is unusual too in providing a comprehensive methodology as well as a set of measuring tools. The main competitor to the social quality approach in the West is the notion of quality of life, but, as has been demonstrated elsewhere, this notion is too flexible and amorphous to be of much value in either social policy or comparative research (Walker and van der Maesen 2004). In the East, and especially in development policy and practice, the idea of human development and security has a high value, and joint work with colleagues at the Institute for Social Studies in the Netherlands has indicated the synergies between the two concepts and the potential for cross-over (Gasper et al. 2008). In particular they share:

- a human focus on the well-being of people, rather than a primary focus on the economy, the sphere of monetary values.
- an explicit normative basis, beyond values expressed only through wants or demands backed by purchasing power in markets.
- a strong multidimensionality in their conception of human well-being, rather than a reduction for a single denominator of money or "utility."
- a holistic analytical approach, which leads to concerns about interconnections that can cut across boundaries and threaten sustainability.
- a dissatisfaction with the nineteenth-century pattern of disciplinary and professional divisions.
- an underlying preoccupation with relationality: an open or implicit recognition that every person is a nexus of relations that are mutually constitutive (Gasper et al. 2008: 25–26).

This identification of mutuality is not intended to skate over their very different origins and orientations: social quality from within the EU, based on long established welfare systems and ideas about what constitutes "the good society," and human development and security from a contrasting environment of far less developed societies where the primary focus is on critical threats and risks of life-destroying crises. The social quality approach also is avowedly preoccupied with the social while human development and security focuses on the human (Gasper et al. 2008: 26). The challenge for the social quality approach is to employ the insights of human security in adapting itself to non-Western, including less developed societies. For its part, the human development and security approach needs to take on board some of the social orientation identified with social quality. This represents a significant future challenge for the application of social quality to less developed societies. The remainder of this chapter focuses on sustainability.

Sustainability: The Missing Dimension

Sustainability has been a term associated with development since the Brutland Commission twenty years ago. In that field it is now commonly perceived in terms of three pillars—environmental/ecological, economic and social—and this tripartite approach has been accepted widely, including by international governmental organizations (IGOs) (OECD 2001; EC 2000). In practice, however, it is the ecological and economic and the trade-offs between them that dominate discussions of sustainability. As a result of its subordinate position, the social dimension remains undefined (Lehtonen 2004). The main contender to fill this void has been the concept of social capital (Bourdieu 1986; Coleman 1988; Putnam 2000), itself a quasi-economic term and one which may be criticized on various grounds (Phillips 2006). As will be discussed later, social quality offers a more holistic basis on which to consider sustainable development.

The application of sustainability to the welfare field is almost exclusively in economic terms, although there have been some attempts to integrate questions concerning environmental sustainability into social policy (Cahill and Fitzpatrick 2002; Fitzpatrick and Cahill 2002). The fact that the sustainability of welfare systems has become a global issue and that this is constructed in very narrow economic terms must be attributed, at least to some extent, to the influence of the IGOs in the economic and financial fields, which are the institutions of globalism (Deacon et al. 1997), the OECD, World Bank, IMF and WTO. As with globalization itself, these institutions have played important roles in framing the discourse on sustainability (Stone 2004) as well as in the application of one-dimensional policy prescriptions, for example, in the Eurasian transition countries and Latin America (World Bank 1994).

These two critical dimensions of the policy work of the IGOs are founded within the same economic paradigm: the Transatlantic Consensus on globalization. This "consensus" holds uncritically that free markets and trade liberalization are the only ways to promote growth and raise living standards globally. It is a neo-liberal position in that it idealizes the market and seeks to minimize the role of the state. Again it is impervious to evidence, such as the failure of these policy prescriptions at national level, for example, in the United Kingdom, and in the ex-Communist bloc states of Central and Eastern Europe. How has this global discourse influenced welfare policy in the EU and East Asia?

Welfare Sustainability in Europe

As far as the EU is concerned, the issue of sustainability first emerged very recently and only in its economic and ecological forms. There have been a large number of social protection system reforms, especially with regard to pensions because it is there that questions of economic and welfare system sustainability are posed most sharply. However, these are mostly parametric reforms with the main exceptions being the liberal welfare regimes and the transitional ones of Central and Eastern Europe. Moreover, there is a powerful scientific consensus that globalization per se has played no direct role in these reforms (Leibfried and Reiger 1998; Pierson 2000; Soderstein 2004; Vobruba 2004). In practice, therefore, reform and retrenchment have been mainly matters of national policy preferences rather than necessities created by globalization. We must not underestimate, however, neither the power of the IGOs in shaping the global discourse within which national policy makers act nor their more direct roles as experts and advisers to governments (Deacon 2000; Stone 2004). Certainly globalization and sustainability have figured centrally in the legitimization of welfare reforms.

The EU itself plays a pivotal role in framing the European debate on welfare sustainability. At the moment we can discern two potentially conflicting tendencies. On the one hand there is an uncritical acceptance of the neo-liberal Transatlantic Consensus on globalization (Walker 2005). This is reflected starkly in the "Lisbon priority" set out in 2000 "to become the most competitive and dynamic knowledge-based economy in the world capable of sustainable economic growth with more and better jobs and greater social cohesion" (European Council 2000: 2) and recently reinforced by the 2020 strategy. This approach is translated into the welfare field in the form of a productivist approach to social policy (European Commission 2001). The idea of social policy as a productive factor bears more than passing similarity to the welfare orientation in some East Asian countries, such as Japan. On the other hand there are opposing tendencies, although whether they are recognized as such by the main players is not possible to say. At the very least they are suggestive of some ambivalence within the EU toward the Transatlantic Consensus. Examples include the emphasis on the function of economic growth, the inclusion of references to social quality in the EU's first Social Policy Agenda (European Commission 2000) and the approach adopted toward the long-term sustainability of Europe's pension systems. This suggests that economic or financial sustainability is one part of a much more comprehensive interpretation of sustainability, which includes key social items such as living standards, intergenerational solidarity, gender equality and governance. Specifically, the European Council has set out three broad principles for securing pension system sustainability: safeguarding the capacity of systems to meet their social objectives (adequacy), maintaining their financial sustainability (financial sustainability) and meeting changing societal needs (modernization) (European Commission 2002).

As far as the EU is concerned, therefore, there are no indications, as yet, of a mass transition from the variety of existing welfare regimes toward a residual neo-liberal one. In fact, what restructuring that has taken place so far under banners such as "modernization" and "activation" have not undermined the institutional design and core principles of the European welfare states. There are no signs, in other words, of a significant shift on the welfare state/welfare society continuum. This is definitely not to say that the Western European social model is immune from radical change in the future: there are obvious risks to it in the dominant role being played by neo-liberal ideas and policy prescriptions in the current debates about globalization and sustainability; the key place of the UK in recent years as the brand leader in welfare modernization and production-orientated social policy (Cox 1998); and the growing influence of the former Communist-bloc countries that underwent a neo-liberal transformation under the guiding hands of the IMF and World Bank, which are now members of the EU (Ferge 2002; Juhasz 2006). The first wave of policies from the Coalition Government, elected in the UK in 2010, suggest a distinct shift toward residualization (Yeates et al. 2011).

Welfare Sustainability in East Asia

Welfare sustainability is not a new concept to East Asia, and there too the focus has been primarily economic. Reflecting the nature of this region's welfare regimes and their path dependency, the discourse is often shaped in terms of welfare societies rather than welfare states. In practice, however, there is a wide range of policy responses. Most of the welfare regimes (excluding China) are of a liberal kind, albeit with Bismarckian tendencies in Japan, Korea and Taiwan (Ahn and Lee 2005; Takegawa 2005). The Asian financial crisis and the neo-liberal globalization prescriptions that followed it have had a direct impact on welfare in the region. Not surprisingly, liberal welfare regimes have taken readily to neo-liberal policy prescriptions. Reforms to ensure pension system sustainability range from minor changes in social insurance contribution rates and pension ages in Korea to the replacement of a defined benefit pension system with a defined contribution one in Taiwan (Goodman et al. 1998). In contrast, China has recently undertaken a progressive expansion of its pension system, and there is a crucial debate about the choice between universalism and selectivity in social protection.

In sum, in both the EU and East Asia, the current political discourses on welfare sustainability reflect their different social models and the historical paths of development behind them (Walker and Wong 2005). But there are similarities too, not surprisingly given the global power of neo-liberalism and the influential role played by the IGOs in both regions. In both places global competition is portrayed as a key reason for welfare reform with the economic sustainability of welfare systems being called into question by it and socio-demographic changes. In both regions the concept of sustainability is interpreted in equally narrow economic and financial terms. Whether we look east or west, the social dimension of sustainability is consistently missing. Three critical consequences flow from this lacuna.

First of all, attention is diverted from the need for systemic reforms in welfare regimes East and West to tackle inequalities, such as those based on gender, class and race, or to promote social quality. In other words, sustainability is often concerned with the maintenance or narrowing of a particular regime and excludes more progressive options. Second, it means that the perspectives of citizens, especially those reliant on a particular welfare regime, are also absent. Yet in both regions there are questions about the legitimacy of welfare institutions from the perspectives of citizens demanding a response (Taylor-Gooby 1998, 2004). Third, in both East and West, there is a supreme economistic doctrine of government, which holds that the promotion of higher and higher consumption is the only route to a better society: an approach once called "growth-mania" (Sears 1969; Walker 1984). In other words, in both the EU and East Asia, there is an urgent need for a new holistic approach to sustainability, which brings in from the cold the missing social dimension. Social quality could provide a conceptual vehicle to achieve this transformation in the understanding and application of sustainability.

Social Quality and Welfare System Sustainability

The social quality paradigm raises critical questions about the nature of the present global discourse on welfare sustainability and especially about the weak conceptual foundations underlying it. In particular it questions the tripartite construction of sustainability, which suggests either that there are separate pillars—economic, ecological and social—or, more commonly, that these three factors exist in a hierarchical relationship with the economic one preeminent (Lehtonen 2004; Coenen et al. 2000). This is identical to the critique of the subordination of social policy to the economy and economic policy that first led to the development of the social quality approach and may now be applied to the concept of sustainability. Globally this false and manufactured separation between the "economic" and the "social" performs exactly the same functions as it does nationally: it purveys the superiority of economism and production over social relations and, crucially, maintains the illusion that these are detached from their social context (Walker 1984). This serious conceptual deficiency has had important practical spin-offs such as the lack of attention paid to understanding and measuring the social dimension of sustainability, in contrast to the huge concentration on the economic and ecological ones. Also, too little attention has been paid to the trade-offs between these two dimensions and their social sister. The social quality paradigm questions not only the tripartite model of sustainability but also the concept itself. In addition to its narrow construction, there is also the danger that it exerts a conservative influence on policy making by emphasizing only the maintenance of existing institutions and priorities (Lehtonen 2004: 3).

How can social quality contribute productively to the debate about welfare system sustainability, particularly in Asia? There are four elements of its potential contribution that could also help to establish a framework for a new approach to sustainability. First, in contrast to the present tripartite approach to sustainability and largely economic one toward welfare sustainability, social quality provides a holistic conception. Thus, the economic and ecological dimensions are embedded in social relations and, therefore, within social quality. With social quality as the goal, it is self-evident that a combination of ecological, economic and social policies are required: only such a comprehensive approach will deliver the developments necessary to achieve sustainable social quality. In other words, it may be possible to liberate discourses on welfare sustainability (and globalization) from their economistic straitjacket that offers little other than a race to the bottom in welfare terms. This paradigm shift would be particularly helpful in an Asian context because institutional welfare has negative associations in many parts of the continent (Gough 1999; Chau and Yu 2005). Although it originated in a European context, social quality does not privilege any particular form of welfare production, providing it leads to positive outcomes, in terms of social quality, and meets its normative prescriptions. So, the idea of a "welfare society," as opposed to a "welfare state," is not necessarily problematic within this paradigm. It would depend on the nature of the welfare arrangements. Unfortunately, at the present time, the term "welfare society" to many policy makers means a residual welfare regime that may aspire, at best, to minimum standards, not social quality (Walker 2005).

Second, a social quality perspective opens up a discussion about the conflicts between the ecological, economic and social dimensions of sustainability and sets an agenda for policy makers in terms of the impact of all three on levels of social quality. For example, it may be appropriate to determine normatively optimum social quality guidelines based on a combination of ecological, economic and social sustainability criteria.

Third, this paradigm emphasizes the outcomes for citizens (in terms of socio-economic security, inclusion and so on), which brings in a democratic dimension to development and the policy-making process concerning sustainability. As citizens gain access to the tools to understand and measure their conditions and well-being, within societies and between them, so we may expect the policy-making process to be transformed. This would also add a fully fledged fourth dimension to sustainability: a political one.

Fourth, social quality transcends the inherent conservatism of welfare sustainability discourses by raising questions about what is being sustained (Coenen et al. 2000). From this perspective it is first a matter of the outcomes of different welfare arrangement, in terms of social quality, and, second, how to sustain them. Of course this opens the door to a wide range of normative issues, for example, concerning the basis for distribution and redistribution in any society. As we have seen, social quality theory is completely open about its normative dimension, in stark contrast to most of the concepts used for debates about welfare sustainability. This allows for variations in judgments about which social quality goals to aim for according to stages of development and national culture and values. Thus, both the measurement of social quality and the policy goals arising from its application differ between regions of the globe. In other words, while the core theory and conditional factors remain the same, their measurement and policy implications are subject to developmental and cultural contexts.

These four elements suggest that social quality has significant potential to transform the present discourses on both sustainability and welfare sustainability from their present narrow and compartmentalized boxes into a more holistic and participative framework. Rather than focusing factors only on economic or environmental policies and their trade-offs, policy makers would need to subject all policies to the test of social quality impact and to engage with citizens in discussions concerning the ways to achieve social quality and the costs of failing to reach sufficient levels. Rather than dominating this debate, the question of financial sustainability becomes an important one among several focusing on the nature of society and well-being of its citizens. This would not be an easy task as it would entail a paradigm shift not only in social policy analysis but also in the policy-making process. This is as true in Asia as it is in Europe and as necessary. In both places and in countries at opposite ends of the development spectrum, social priorities are constantly subverted to the economy (Walker 1984; Beck et al. 1997; Yang 2003).

Not only would the understanding of and approach to the implementation of sustainability be transformed by the goal of social quality, but the outcomes would also have a high chance of being sustainable in terms of their public and political legitimacy. Within a social quality paradigm, citizens in Asia might be expected to adjust their motivation for supporting welfare from empathy to mutual self-interest or solidarity (Wong et al. 2006). In turn this would alter the nature of the financial sustainability question by subjecting it to normative considerations about the sort of society that people want to live in. These considerations are as relevant in Asia as they are in Europe, but, at present in both regions, they are largely invisible. While social quality provides a mechanism to put them on the policy agenda, it does not mean that state welfare is a sufficient condition for social quality. Investigation of the scope for social quality in Asia is necessary to reveal what is the appropriate mix of sources for its conditional components in that region (Yee and Chang 2009).

Conclusion

This chapter has provided a broad overview of the relationship between social quality and welfare sustainability by examining the global discourse on welfare sustainability and summarizing how this plays out in the two regions of East and West; emphasizing the importance of the missing social (and political) dimension in sustainability discourses; and then, finally, showing how social quality could provide a scientific and normative vehicle with which to rescue current welfare sustainability discourses from a neo-liberal inspired race to the bottom. This does not mean that Asian welfare systems must mirror European ones or vice versa: that debate is a sterile one serving only the narrowest of political purposes. A scientific perspective tells us that welfare systems in both regions will, above all, respect their cultural and historical paths and reflect their different political and institutional processes. The big challenge for research is to find a common template by which the everyday circumstances and well-being of citizens in both regions can be assessed and appropriate policies developed. If the theoretical foundations of the social quality paradigm are broadly accepted, then the rest is a matter of rather mundane research methods and indictor selection. In this endeavor it is vital that a close dialogue is maintained between Asia and Europe so that we can learn from each other's cultures and histories and, thereby, know what is feasible, in policy terms, in each region.

Alan Walker, CBE, is Professor of Social Policy and Social Gerontology at the University of Sheffield. He is currently Director of the New Dynamics of Ageing funded by five UK research councils, Mobilising the Potential of Active Ageing in Europe and Social Innovations for an Ageing Population funded by the European Union. Previously, he directed the European Research Area in Ageing. In the 1990s, with Wolfgang Beck and Laurent van der Maesen, he originated the concept of social quality and established the European Foundation on Social Quality.

References

Ahn, S. and S. Lee. 2005. "The Development of the South Korean Welfare Regime." pp. 165–186 in *East Asian Welfare Regimes in Transition*, Walker and Wong.

Archer, M. 1995. *Realist Social Theory: The Morphogenetic Approach*. Cambridge: Cambridge University Press.

Beck, W., L. van der Maesen and A. Walker, eds. 1997. *The Social Quality of Europe*. The Hague: Kluwer International.

Beck, W., L. van der Maesen, F. Thomése and A. Walker, eds. 2001. *Social Quality: A Vision for Europe*. The Hague: Kluwer International.

Bourdieu, P. 1986. "Forms of Capital." pp. 241–258 in *Handbook of Theory and Research for the Sociology of Education*, ed. J. Richardson. New York: Greenwood Press.

Cahill, M. and T. Fitzpatrick. 2002. *Environmental Issues and Social Welfare*. Oxford: Blackwell.

Chau, R. and W. Yu. 2005. "Is Welfare UnAsian?" pp. 21–45 in *East Asian Welfare Regimes in Transition*, Walker and Wong.

Coenen, F., D. Fuchs and R. van de Peppel. 2000. *The Environment and Social Well-being: An Exploration of Facts and Figures and Possible Relationships*. The Hague: Centre for Clean Technology and Environmental Policy.

Coleman, J. 1988. "Social Capital in the Creation of Human Capital." *American Journal of Sociology* 94: 95–120.

Cox, R.H. 1998. "The Consequences of Welfare Reform: How Conceptions of Social Rights Are Changing." *Journal of Social Policy* 27(1): 1–16.

Deacon, B. 2000. *Globalization and Social Policy*. UNRISD Occasional Paper 5, Geneva: United Nations Research Institute for Social Development.

Deacon, B., M. Hulse and P. Stubbs. 1997. *Global Social Policy: International Organizations and the Future of Welfare*. London: Sage.

Esping-Andersen, G. 1990. *The Three Worlds of Welfare Capitalism*. Cambridge: Polity Press.

Esping-Andersen, G. 1999. *Social Foundations of Post-industrial Economies*. Oxford: Oxford University Press.

European Commission. 2000. *The Social Policy Agenda*. Brussels: European Commission.

European Commission. 2001. *The Social Situation in the European Union*. Luxemburg: Office for Official Publications of the European Communities.

European Commission. 2002. *Joint Report on Social Inclusion*. Brussels: European Commission.

European Council. 2000. *A Sustainable Europe for a Better World*. Brussels: Commission of the European Communities.

Ferge, Z. 2002. "European Integration and the Reform of Social Security in the Accession Countries." *European Journal of Social Quality* 3(1/2): 159–174.

Fitzpatrick, T. and M. Cahill, eds. 2002. *Environment and Welfare: Towards a Green Social Policy*. Basingstoke: Palgrave Macmillan.

Gasper, D., L. van der Maesen, T.D. Truong and A. Walker. 2008. *Human Security and Social Quality: Contrasts and Complementarities*. Working Paper no. 462. The Hague: Institute of Social Studies.

Goodman, R., G. White and H.J. Kwon. 1998. *The East Asian Welfare Model: Welfare Orientalism and the State*. London: Routledge.

Gough, I. 1999. *Welfare Regimes: On Adapting the Framework to Developing Countries*. University of Bath: Institute for International Policy Analysis, Global Social Policy Programme.

Juhasz, G. 2006. "Exporting or Pulling Down? The European Social Model and Eastern Enlargement of the EU." *European Journal of Social Quality* 6(1): 82–108.

Lehtonen, M. 2004. "The Environmental—Social Interface of Sustainable Development: Capabilities, Social Capital, Institutions." *Ecological Economics* 49(2): 199–214.

Leibfried, S. and E. Rieger. 1998. "Welfare State Limits to Globalization." *Politics and Society* 26(4): 363–390.

Lewis, J. 1992. "Gender and the Development of Welfare Regimes." *Journal of European Social Policy* 2(3): 159–174.

OECD. 2001. *Sustainable Development: Critical Issues*. Paris: OECD.

Phillips, D. 2006. *Quality of Life*. London: Routledge.

Pierson, P. 2000. *The New Politics of the Welfare State*. Oxford: Oxford University Press.

Putnam, R. 2000. *Bowling Alone: The Collapse and Revival of American Community*. New York: Simon & Schuster.

Sears, D. 1969. "The Meaning of Development." *International Development Review* 6: 2–6.

Södersten, B., ed. 2004. *Globalization and the Welfare State*. Bakingstoke: Palgrave Macmillan.

Stone, D. 2004. "Transfer Agents and Global Networks in the Transnationalisation of Policy." *Journal of European Public Policy* 3: 546–566.

Takegawa, S. 2005. "Japan's Welfare-State Regime: Welfare Politics, Provider and Regulator." *Development and Society* 34(2): 169–190.

Taylor-Gooby, P. 1998. "Commitment to the Welfare State." pp. 57–76 in *British and European Social Attitudes*, eds. R. Jowell, J. Curtice, A. Park, L. Brock, K. Thomson and C. Bryson. Aldershot: Ashgate.

Taylor-Gooby, P. 2004. "Open Markets and Welfare Values." *European Societies* 6(1): 9–48.

Vobruba, G. 2004. "Globalization versus the European Social Model?" *Czech Sociological Review* 40(3): 261–276.

Walker, A. 1984. *Social Planning*. Oxford: Blackwell.

Walker, A. 2005. "Which Way for the European Social Model: Minimum Standards on Social Quality?" pp. 33–53 in *The Changing Face of Welfare*, eds. J. Goul Andersen, A.M. Guillemard, P. Jensen and B. Pfau-Effinger. Bristol: Policy Press.

Walker, A. and L. van der Maesen. 2004. "Social Quality and Quality of Life." pp. 13–31 in *Challenges for Quality of Life in the Contemporary World*, eds. W. Glatzer, S. von Below and M. Stoffregen. The Hague: Kluwer Academic Publishers.

Walker, A. and C.K. Wong, eds. 2005. *East Asian Welfare Regimes in Transition: From Confucianism to Globalisation*. Bristol: Policy Press.

Wong, C.K., K.Y. Wong and B.H. Mok. 2006. "Emotions, Self-interest and Support for Social Welfare in a Chinese Society with Reference to a Dutch Study on Welfare Legitimacy." *International Journal of Social Welfare* 15(4): 302–313.

World Bank. 1994. *Averting the Old Age Crisis: Policies to Protect the Old and Promote Growth*. Oxford: Oxford University Press.

Yang, T. 2003, ed. *Social Policy in China*. Beijing: Social Policy Research Centre.

Yeates, N., T. Haus, R. Jawad, and M. Kilkey, eds. 2011. *In Defence of Welfare*. London: Social Policy Association.

Yee, J. and D. Chang. 2011. "Social Quality as a Measure for Social Progress." *Development and Society* 40(2): 153–172.

CHAPTER 4

The Prototype of Social Quality Theory and Its Applicability to Asian Societies

Ka Lin

Introduction

Modern European social scientists have contributed a great deal toward laying the foundations of academic disciplines. In the field of social policy, for instance, the works of Titmuss, Townsend, Taylor-Gooby, George and Wilding and others, established new perceptions, assumptions and the analytic frameworks grounding the theoretical development for modern social policy theories. However, when these European-initiated theories spread to non-European societies, they underwent a process of adaptation, modification and revision. In this process of transmission, the "dialogue" between European and non-European investigators was and remains essential for development. These transformations of the social policy theories from European perspectives into international ones help to break the theoretical limits imposed by European contexts, but also leave room for non-European scholars to develop the theories further. This also applies to the social quality theory (hereafter SQ theory).

In social quality theory, the original intention of this European initiative was to address the trend that saw the development of the European Union (EU) in terms of economic integration rather than as a social project. The theory emphasized the side effects of a neo-liberal and individualistic interpretation of social progress and proposed an interpretation based on "social relationship." As the first group of the advocates for the SQ theory claimed (Beck et al. 1997: 2), the asymmetrical relationship between economic policy and other policies was a major reason for the ongoing crises of the European states. Accordingly, the measures proposed for resolving the problems of the European states were policies that empowered their citizens to cope with daily life. This became an essential factor in the generation of SQ theory.

These policies implied citizenship-focused proposals that certainly undermined the principle of market-oriented development prevailing in the United States of America. As argued by Herrmann (2005: 25), Europeans do not share the same dream as Americans for their social development, so the development of "social Europe" would be a striking alternative to the global development. This view is also reflected in SQ theory, since in this theory the condition of social quality is measured by the extent to which citizens are able to participate in the social and economic life of their communities (Beck et al. 2001: 7).

With the efforts of the European Foundation on Social Quality, this theory has extended its influence into Asian societies since the early twenty-first century. For Asian adopters, difficult questions arose concerning whether this imported theory could be reconciled to their own contexts. If so, could it effectively meet their practical needs? This situation leads our attention to the initial forms and adaptations of this theory, given the different stresses and indignation generated during this process. Thus, we have to study the impacts of diverse institutional and normative contexts between the European and Asian states, for understanding and emphasizing the SQ theory and subsequent policy ideas. This study will undertake this task by conducting a contextual analysis through cross-regional comparisons. The chapter is organized in the following ways, given below.

First, it will test the context and the background of SQ theory in Europe as the basis for Asian adaptation, which may either support or discourage the growth of SQ theory at particular localities. Second, it will examine the ideas presented by the SQ theory to see how suitable this theory is for adoption by Asians. Third, it will propose a strategy of research to treat SQ theory in the sense of meta-theory, in order to cope with the complications caused by different ideas and institutional contexts. Fourth, the study suggests using four approaches based on the data concerning four-set "conditional factors." Such data will help us to apply the general SQ theory (as a meta-theory) to any particular society for producing any policy advice. Fifth, from the four approaches used in analysis, the study evaluates the general condition of SQ discussion in Asia and its policy orientation. In the conclusive part, this study will assess theoretical meanings and practical implications for the extension of SQ theory worldwide.

On the Original Purpose of the Theory

By its origin, social quality theory developed from a need to create an image for the European future, which demands a "scientific" and theoretical basis to facilitate it. According to Beck et al. (1997), the first book published by the European Foundation of Social Quality was stimulated by a debate about the future of the EU. The process of European integration necessitates some kind of ideological glue, or banner, to enable European citizens and the states to stand together against the challenge of global competition. Keeping this in mind, the birth of SQ theory can be seen as the reflection for a strategy of developing European societies based on a new interpretation about the concept of "the social" (Beck et al. 2001: 15). Its attitude toward the key factors that affect the European future was and is to stress the need to cultivate new types of citizens, with new ideas about their societies and their lives. This orientation reflects a general consensus among European policy makers.

Accordingly, European states were advised to pursue social quality goals. This may offer a new alternative for world development to the American approach that values market-oriented management (Beck et al. 2001: 64). For instance, Blair stated that he "would never accept a Europe that was simply an economic market," although he did not speak further on how to go beyond the limit of the market-oriented approach (Herrmann 2005: 25). Despite the notion that a social Europe often remains an empty conception or an artificial political construction as commented by critics of the "European Social Model" against its weak theoretical foundation (see Walker 2007), this notion and its associated policy ideas provided a strong motive to generate SQ theory.

Once this theory spreads to Asian societies, however, this motive vanishes. In Asia, there is a lack of regional consensus as there is in the European region, and the far-reaching diversities of Asian political, historical, cultural and ethnic backgrounds dispose of any ambitions to reach a strong regional consensus in social development. This situation is reinforced by different paths of institutional evolution. For instance, both Japan and China are leading economies of the present world, but they are representatives of capitalism and socialism, respectively. Interactions between countries of this region are increasingly frequent, but there is still a lack of strong organizational power to support social development processes in this region. This makes it difficult to create a common image for the region's future.

Meanwhile, a large number of Asian countries in this region are developing countries or newly industrialized countries. They were and are used to pursue rising GDP levels and strengthen their national economies as the principal orientations of social policy making (up to the early 1990s; see Lin 2008), while discouraging other ideas, including welfare rights. Thus, once SQ theory in Europe emphasized the policy goal of empowering citizens, such consequences were hardly discernible in these Asian states. Thus, the dynamics for the development of SQ theory in Asian states are dissimilar to those in European states. Under such circumstances, we have to question the application of SQ theory to the Asian context, both in its inspiration and desires, and by the institutional contexts that determine how open these societies are to accepting such ideas. In making comparisons, it is essential to study the institutional features and the cognitive codes of the theory in order to evaluate whether they are applicable to Asian societies.

The Inspiration of SQ Policy Ideas

In their struggle for the harmonious future of European states, the SQ scholars presented an idea of "sustainable welfare society" as an alternative for the idea of "welfare state." This brought the debate on the idea of "welfare society" back to 1980s (see OECD 1981), but in SQ theory, this idea is rephrased with its contained policy implications re-evaluated. In SQ theory, the idea "welfare society" was originally defined as relying on welfare provision by a complex of networks of citizens, families, companies, private and public organizations and state departments. Therefore, this approach intends to create a "welfare mix formula" (Nectoux 1999) against an old version of the "welfare state" model; on the other hand, "welfare society" ideas also function against an individualistic liberal model of privatization. Accordingly, the idea of "welfare society" seems a model caught between a model of state welfare and a neo-liberal model of privatization endorsed by the ethics of individualistic liberalism.

To make a comparison with Asia, the idea of "welfare society" was discussed in Japan in the mid-1980s, regarding it as an alternative model to the "welfare state" (Rose and Shiratori 1986). These discussions often refer "welfare society" to the traditional Asian family networks of interpersonal relationships. For this sake, European scholars used to accent this "welfare society" idea as an "Asian idea." However, in a practical sense, this idea often connotes residual welfare in Asia. Criticism of this idea also comes from China. With the expansion of state welfare in many East Asian societies, especially in the last decade, the impetus to address the "welfare society" was further weakened.

Thus, the above observation through cross-regional comparison gives us an interesting point of discussion: in Europe, the over-extended welfare state system and its liberalism-oriented reform stems from a desire for a "welfare society" model, as advised by European SQ scholars, whereas in Asia its connotation of residual welfare creates less desire for this model. Thus, when European scholars are interested to learn the Asian experience of "welfare society," regarding it as in affiliation with Asian values (Phillips and Berman 2008), Asian scholars are more interested to learn from the European experience of state welfare, especially that of income redistribution and social protection. Consequently, the Asian experience seems to inspire European SQ scholars to develop social quality theories but seems unable to give much inspiration to Asian countries. Instead, the interest of Asian scholars in SQ theory is mainly in its theoretical framework of social analysis and its ideological emphasis on improving social harmony rather than in its policy proposal of a "welfare society."

A similar situation also occurs in the discussion about "sustainability." In SQ theory—in reference to its goal of "sustainable welfare society"—it is important to know how to integrate the environmental, economic, social and welfare aspects of the overall sustainability (van der Maesen 2009). Given these perspectives, the sustainability of the operated welfare state system (especially on finance and legitimacy) is a central issue of "sustainability." In Asia, by contrast, the environmental and economic perspectives of sustainability are the main concerns. Due to few social security programs and many existing programs that have not yet reached maturity, many Asian countries do not have a heavy burden of public welfare, which makes the "sustainable" issue of state welfare provisions less troubling.

Thus, we observe different ideas, purposes and desires for social development, which also influence the elaboration of the SQ theory. Even when both European and Asian scholars address the idea of "welfare society" in a positive sense, the content of this idea may still be understood in dissimilar ways. As Hiroi (2007) noted, "the agenda for a sustainable welfare society takes different forms in Europe and Asia, although there are commonalities as well." For instance, in SQ theory, European scholars promoted the notions of social rights and responsible citizens, as well as democracy (see Therborn 2001: 19–30); these elements, however, could hardly be distinguished in the accents of Asian scholars. These differences may hinder theorizing the differences between the European welfare state approaches and the Asian developmentalist application of this theory. Nevertheless, these differences do not discourage the interest of Asian scholars in SQ theory. Thus, we need to consider how useful it is to apply the SQ theory to Asian societies and the adaptability of the SQ theory for these societies.

The Theoretical Meaning of SQ Theory for Social Analysis

When we apply SQ theory into the study of non-European societies, it shows how the theory is embedded in its European context. This context may limit its power of explanation for non-European societies and generate the debate over indigenization or regionalization when applied beyond Europe. In order to increase its applicability to non-European states, a basic strategy for universal application of this theory is to reduce the influence of specific European contexts on the content of SQ theory. The practical way to achieve this goal is to uproot the institutional context of the SQ debate and set up the research footing on an abstract level, broadening the scope of its explanation (see Figure 4.1 below).

To conduct this work strategy, it is necessary to treat this theory as a meta-theory of social analysis. The SQ theory embodies rich social-philosophical characteristics—ontological, epistemological and ideological—which enable reflection on the conditions of social quality (Beck et al. 2001: 307–360). This provides the opportunity to accent SQ theory in the sense of meta-theory. Thus, by using meta-theory, SQ theory can be used as a general model of social analysis despite institutional diversities. As this theory uses a comprehensive framework for analysis and embraces a number of factors in a wide range of spheres, its conceptual and methodological underpinning allows us to engage in a deeper study.

In this study, "social quality" can be used in various terms: as a concept, a theory, an approach, a policy instrument (Beck et al. 2001: 148) or a perspective (Taylor-Gooby 2006: 121). Studies of social quality can be used to analyze the interrelations among different parts, factors and institutions—the logical ground of social systems at a general level—to give a better explanation about the nature, features and function

The prototype of SQ theory entangled with European contexts (step one)
↓
SQ theory as a theoretical and methodological instrument of analysis
(leaving particular European contexts out, step two)
↓

	→ Asian societies
Using this instrument to apply to the analysis of	→ European societies
(step three)	→ Other societies

Figure 4.1. Uprooting the SQ Theory from European Contexts

of the theory. In this way, this theoretical work can help reveal both possibilities and barriers in the spread of SQ theory in Asia.

Besides its meta-theory function, the value of SQ theory can still be asserted in a sense of the normative guide and the policy-making guide. Against the institutional diversities of various analyzed societies, SQ theory establishes its normative basis for judging the appropriateness and outcomes of policy actions, recognizing the values of solidarity, social justice, equal value and human dignity (Walker 2007; van der Maesen 2000). Following the European legacy of Durkheimian sociology, the SQ theory holds to its collective priorities, ethical values and the principles of justice, social innovation and emancipatory process (Bouget 2001b: 118). The theory is antithetical to individualistic liberal ideology, as prevalent in Anglo-Saxon countries, as it stresses the notions of social cohesion and social harmony. Given this normative basis, SQ theory can function as a policy-making guide and provide a better perspective for policy analyzers within this theoretical construction.

As a policy guide, this theory can connect with various theories of social analysis, such as social indicator studies, the quality of life, the social capital theory and human security approach (van der Maesen and Walker 2003), and can therefore present various policy ideas by rephrasing them from a perspective of social quality analysis. It should be noted that this theory puts its emphasis on social cohesion and solidarity and the significance of citizenship and democracy. This makes the theory welcome in both European and Asian states (Walker and Wong 2005). In most Asian countries, the notion of corporatism is not a practical right but rather an orientation of collectivism within civil society that makes it easier for this theory to be accepted. In China, for instance, economic growth enhances people's living standards, so SQ theory gives increased emphasis to a need for all-round development targeted at a goal of general improvement.

On the Contextual Analysis

To analyze the applicability of SQ theory to certain societies, we need to return to our understanding of SQ studies, going from meta-theory back to contextual analysis. As Gordon (2005: 3) maintained, comparative studies often failed to achieve their goals due to inadequate knowledge of particular contexts and due to inadequate data. This implies a need to examine the roots of social conduct, putting aside the previous SQ studies. As commented by Filipovic et al., social quality theory permits a number of new social issues to be addressed, which were often articulated in a specific context (2005: 227). In contextual analysis, we should investigate the social norms and institutional arrangements of different societies, referring also to their structural, normative and cultural contexts.

With a framework of three-sets factors, namely conditional factors, constitutional factors and normative factors, SQ theory can effectively reflect social realities. We can reveal the essential relationships among different SQ factors and demonstrate the explanatory power of this theory at the theoretical and abstract level: what is "social quality," and how should we divide its domain, using which indicators to reflect "social quality"? At present, the SQ analysis is mostly based on "conditional factors," although there are constitutive factors and normative factors as well. These conditional factors refer to four socio-economic dimensions: security, social cohesion, social inclusion and social empowerment. However, to use these factors to investigate the social quality of any particular society still seems problematic. There are three major questions.

First, what are the interrelations between the conditional factors, constitutional and normative factors? So far, the division between the constitutive factors and normative factors are philosophically accented, but they are hardly divided along any clear line of classification in a practical sense. Second, what are the appropriate, coherent and adequate social quality indicators in all four domains that reflect SQ realities, and what are the fundamental differences between the various conditional factors of the four domains (Bouget 2001a: 49)? Third, could the same sort of "conditional factors" exist in different domains? This relates to an essential question: the overlapping of the "conditional factors" with the constitutive factors and normative factors. For instance, social cohesion is a normative factor but also a "conditional factor." Bouget addresses this problem by saying "this overlap is reinforced because we do not exactly know what the articulations between them are."

When the division between various sorts of conditional factors and their relations remain vague, we can suggest extending the contextual analysis of SQ data to "conditional factors." This extension can result in four analytical approaches that go beyond the descriptions of "conditional factors." These approaches are a material life approach, a normative approach, an institutional approach and an agent/actor- approach.

A material life approach can reflect the economic basis of social quality. Indicators reflecting the conditions of material life can be both objective and subjective, referring to the spheres of income security, education, housing employment and other kinds of social policy provisions. It can give us reasons to explain people's material well-being and help us to perceive people's satisfaction with their lives. With this approach, studies made are mostly descriptive rather than interpretive, but they can establish the empirical basis of cross-system comparisons. Accordingly, we can draw on many social studies when using this approach in connection with human security theory and developmental studies, which may allow us some empirical basis for developing interpretative or comparative work.

A normative approach, meanwhile, can be developed with the help of data from the domain of social cohesion. In SQ theory, "conditional factors" in the domain of social cohesion are closely associated with values and ethics. Work that exposes the normative basis of a society must refer to the notions of solidarity and social trust (Ward et al. 2006: 10), which touch the core of people's everyday lives. Since social cohesion can strengthen the bonds between values, social networks and identities (Berman and Phillip 2003), it is also the constitutive code for people's interaction in communities, configurations in groups and the development of society. Thus, as this dimension of work influences the rationality of people's behavior and their group actions, the constitutional and cognitive factors interact. Therefore, a normative "social cohesion" approach enhances, applies and contributes to the processes of recognition in the interactive setting between societal development and the world of daily life (Herrmann 2005: 21).

Table 4.1. Four Types of "Conditional Factors" and Four Approaches to SQ Studies

Approaches	Topical Areas	Key Notions	Conditional Factors
material life (descriptive)	social indicators economic and social conditions	income level social security	socio-economic life
normative	ethics and ideology cultural studies	solidarity trust	social cohesion
institutional	institutions and social stratification	social network	social inclusion/ exclusion
actor/agent -oriented	civil society social capital	democracy participation	social empowerment

An institutional approach relates to the "conditional factors" in the domain of social inclusion. In SQ theory, social inclusion is defined as the degree to which people are integrated in different social relations (systems, institutions, organizations and structures) that constitute everyday life (Walker and Wigfield 2003). Its opposite, social exclusion, should be accounted for by some institutional factors. Thus, institutional analysis will help to reveal social networks, community and class stratification in society and give reasons for social inclusion and/or exclusion. For instance, on the issue of democracy, there is a general absence of democratic notions as well as the institutions in the Western sense that support the notion of social inclusion. Thus, social inclusion and exclusion are formed by the social structures, social stratification and social institutions of certain societies.

The agent/actor approach can be associated with the fourth set of "conditional factors" in the domain of social empowerment. In theory, "social empowerment" connotes "developing the competences of citizens in order to participate in processes determining daily life" (Beck et al. 1997: 290). With this understanding, we can develop social quality studies from the agent approach, involving welfare agents, companies, communities, minority groups and gender groups. Thus, social actions that uphold SQ conditions are subject to the social agents, for which an agent/actor approach would be essential. Since social processes "are continuously negotiated by actors who have different or, even, opposite values and interests" (Bouget 2001b: 121), the improvement of social quality conditions would be the outcome of political interests, representing those who are losing and those who are gaining. This effect also appears in the process of policy making and performance. The field of industrial policies, for instance, involves various actors engaging in dialogue, including trade unions, employers and governments, aimed at improving the social quality of citizens' daily circumstances (Ojeda-Aviles 2001: 31–45). Thus, if we look at the dynamics of promoting SQ in society, we have to study the motives and roles of social agents and their mutual relationships.

The Applicability of the SQ Approaches to Asian Societies

With this theoretical construction, we can further analyze Asian situations. With regard to material life, the Asian region has a wide range of variation: some countries have a high standard of living and well-developed social security programs, whereas many others still depend on the protection by informal networks of social assistance. However, through a regional view, we can observe two phases of development before and after the 1980s. In the early stage, the GDP-oriented pursuit of many Asian countries meant that their social security systems were weakly installed. In the second stage, economic growth resulted in an increased income gap and inequality (Oishi 2007; Lin 2009), and the pressure of democracy was and is helpful for welfare extension.

This welfare extension is observable in mainland China, Taiwan and Hong Kong, as well as in South Korea and Malaysia. There has been a remarkable increase of public welfare in these countries and regions, and the foci of the policy discussions are on how to design new programs, how to promote actions by the government and other welfare suppliers. Since SQ theory demands societal development as a measure to overcome the increase of "(income) gaps within society" (Herrmann 2005: 22–23), conducting SQ studies can disclose the real need for social protection policy in Asian countries and to enhance socio-economic security for the majority of people.

Taking a normative approach, the European SQ scholars (e.g., Cook and Kwon 2007) regard Asian people as culturally inclined toward a society-oriented rather than an individualistic outlook. Since social cohesion and collective morale are surely welcomed by Asians, this makes it easy to use the ideas of social cohesion and social harmony in SQ theory. However, when it comes to "welfare society," the Asian response is mixed: on one hand, this idea may function as an ideology that supports a residual model of welfare, or a model of civil self-regulation, while on the other hand, this idea underlines the significance of "welfare" goals for social development. Thus, the ideal of a "welfare society" is not strange for Asians, but its meaning and usage needs to be further clarified (Lin 2004).

When addressing the potential for Asians to adopt SQ theory, some crucial aspects should not be ignored. In many Asian states (typically in East Asia), the fast growth of market economy enlarges the income gap. Thus, the Asian states have a strong need to look for any theory that can work as the ideology of social harmony. This is particularly true in the case of mainland China, where the government promotes the idea of a "harmonious society" as a coping strategy to moderate the potential social risk it generates. Meanwhile, since the late 1980s, the surge of democratic movements intensifies the strains between social and political groups. This is particularly true in the cases of Japan, Korea, Taiwan and recently Thailand. This again produces a large need to strengthen social harmony. Since "social quality can be a general reference to narrow the gap between ethics and politics, i.e., the difference between general principles of ethics and realistic politics" (Bouget 2001b: 121), we may see the normative approach of SQ theory used within Asian societies to increase the degree of social harmony.

From an institutional approach, in many Asian developing countries, less developed market power does not lead to a sharp division between social classes (unlike that of liberal capitalism), although income gaps and unemployment rates are consistently rising. Strong network connections have a positive impact on maintaining social order. Thus, in Asia, we do not encounter such a sharp (but vague) division between the public domain and the private domain. There is coexistence between an authoritarian order and a self-regulated civil society (typically in South Asia). This institutional context has gradually changed in the process of industrialization and urbanization, which increases population mobility, making a large part of the population exposed to the risk of social exclusion. This makes Asian states favorably inclined to adopt SQ theory. Accordingly, this institutional context may have a substantial influence on social institutions. The institutional integration remains to go through a cluster of informal contacts and networks.

Still, underlining an agent/actor approach, the SQ theory promotes a notion of "people's-citizens" (Herrmann 2005: 31) or citizen's participation. It refers to the means, processes and relations necessary for people's participation that has active influence over the social and physical environment. In the European context, social empowerment goes from political participation to the enabling of citizens and enrichment of their capacity (by knowledge, skills, experience and so on) (Walker 2007). In Asia, although people are active in civil society, the notion of "people-citizens" is not popular because there is little emphasis on the individualist citizenship approach, which is endorsed by democracy. In this respect, what Asian states may learn from European states is how to mobilize people to involve themselves in public affairs in a democratic manner. This demands that these societies establish some corresponding institutions and create more access to people for the knowledge base, institutional supportiveness, access to collective action and cultural activities and so on (Gordon 2005: 2). So far, Asians have adopted some notions of social empowerment with dissimilar motivation and stresses, but, from a future perspective, they would increasingly learn from the European experiences of empowering people as political citizens. This makes SQ theory valuable for Asian societies, as it demands the promotion of activities of civil agents and the cultivation of a proactive society.

Conclusions

The extension of the SQ theory to Asia can be the first attempt to extend this theory from a European one to a global one. This attempt will help to break down its existing limitations in a number of aspects: its focus, concept, institutional presumption and theoretical orientation, as well as the claims made for the value of SQ theory. The Asian cases would be a good test for the global applicability of the theory. These societies contain large institutional variations, from the developed capitalist states to the "transitional" and developing countries. This varied context makes it possible to estimate how effectively the SQ theory could serve the need of a global social policy. Through a comparative study, this analysis reveals the influence of socio-cultural and institutional contexts in Europe and Asia on the development of SQ theory. It suggests a strategy of the theoretical development so as to lift up the level of abstraction in order to render it applicable to non-European societies. Such studies will eventually enrich the content of this general theory.

Meanwhile, as the framework of the contextual analysis, this chapter also calls for the re-articulation of the four conditional factors of SQ studies in terms of four different approaches: a material life approach, a normative approach, an institutional approach and an actor/agent-oriented approach. Work done in each individual approach may have its own purposes and aims, but the accumulation of these studies across various dimensions will facilitate the development of SQ theory. These analyses should not be totally separated since they reflect the same realities from different aspects. Instead, the coordination and integration of these factors are needed in order to present a general profile of the social qualities in certain societies.

In the light of the normative guide and its developmental aims, we find complexity when using the theory in a cross-regional comparison. In Europe, promoting the idea of "welfare society" is the way for European states to go beyond the idea of "welfare state." In Asia, where a system of state welfare needs to be developed, to raise the amount of social expenditure on welfare would be the basic way of promoting social quality there. This comparison of norms and ideas produces interesting observations: some elements that suit the Asian contexts would make the theory more acceptable for the Asian region but less inspirational; other elements may seem strange to local people but are more inspirational. Thus, our concern should not be focused on making a general statement about whether the SQ theory is acceptable for Asians but rather on the impacts, consequences or implications of this theory for Asians.

Thus, these diverse contexts can be helpful for social researchers by stimulating the debate needed to generate the theory's further development. This diversity provides the potential for adaptation from the European model to the Asian one through "adaptive learning," resulting in the modification of the theory. The theory itself will be also modified but could still contribute to the theory's transformation from a European one to an Asian one and, eventually, a global one. Thus, the purpose of this analysis is not targeted at revealing the particular features of different societal systems but is rather a theoretical exploration of what features can be compared, with what implications. Eventually, this work illuminating the common features of the different systems will help us to test the general applicability of SQ theory, thereby enabling its future extension.

To adopt the general SQ theory in global contexts, we must still address its policy implications. The SQ theory demands that no form of policy should be subordinated to economic policy. This is particularly meaningful for Asian policy makers, as in the past two decades, these states adopted the productivist strategy of development, with the successful performance of economies achieved through certain costs for social relationships and societal structures (including low labor costs and cheap goods for export). This strategy increases social stress. SQ theory could work as an ideological vehicle to accommodate these developments. Thus, the theory contains a number of policy options, which may arouse increased sensitivity in policy makers to social harmony, labor interests, welfare rights and civil mobilization.

Consequently, SQ theory can make its contribution in two ways. One way is to provide perceptions, assumptions and analytic methods for policy analysis; the other way is to look for its policy implications, for example, in the processes of policy articulation, implementation, monitoring and evaluation. There might be a suggestion that increasing discussions among people would promote social solidarity (Filipovic et al. 2003: 227). The benefits of such comparative studies rely on their contextual analyses. These analyses will not only expose the essential features of the SQ theory, or deepen our understanding about its content, but will also enrich comparative studies of social quality. This chapter examines the problems and obstacles encountered by the SQ theory when applied to the international context; these Asian examples provide the first set of test cases for identifying the original features of this theory and the potential for it to be adopted in other regions.

Ka Lin is Docent at the University of Tampere, Senior Researcher and Docent at the University of Turku, Professor and Director of the Social Policy Research Center at Nanjing University, Professor and Executive Director of the MSW Center of Zhejiang University and Deputy Director of the Center for European Studies at Zhejiang University. He is also Vice President of the International Association on Social Quality and Editor of the *International Journal of Social Quality*.

References

Beck, W., L. van der Maesen, F. Thomése and A. Walker. 2001. "Introduction: Who and What Is the European Union For?" pp. 1–17 in *Social Quality*, Beck et al.

Beck, W., L. van der Maesen and A. Walker. 1997. "Social Quality: From Issue to Concept." pp. 301–340 in *The Social Quality of Europe*, eds. W. Beck, L. van der Maesen and A. Walker. The Hague: Kluwer Law International.

Beck, W., L. van der Maesen, F. Thomése and A. Walker, eds. 2001. *Social Quality: A Vision for Europe*. The Hague: Kluwer Law International.

Berman, Y. and D. Phillips. 2003. "Social Quality and Ethnos Communities: Concepts and Indicators." *Community Development Journal* 38(4): 344–357.

Bouget, D. 2001a. "Identification of the 'Problematique.'" pp. 47–67 in *Social Quality*, Beck et al.

Bouget, D. 2001b. "The Empirical and Policy Relevance of Social Quality." pp.105–124 in *Social Quality*, Beck et al.

Cook, S. and H.J. Kwon. 2007. "Regional Perspective: Social Protection in East Asia." pp. 5–18 in *The Second Asian Conference on Social Quality and Sustainable Welfare Societies*. Taipei: National Taiwan University.

Filipovic, M, S. Mandic and R. Boskic. 2005. "Social Quality in Slovenia: Emergent Individual Risks and Disappearing to Discuss Them." *European Journal of Social Quality* 5(1/2): 216–230.

Gordon, D. 2005. "Indicators of Social Quality." *European Journal of Social Quality* 5(1/2): 4–6.

Herrmann, P. 2005. "Social Quality and the European Social Model: Opening Individual Well-Being for a Social Perspective." *Alternatives: Turkish Journal of International Relations* 4(4): 16–32.

Hiroi, Y. 2007. "Possibilities of Sustainable Welfare Societies in Asia." pp. 51–72 in *The Second Asian Conference on Social Quality and Sustainable Welfare Societies*. Taipei: National Taiwan University.

Lin, K. 2004. "Sectors, Agents and Rationale: A Study of the Scandinavian Welfare States with Special Reference to the Welfare Society Model." *Acta Sociologica* 47(2): 141–157.

Lin, K., L. van der Maesen and P. Ward. 2009. "Social Quality Theory in Perspective." *Development and Society* 38(2): 201–208.

van der Maesen, L. 2000. "Social Quality: A New Vision for Europe." *European Journal of Social Quality* 2(2): 139.

van der Maesen, L. and A. Walker. 2003. "Indicators of Social Quality: Outcomes of the European Scientific Network." *European Journal of Social Quality* 5(1/2): 8–24.

Nectoux, F. 1999. "Editorial." *European Journal of Social Quality* 1(1/2): 3–11.

OECD. 1981. *The Welfare State in Crisis: An Account of the Conference on Social Policies in the 1980s.* Paris: OECD.

Oishi, A . 2007. "Indicators of Social Quality in Japan." pp. 85–110 in *The Second Asian Conference on Social Quality and Sustainable Welfare Societies.* Taipei: National Taiwan University.

Ojeda-Aviles, A. 2001. "A Juridical Approach to the European Model of Social Quality." pp. 31–45 in *Social Quality*, Beck et al.

Phillips, D. and Y. Berman. 2001. "Definitional, Conceptual and Operational Issues." pp. 125–146 in *Social Quality*, Beck et al.

Rose, R. and R. Shiratori, eds. 1986. *The Welfare State East and West.* New York: Oxford University Press.

Taylor-Gooby, P. 2006. "The Rational Actor Reform Paradigm: Delivering the Goods but Destroying Public Trust?" *European Journal of Social Quality* 6(2): 121–141.

Therborn, G. 2001. "On the Politics and Policy of Social Quality." pp. 19–30 in *Social Quality*, Beck et al.

Walker, A. 2007. "Society Quality and Sustainable Welfare Regimes." pp. 1–4 in *The Second Asian Conference on Social Quality and Sustainable Welfare Societies.* Taipei: National Taiwan University.

Walker, A. and A. Wigfield. 2003, "The Social Inclusion Component of Social Quality. European Network on Indicators of Social Quality." *European Journal of Social Quality* 3(1/2): 1–31.

Ward, P., P. Redgrave and C. Read. 2006. "Operationalizing the Theory of Social Quality: Theoretical and Experiential Reflections from the Development and Implementation of a Public Health Programme in the UK." *European Journal of Social Quality* 6(2): 9–18.

CHAPTER 5

Economic Performance, Social Progress and Social Quality

Peter Herrmann

━━━━━━━━━━━━◄O►━━━━━━━━━━━◄O►━━━━━━━━━━◄O►━━━━━━━━━━━━

Introduction: Indicators and Social Progress

If we explore immediately some challenges that are too obvious to be ignored, we may refer to increasing inequality, disintegration on grounds of precarious labor market integration and political tensions in many parts of the world. It is also apparent that while some traditional economic measures (like GDP) fail to provide valuable information, many considerations and proposals are able to go beyond offering a rag rug—a toolbox for filling one gap by using the mortar from the gap opened at another spot. Thus, in regard to the measurement of social progress, researchers often accent the failure of indicators on economic growth and industrialization to respond to the global challenges in the contemporary world (see Stiglitz et al. 2009). This critical view leads them to claim a need to go beyond GDP. This is the case for the European Commission (2015) that evokes a problem of a simplified and mechanical understanding about the significance of economic growth, and this understanding may not help the policy-making process to address the virtual issues in people's daily life. Thus, it seems to be cyclical: policy makers can neither well answer the concerns raised by social demands with "popular moods," nor are they able to acknowledge the limitations of the traditional model of societal analysis to reflect the outcomes of societal changes. Therefore, new approaches looking for alternative ways to understand the nature of progress and to measure its changes are needed.

These approaches should go beyond the traditional strategies of development studies in order to reflect the condition of societal changes and the living situation of general individuals in a better way (see van der Maesen and Walker 2012). This raises a new task for the work of indicators along the following lines: (a) to overcome the disjuncture between the purposes of economic and social processes, (b) to find new ways to match indicator measures with real practices and (c) to investigate if we could still distinguish (or borrow) new ideas from the natural and social sciences to enrich indicator research. We must reconceptualize these indicators that are not measurement instruments sui generis. Rather, they are instruments to develop an understanding of complex issues and trends, and as such they need to be guided by a sound conceptual reflection of what they are looking for. For instance, we need to work on securing the basic means for existence for human society and to take action on both aspects of reserving natural resources and self-restriction on consumer behaviors.

This concern for a plea for "better indicators" refers to the work of the Commission on the Measurement of Economic Performance and Social Progress, conventionally known as the "Stiglitz, Sen and Fitoussi report" (called "the report" hereafter). Its aim is to check the limitations defined by the scope of conceptual eclecticism and also to look for pragmatic solutions (see Stiglitz et al. 2009). This chapter's question asks whether this report enables an understanding of complex issues and societal trends, and whether it will contribute to the development of an analytically founded paradigm that can accommodate economic and environmental issues.

The Meaning of "the Report"

In 2008, the Commission on the Measurement of Economic Performance and Social Progress was created on the initiative of the French government. The Commission, according to its website that presents the background of the work, refers to increasing concerns in assessing the traditional mainstream measures as they are in particular based on GDP. The broader orientation is geared toward a set of questions, highlighted by concerns raised by former President Sarkozy (see Stiglitz et al. 2009), namely:

> to identify the limits of GDP as an indicator of economic performance and social progress, to consider additional information required for the production of a more relevant picture, to discuss how to present this information in the most appropriate way, and to check the feasibility of measurement tools proposed by the Commission.

Looking at this statement it is easy to see that the approach is more nurtured by a general sense of discontent with respect to recent developments rather than being based on a strategic vision. Furthermore, it implicitly refers to the traditional usage of social indicators as descriptive measures of societal realities rather than as measures to generate a strategy of policy actions. Of course, the demands for going beyond the traditional mainstream thinking that measures social progress mainly with indicators of economic performance—without defining what "social progress" really means—have existed for a long time.[1] The limitations of the "disintegrated," "disjoined" views of social progress in traditional thinking are apparent, and a claim is heard to reorient toward the line of inclusive development. This claim pursues the reflection of societal integrity with different measures and from different disciplinary areas.

One must acknowledge that GDP indicator does not simply provide a measurement instrument but rather considers a certain combination of figures that would be able to reflect the general economic development by assuming that (1) the goods and services produced for the market would (2) express overall economic performance (3) as such express also the wealth, and with this (4) represent the overall standard as living and social standard alike. Admittedly, the social standard would be not necessarily (only) a direct representation of living standard but also an indirect correlation, because it supposes to transform or to translate material wealth into conditions of social wealth (and again, without explaining what "social wealth" really means).

We may recognize two interesting characteristics of "the report." First, "the report" stands side by side with many works in the same vein, for example, the European Commission's work aiming to go "Beyond GDP" (European Commission 2015). In this work, ideas from various international organizations (such as the OECD, IMF, World Bank, etc.) are discussed, which resulted in ideas being set up by the Pittsburgh G20-summit that looked for a framework for strong, sustainable and balanced growth (G20 2009). The initiatives of "Beyond GDP" also come from some private research institutes (e.g., the New Economic Foundation, Forschungsstätte der Evangelischen Studiengemeinschaft [Research Institute of the Protestant Study Community], Institut für Interdisziplinäre Forschung [Institute for Interdisciplinary Research]). Not least, the debate on the Green Deal belongs in this row.

Second, the debate in "the report" takes place by spanning across a wide ideological range. It brings together highly different economic schools as represented by Joseph Stiglitz on the one hand and Amartya Sen on the other. A review on a set of studies made on the basis of the European Commission's work since 2007 shows that they are looking for answers to deal with the current multiple crises in Europe with a broad range of presumptions. In many cases, these presumptions even contradict each other. They desire to find some "perfect technical" solutions to respond to certain problems but seem to fail to recognize the challenges on the crosscutting settings. Since this work appears to be restricted to certain particular issues, the European Commission seems to have difficulties realizing its ambition of reaching an overall solution.

With regard to their theoretical underpinnings, "the report" approaches economic issues with different underlying theories. They differ not so much by whether to be in favor of the laissez-faire principle but rather on the objective of steering (steering demand versus steering supply) and the means of steering (political and technical steering versus moral standards and virtues). For example, it relies on classical economics regarding the demand from the market as a driving force, but on the supply side, it uses the Keynesian concept of supply as a driving force of economic growth. To further discuss the issues of this report made in the above-mentioned context, we will refer to its three key themes, namely "Traditional GDP Issues," "Quality of Life" and "Sustainable Development and Environment." It is important to conclude here that rather than starting from a specific "real model of society" or acceptable perspective, it discusses the mainstream discourses on these three burning issues of contemporary development from a so-called pragmatic point of view.

A Discussion about "the Report"

Any change must start from the presumption that the present is just one option from a horizon of different, other possibilities. The authors, by isolating the three key themes systematically from each other, undermine such a widened integrated view. These themes are crucial when it comes to the proposed analytical view on reality. The separation from one another can only feed the need for a technical rapprochement. This will prevent critical answers to cope with global challenges, a limitation demonstrated by "the report" in its own way. As said, it pleads for "a pragmatic approach that combines limited-scope 'synthetic' indicators" (Stiglitz et al. 2009: 59).

Accordingly, "the report" remains a limited framework to confirm the fundamental parameters of the present systems. It fundamentally leaves unquestioned what we can do on incremental changes and improvements and why. This point of departure also influences the view of policy makers. They are interested in better (and more effective) measures of administration with the help of new technical measures but less concerned with real change in people's living conditions. They prefer to see policy development from pragmatic (and indeed fragmented) approaches, which contradicts their actual claims for empowering people to achieve better ways of managing their lives (see Herrmann 2012). This technical-oriented nature of societal change may undermine the potential of development at the system level, which needs to be reorganized and to coordinate various interests of actors in societies.

As such, this approach undermines any systematic and holistic policy development because of its technical nature. Governance and evidence-based or indicator-oriented political practice are then very much an issue of helplessly dealing with existing and recognized complexities, proposing a misleading understanding of indicators as measurement instruments per se. Seen from this perspective, we can comment on "the report" by three issues. First, the studies on the orientation of the development are restricted to maintaining the structure of the current system. Within this context, topics of economy, quality of life and environment are regarded to be located in different subsystems, and they are seen as relatively independent factors or dimensions. This emphasis refers to the functional perspective of autopoietic systems. Moreover, it fails to acknowledge the distinct functional role of the political system as a "power system," reaching well beyond a self-referential system.

Second, and more fundamentally, "the report" presents a desire to improve the internal functionality of the systems, which are in their own terms considered to be stable. However, this does not even allow asking whether and in which way these systems—the economic system, the sphere of management of lives and the natural environment—are actually worth being maintained. Sustainability as an overarching concept remains bound to the functionality of these systems. The point brought forward in "the report" is the search for mechanisms that allow a reduction of the production of externalities. However, the core question—do we want to maintain the complexities of actual systems—remains unanswered. The segmented approach does not even allow serious engagement in debates on economic development without growth. Taking another example, it does not allow looking honestly into questions around lifestyles and their relevant patterns and how they are systematically rooted in the specific shape of a given accumulation regime (Lipietz 1986).

Any "good will" to change lifestyles or to act more responsibly, to develop a caring approach toward environment and act in a societal-responsible way, can only be as valuable as the politico-economic system itself and requires this orientation. To put it boldly, the separation of the different realms of societal existence—economic activity, living conditions and environment—as it is maintained in "the report" runs into danger of not only perpetuating the given patterns but moreover moving them toward serious mal-developments: better management as further segmentation, tight-fastening the borders between the different segments. Thus, although the report is valuable, it lacks coherence and a theoretical supportive concept.

The third issue is on the social indicators. The commentators of the *Financial Times*, who wrote under a headline "De-fetishising GDP," ask "not [to] pretend to engineer a figure that will tell us how important economic production and wealth are relative to other values." It is emphasized that such orientation is not about queer focusing on "happiness" but has to "elevate other objective indicators of human well-being (such as already existing health, education and environmental sustainability measures) to the status now enjoyed by GDP" (*Financial Times* 2009). Similarly, the German newspaper *Die Zeit* uses the headline "Die Mängel der Statistik" [The Flaws of the Statistics] as if all this debate is based on the problem of measurement. The referrals above question the way to use social indicators to reflect social progress (or better: societal progress) and therefore ask what we mean by "social progress" (or better: societal progress).

The answer to the last question is a condition for applying indicators with which to understand this progress. But as usual in European discourses, the attention for conceptual clarity of social cohesion, social inclusion, social progress and sustainability, among other factors, is lacking. Due to the worldwide desire "to be as pragmatic as possible," the work on conceptual clarity in European discourses has faded since World War II (van der Maesen and Walker 2012). The essential issue of this chapter is not about measuring, however, but how to find a positive outlook. In this regard we can quote two mottoes about measurement. One comes from Bill Hewlett (cofounder of the Hewlett-Packard Company), who states, "You cannot manage what you cannot measure." The other is attributed to a sign that hung on Einstein's office wall: "Not everything that counts can be counted, and not everything that can be counted counts."[2]

The Social Quality Approach (SQA) and Its Indicators

"The report" addresses the function of statistical indicators, not just of measurement but also for planning social progress. It underscores the significance of social indicators to understand a complexity of societal relationships and raises the task of interpreting them as part of complex politico-economic-ecological relationships. However, since "the report" adopts indicators with a GDP-centered orientation, its studies made on indicators did not reveal many valuable observations about social or societal progress. In this respect the SQA presents an indicator system that reflects a societal-focused orientation. This approach starts from a notion of "the social," which connotes a feature of interconnectedness in human relationships and societal organizations.

We may see the SQA's point of departure more or less as a shorthand paradigm for a better, "more social Europe," which implies the connection of the adjective "social" with the noun "the social" as elaborated in the SQA. At the end of the 1990s, it was developed as a rather academic strand of debates, having first only a vague understanding of what "the social" is really about. Although it was not divorced from societal reality, the main orientation had been employed by the need for revisiting the traditional understanding of "social policy" by way of complex methodological considerations. The aim can be described as a search for a more complex methodologically guided understanding of policy making. It may be worthwhile to note that at that stage the use of the terms "social," "social policy" and the like still needed to be systematically elaborated and renewed (Beck et al. 2001). This is a challenging task and surely not yet fully taken up.

With this perception underscored, the SQA developed a framework of analysis with interplay of three sets of factors: the constitutional, the conditional and the normative. Dynamics to push the development of this approach come from a critical discussion on the quality of life approach, as well as the social capital, social development and capability approaches (van der Maesen and Walker 2012). It comes also from the field of urban studies carried out in the city of The Hague (van der Maesen 2012). With full recognition of the significance of indicator studies, researchers working on the SQA insist that the crucial point is to see indicators not only as measurement instruments of the conditional factors—socio-economic security, social cohesion, social inclusion and social empowerment—but also as instruments for analyzing complexities and for revealing the trends of societal change, their contradictions and their challenges. This extension of the meaning of social quality indicators will be realized in confrontation with the outcomes of their application with studies on the nature and change of the constitutional and normative factors.

With reference to the SQA, we regard social quality indicators as different from the view on indicators in mainstream thinking. First of all, at stake is the emphasis on the nature of "the social" and on its developmental character. "The social" emerges at the intersection of relations, defined as opportunities and contingencies, being developed and changed in processes. The orientation for both emerges from the interaction between the two, however, and also from having an "independent" meaning by way of externally defined norms. This should be examined in social quality studies about the interplay of the conditional, constitutional and normative factors and their determinants and assessment (Herrmann 2010: 14). This paves the way for a second argument. We need to apply profiles and criteria as instruments of, respectively, the constitutional and normative factors and to link the results with the application of social quality indicators in order to fully understand the change of the conditional factors itself. This linking will deliver our points of departure to understand the change and consequences of societal complexities. Social quality indicators are necessary (though insufficient) for understanding these complexities and to determine their features of social quality at a specific time and a specific place of society. The presumptions of the SQA differ from the presumptions of quality of life, social capital or capability approaches (van der Maesen and Walker 2012).

In the SQA, if the interpretation of "the social" is understood as a guiding notion, it has also been completed on some normative ground. There is a difficulty in making value judgments due to the danger of its tautological character. Something will be considered to be good because it is considered to be good. There are at least three endeavors to overcome this limitation. Ostrom, coming from an economic perspective, calls for the need to consider normative reasons as part of actions analysis and the consequence evaluation. She contends that we are concerned with "commitments to the norms and rules of a community, not from the incorporation of other's payoffs into one's own payoff" (Ostrom 2005: 173). From a legal perspective, on the other hand, Simmonds underlines the ambiguity of law as it represents an established institution that also acts as a guiding ideal (2007: 21) and that this stands against what Simmonds sees as actual fact, namely that "men and women create their oral identities and values as by-product of interaction and mutual acknowledgement, just as they create culture, language and the structures of thought" (2007: 7). A further inspiring fulcrum has been brought forward by Slife, who emphasizes the importance of looking at rationality, demanding that it be understood as "an ontological rationality" and as such concerned with the fact that "each thing, including each person, is first and always a nexus of relations" (2004: 159).

Thus, while maintaining the orientation on the interdependencies of the application of indicators, profiles and criteria in order to elaborate the SQA, our attention should be paid also to (1) processes that are reflected in the personalities and their active constitution, (2) the practice that is reflected in particular in the productive process and (3) the structure or structuration reflected in the rules, and not least the legal regulations of any society. This argument disfavors a segmented approach of societal issues as happens in "the report," as well as to restrict our attention to social quality indicators' research. Without a further elaboration of the interdependencies of the SQA, the exploration of the three factors remains to a large extent within the framework of traditional perspectives on "social policies" and perhaps even more so of the traditional epistemology of social science. Reading it in a conservative way, the factors mentioned above do not bring anything into the debate that is as such fundamentally new. Therefore we have to make new steps.

Considerations of Productive and Reproductive Interrelationships for the Elaboration of the SQA

The productivist-industrialist paradigm is by and large carried forward, also in recent debates on sustainability. On a tentative level it merged with the biased, middle-class "post-materialist" value orientation and stands behind the danger of falling into some romanticist, uncritical convergence with communitarian ideas. In other words, what is still very much needed is to drive the SQA further, beyond the boundaries of what Giri (2011) recently with some justification called anthropocentrism, Eurocentrism and dualism.

At this stage the difference with mainstream approaches—and also with the core arguments of "the report"—is that the SQA investigates how different moments are constituted in an interactive way by three sets of interacting, conflating dimensions, namely the cognitive and emotional dimension, the objective dimension and the ethical dimension. It is important then to look at how this can be used in order to elaborate an understanding of "the social" as the demonstration of the productive and reproductive human interrelationships. The nature of these interrelationships determines the possibility for development toward sustainability (van Renswoude et al. 2012). The important point for moving forward must be seen in the fact that production is not rejected as a point of reference. However, production gains an entirely new understanding. We can define production—seeing it as a core moment of the definition of "the social"—as a process of relational appropriation.

The real challenge becomes especially clear on the basis of confronting the European approach with realities in Asian countries over the recent years and the analysis and reflections by Asian scholars on the situation in their region. It is important to emphasize that these reflections are only to some extent centrally driven by different philosophies. Rather, as important as different ideologies in the widest sense may be, more important is a fundamentally different reality. Lin elaborates this further. He discusses a Western celebration of "welfare society model" and Asian reluctance toward it and sees on both sides the desire to learn from each other's differences (Lin 2011).

It is important, however, for this learning to look for more abstract references. Terms of welfare society, welfare state, social state and the like must be fundamentally questioned, as the use in different contexts may easily cause confusion. The confrontation with different understandings and contexts actually opens space for new understandings. Still, there is an underlying, implicit shift, made possible by following the arguments for which the SQA provides the seedbed. The focus on production as a process of relational appropriation opens a new perspective on economic processes that are now themselves emerging as going beyond being concerned with the GDP (and the related traditional "social indicators").

A Relational Appraisal

Looking back at "the report," it shows its eclectic approach, namely the justification for a separation of economic, social life and ecological issues. It fails to go beyond GDP and similar traditional measures. In this context, "social life" remains in a bin liner of all aspects of society outside of the economic and ecological realms that are artificially separated. On the other hand, the implicit based notion of "the social" is applied very much in an individualistic sense. This is clearly problematic as demonstrated in the theory of quality of life. We can observe such a combination of the economic understanding of society and the individualistic understanding about people's lives on the website of the third OECD World Forum Measuring the Progress of Societies. We find under the site heading "Main Conclusions of the 3rd OECD World Forum and Proposals for Future Work" (OECD 2009) various documents, one nearly juxtaposing "the social" as an institutional realm. Apparently it is freed from human beings and the personal as space of real people.

At least one contribution's subtitle, *From Measures of a Nation's Progress to Measures of a People's Progress* (Pink 2009), may cause some mystification. Mainstream debates on social policy and its relationship to economy as they are implicitly incorporated in "the report" are characterized by two perspectives. On the one hand—and dominantly—we find the emphasis of economy. It is suggested that we first need to produce the material resources that are then, via social policy, (re)distributed. On the other hand, the productive role of social policy is emphasized. Both perspectives are caught in a traditional model that in no way questions the market as dominant and only a pattern of a productive system. Already this formulation shows the problematic. Generating values is not seen as a matter of what people are doing, as core of the productive process itself and as such linked to use values. Rather, such arguments propose that generating value is equal to generating money.

"The report" problematizes this point too, asking for comprehensive information, integrating the different areas of life and society (Stiglitz et al. 2009: 14). But considerations around different material/monetary dimensions should be better seen as closely embedded in a wider approach to the political economy of societies. In modern times, industrialization and economic growth should no longer be limited to the aspect of productivity or for generating resources for distribution. Thus, we should see these issues in a more general framework of analysis from a view of political economy, with reference to four politico-economic regimes, namely, the accumulation regime, the mode of regulation, the life regime and the mode of life (Herrmann 2009: 44ff.; Boyer and Saillard 2002).

Viewing the SQA, we may say that the present critical view on "the report" is also about stating self-critically that the SQA did have the ambition, made some attempts of overcoming the limitations but was nevertheless caught in the methodological cage of focusing on a traditional understanding of society, namely, carving a "specific social" out of the wider array of living and practicing together. Furthermore, these four forms are also characterized by their contingent character. However, contingency has to be qualified. It is not about arbitrariness. Rather, it goes hand in hand—and even reinforces—the meaning of the relationship between basis and superstructure.

Understanding societal practice, and centrally the productive relationship as a "social relationship"—as presented in the recent SQA (see the new interpretation of the noun "the social")—we have to acknowledge also that they are systems concerned with practice. On danger of oversimplification, we can say that the determination within systems is stronger than the determination of systems. Contingency is then about possibilities of arranging the variations of at least the four different though interdependent relationalities: those between individuals and the (non-social/natural) environment and those existing between groups and classes and the (non-social/natural) environment. We can also say contingency is about the complexity and multitude of possible combinations and the arising interferences.

For the SQA this poses the need to engage more in questions of genuine political economy rather than restricting its economic considerations to areas as welfare economics. This relational view of interpretation about the production process can even be traced back to the Marxian approach that understands capital itself as a process of reproducing social relations between antagonistic forces (Callinicos 2010: 18). The economy is now not only about enhancing productivity and/or pooling resources for distribution. It is fundamentally different, namely, about being by itself a social relationship. The social itself, for the first time, is now approachable as being crucially a matter of sustainability and vice versa.

Moving Forward

The first issue inspired by the debate on "the report" concerns the understanding of "multidimensionality." In "the report" we read for instance about the multifactorial character of quality of life. We are told that "the multi-dimensional nature of quality of life (as opposed to the scalar nature of income) increases the complexity of the analyses and raises a number of measurement issues" (Stiglitz et al. 2009: 144f). However, for assessing the effect of multidimensionality, we need to enter a wider scope of debate and reassess the relations between them. Such work needs to be made in both normative and technological aspects, but it requires an orientation more on societal practices rather than on technocratic reforms. It is certainly true that we can consider these matters in terms of the psychological and personal relations, but even more significant are social relationships in terms of the SQA.

Equally important is to develop an understanding of multidimensionality that does not serve as an excuse for lacking the ability and readiness to make decisions. To elaborate, the SQA will allow us to develop the basis of actions with societal agents playing decisive roles. The Asian debates are in this context of particular interest, confirming the point taken in the present exploration. Lin, for instance, underlines the necessity of looking at the entirety of the production of the social rather than dealing only with the production of goods. This argument is of interest and underlined by Lin's remark to explore the change of the meaning of the institutional context in connection with industrialization and urbanization. This recognition on the meaning of institutional change in assessing social quality is meaningful for individuals and societal agents to actively engage in the act of reconstructing the organic. This underpins the rationale of the SQA, allowing the development of new societal policies (Lin 2011).

What at first glance appears complementary with different kinds of capital in the understanding of Bourdieu is qualified by pointing out that such an exchange of types of capital depends itself on certain power structures that can only be grasped in a wider context. The same meaning is also addressed by Joshi's analysis (2011) of elderly care in India. However, the SQA should be oriented on especial societal practices instead of technocratic reforms in order to take a step forward. The proposal of looking at different sub-approaches of social quality analysis—namely a material-life and institutional approach (conditional factors), an actor/agent-oriented approach (constitutional factors) and an ethical/value-oriented approach (normative factors)—is indeed in heuristic terms a major step forward. But at the same time more effort is needed to explore these different approaches as aspects of a whole. For determining the nature of social quality, we need an understanding of the outcomes of their interdependencies. Therefore, the application of social quality indicators—to understand the nature and changes of the conditional factors—is a necessary but insufficient part of the SQA, which is oriented on this comprehensive whole of interdependencies.

There is also another aspect of special importance. The SQA suggests—for instance, against utilitarianism—that "the social" itself is the ultimate matter. Utilitarianism, as well known, does not deny the meaning of "the social" as such, but it sees the social as "naturalized" rather than "natural" matter. Mill once emphasized "social feelings" as "a powerful principle in human nature." Although utilitarianism thus attributes a relatively high profile to the social, the crux remains that its understanding is based on the assumption of tying together individual entities that are virtually independent to each other. To quote Mill, we are told that "society between equals can only exist on the understanding that the interests of all are to be regarded equally" ([1863] 1987: 39). Importantly, Mills understands "the interests of all" not as aggregated interests but rather as the individual interests that are ex post entering a process of merger. However, the SQA sees "the social" as a genuine matter that is not constituted as an "external," "quasi-independent" "social fact" based on purposeful action. Thus, "the social" is not an outcome of an invisible hand, neither aggregating individual action nor an aggregate entity or a second nature. Furthermore, it is also wrong to see it as a conscious engagement, bringing people together by a decisive act of drawing up a contract.

Outlook: From Household Economy to Social Market and Social Quality

A second issue inspired by the debate on "the report" concerns the understanding of the relation between the economy and economics. To develop this debate we can start from Aristotle's concept of *oikos*, that is, the household economy. The term can be used for a limited meaning of "micro-economy." In the view of Aristotle, the household is in the centrality of "good management" in terms of the economy, since for Aristotle, "real" economy does not concern a kind of wealth production and thus rejects the relevance of chrematistics. Thus, Aristotle delineates chrematistics in a negative sense as profit-making. For him "real" economic concerns are not about such kind of wealth production. The household is more or less incompatible with today's understanding of microeconomics. It is in itself thought as a generic part of a larger societal framework, and the wealth of the household does not consist of material goods but is centrally seen as a matter of social relationships. In this context the availability of goods is not more than an indispensable condition, itself socially defined. Thus, Aristotle pursues an approach that is deeply rooted in individualism as the matter of the performance of the manager, showing some similarities with Plato's Philosopher King (Aristotle 350 BCE).

Another case of reference here can be seen as renaissance of the work by Adam Smith. It concerns the claim that the principles of economic liberalism are not reflected in or even breached by neo-liberalism. The problem is that, on the one hand, Smith was surely oriented on liberalism. But this was based on the assumption of perfection of the general interest by individual action, seeing the market as central means of steering. The problem, however, is that the aim toward which society should move is defined outside of "the economy," seen as a moral obligation. Under certain "ideal conditions" this can be seen as a valid mechanism. However, taking it as the general rule is highly problematic as the economic system itself is systematically undermining its own criteria. We should never forget that Smith was first a moral philosopher, and only from there did he develop his distinct approach toward economics.

The fundamental flaw of these approaches is that they do not sufficiently consider the meaning of the development of the accumulation regime as a genuine economic variable. Turning this around, if we aim on truly merging the different "elements" of the economic process, we have to overcome the individualist presumption and elaborate what we actually understand under "social production." Karl Marx, especially while elaborating his theory of value, emphasized in particular one part of the production. As well known from the *Grundrisse*, he was well aware that production is a complex issue. However, in the concrete analysis focused in some major way on "manufacturing" at this part of the overall process as it is here where labor functions as a spring for generating value. For our context, namely, the matter of distribution and (productive) consumption is, however, of equal importance or even more important. Here we find the important processes by which social value is actually defined. In different ways we find here, rather than in the array of immediate production, a definition of the constellation of the accumulation regime as explained. It is being concerned with the "allocation of the net product between consumption and accumulation." In other words, particularly in the sphere of distribution we are concerned with the definition of the different qualities: broadly, quality of individual's life on the one hand and social quality on the other.

Distribution is here defined as the matter of defining ex ante the different elements of what is "valued," that is, what is considered to be part of the socially produced value. As such it gives a hint also to reconsider GDP and similar measures. And from what was presented here it should go without saying that we are looking for indicators rather than measurements. A further important moment is that such a stance is not least that the definition of the social character is not left to the market where it is the appreciation of the goods (commodity). Rather, here we are concerned with a much wider understanding without pleading for a process of "planned economy." The planning is a matter of planning the mode of production rather than planning the patterns of (private) consumption. Thus, we may not see the market system as self-regulated but rather as emphasizing the equal importance of the distribution and (productive) consumption. With reference to these social characters, we should not leave too many things to the market as the place of producing goods or commodities. Public goods provided in the principle of decommodification should be handled by the social market. The consumption is not on the private goods or commercial goods but on social goods and public services, which improve the standard of social quality.

Conclusions

This chapter involves the issue of indicators, regarding them not only as measurement instruments but also as instruments for societal change. They are pointers for developing an understanding of complex realities and in many cases even function as a kind of "indirect measurement tool" for societal changes. Thus, when studying social quality indicators, more attention must be spent on the question of integrating the different sets of factors. In the SQA, indicators are often used as instruments to reflect the conditional factors without reflecting their interdependencies with the constitutional and normative factors. But we should realize that this "one-sidedness" of indicator use could easily evolve into a replication of a mechanical understanding of the relationship between base and superstructure. Countering this by building on ontological relationality has two advantages. First, it allows developing the non-mechanical understanding of the complex structure of "the social" and as well its ambiguities. Moreover, it allows countering suggestions of mystifying "the social" by way of subjectivation of meaning. By now it should be clear that meaning evolves and is defined as part of the interactive process rather than as part of a transcendental normative setting. According to Giri, "both Atman-centric and socio-centric approaches have their own limitations: what Day Krishna calls the 'two predicaments': … the socio-centric predicament does not give enough space to self-realization while 'Atman centricity leads a people's attention away from an active concern with society and its betterment'" (2011: 112).

Taking the orientation on a true political economy and the role of rule development as a complex practice into account has to make clear that the actual shortcoming of both approaches so far has been the limitation of relations on a matter of initially independent entities. The complexity and the inherent tendency of lacking calculability does not make these indicators less meaningful for policy making than indicators in other traditions, that is, those that are understanding indicators as technical measurement instruments. On the contrary, with the proposed concept we gain a means that allows overcoming many problems of current processes of society building. Rather than referring to societies as contractual-based entities, understood as abstractions from human action, they can be reestablished as part of constitutive processes, locating personalities also in their natural setting and thus allowing a shift of looking at sustainability. It is now emerging as "social sustainability," the maintenance of conditions that allow the production and reproduction of social quality as process of relational appropriation.

Peter Herrmann is Adjunct Professor in the Department of Social Sciences at the University of Eastern Finland, Honorary Associate Professor in the Department of World Economy at Corvinus University of Budapest, correspondent to the Max Planck Institute for Social Law and Social Policy (Munich), Associate Member of the Eurasian Center for Big History and System Forecasting and Member of the Scientific Committee of Eurispes. He currently lives and works in Rome.

Notes

1. In this context, for instance, already the early social indicator movement in the 1970s or later the work by the European Commission's Social Protection Committee, the latter being symptomatic in reflecting the combination of the search for evidence in an age of uncertainty, merging in a pattern of technico-administrative proposals.
2. I am grateful to Yitzhak Berman who provided me with these two quotes—and over the years also with many inspiring comments based on his personal wisdom.

References

Aristotle. 350 BCE. *Politics*.

Beck, W., L. van der Maesen, F. Thomése and A. Walker, eds. 2001. *Social Quality: A Vision for Europe*. The Hague: Kluwer Law International.

Boyer, R. and Y. Saillard, eds. 2002. *Régulation Theory: The State of the Art*. London and New York: Routledge.

Callinicos, A. 2010. *Bonfire of Illusions: The Twin Crisis of the Liberal World*. Cambridge: Polity.

European Commission. 2015. "Beyond GDP." www.beyond-gdp.eu (accessed 7 March 2015).

Financial Times. 2009. "De-fetishising GDP." *Financial Times*, 31 January (Editorial) www.ft.com/intl/cms/s/0/3535c35e-ee3c-11dd-b791-0000779fd2ac.html?nclick_check=1#axzz1iHloaR8x (accessed 2 January 2012).

G20. 2009. "A Framework for Strong, Sustainable, and Balanced Growth." *G20 Leaders Statement: The Pittsburgh Summit*. www.g20.utoronto.ca/2009/2009communique0925.html (accessed 2 January 2012).

Giri, A.K. 2011. "Rethinking the Human and the Social: Towards a Multiverse of Transformations." *International Journal of Social Quality* 1(1): 109–120.

Herrmann, P. 2009. *Social Quality – Looking for a Global Policy Approach: A Contribution to the Analysis of the Development of Welfare States*. Bremen: Europäischer Hochschulverlag.

Herrmann, P. 2010. *Social Quality – Social Policy and Beyond*. William Thompson Working Paper 19. Aghabullogue: European Social, Organisational and Science Consultancy. wvfs.at/wt-wp_old/WT_WP-19_Herrmann_SQ-beyond_SP.pdf (accessed 7 March 2015).

Herrmann, P. 2012. "Social Empowerment." pp. 198–223 in *Social Quality*, van der Maesen and Walker.

Joshi, A.K. 2011. "Globalisation and Ageing in India." *International Journal of Social Quality* 1(1): 33–44.

Lin, K. 2011. "The Prototype of Social Quality Theory and Its Applicability to Asian Societies." *International Journal of Social Quality* 1(1): 57–69.

Lipietz, A. 1986. "New Tendencies in the International Division of Labor: Regimes of Accumulation and Modes of Regulation." pp. 16–40 in *Production, Work, Territory: The Geographical Anatomy of Industrial Capitalism*, eds. A.J. Scott and M. Storper. Boston, London and Sydney: Allen and Unwin.

van der Maesen, L. 2012. "The Function of Social Quality Indicators." pp. 224–249 in *Social Quality*, van der Maesen and Walker.

van der Maesen, L. and A. Walker, eds. 2012. *Social Quality: From Theory to Indicators*. Bakingstoke: Palgrave Macmillan.

Mill, J.S. [1863] 1987. *Utilitarianism*. London: Penguin.

Organization for Economic Co-operation and Development (OECD). 2009. "Main Conclusions of the 3rd OECD World Forum and Proposals for Future Work." www.oecd.org/

document/53/0,3746,en_40033426_40033828_43963509_1_1_1_1,00.html (accessed 2 January 2012).

Ostrom, E. 2005. *Understanding Institutional Diversity*. Princeton, NJ: Princeton University Press.

Pink, B. 2009. *Maintaining the Momentum in Australia: From Measures of a Nation's Progress to Measures of a People's Progress*. www.oecd.org/dataoecd/55/18/43964070.pdf (accessed 2 January 2012).

Simmonds, N. 2007. *Law as a Moral Idea*. Oxford: Oxford University Press.

Slife, B.F. 2004. "Taking Practice Seriously: Toward a Relational Ontology." *Journal of Theoretical and Philosophical Psychology* 24(2): 157–178.

Stiglitz, J., A. Sen and J.P. Fitoussi. 2009. *The Measurement of Economic Performance and Social Progress Revisited: Reflections and Overview*. www.stiglitz-sen-fi toussi.fr/documents/overview-eng.pdf (accessed 1 February 2011).

van Renswoude, K.J., et. al. 2012. *Development toward Sustainability – The Need for a Comprehensive Conceptual and Methodological Framework for New Politics and Policies: A Social Quality Perspective*. A Report Presented by the International Association on Social Quality (i.s.n.). The Hague, Netherlands.

Vorholz, Fritz. 2009. "Die Mängel der Statistik. In Wahrheit misst das Bruttoinlandsprodukt gar nicht den Wohlstand. Forscher suchen Alternativen." *Die Zeit* 14, 28 March, www.zeit.de/2009/14/BIP (accessed 6 March 2015).

CHAPTER 6

The Human and the Social
A Comparison of the Discourses of Human Development, Human Security and Social Quality

Des Gasper

Introduction

Attempts to extend and use the social quality approach in East and Southeast Asia have raised the question of how it relates, first, to the "human security approach"—which has been prominent in various Asian fora, notably Japan and Thailand, and in the work of some United Nations agencies (UNESCO, the Secretariat, etc.) and development NGOs—and second, to the partner approach led by the United Nations Development Programme (UNDP), the "human development approach," which has become well known since 1990, especially in the form of global, national and local *Human Development Reports*. Both the social quality approach and the human development and security approaches can be seen as reactions to an economy-centered worldview. Both schools try to bring analytical and policy integration across conventional sectoral and disciplinary boundaries, with concern for priority criteria of human well-being (Gasper et al. 2008).[1]

One difference between the approaches is seen in their titles: one school emphasizes the "human," the other the "social." A repeated criticism of the human development approach has been that its picture of personhood is too simple and understates the formation and existence of persons as social products (Apthorpe 1997; Douglas and Ney 1998; Davis 2003). UNDP-sponsored human development writing conceives of "human" mostly in an individualist way, says Apthorpe (2008), who suggests that this conception of "human" fits with a preoccupation with "capacity-building," which UN bodies and similar organizations find less "political" than social reform and "lowering of barriers." Does social quality theory provide an avenue for feasible enrichment of the human development approach?

This chapter takes as given a basic familiarity with social quality theory (see, e.g., Gasper et al. 2008; Phillips 2006). It introduces key themes of the human development and especially human security approaches. It then compares the three approaches by using frameworks developed for clarifying the construction of theories of quality of life like social quality theory (Gasper 2010a) and of broad orienting perspectives like human security analysis (Gasper 2010b).[2] In particular, we will explore the approaches' purposes and roles.

The UN Human Development and Human Security Approaches

The human development approach referred to here was created by a group of socially and development-oriented economists who were working for, with and in the UN system, in reaction against neo-liberal market economics of the 1980s. The leading figure was the Pakistani economist Mahbub ul Haq, who founded the UNDP's Human Development Report Office in 1989. He sought to bring a person-focused reorientation of the centrally important and potent term "development," away from the volume of monetized production, toward the contents and quality of the lives of individuals. Drawing on the thinking of Amartya Sen, the approach (re)interprets "development" to mean expansion of the range of favorably valued life alternatives attainable by ordinary persons.

Haq also initiated the language of "human security," in the *Human Development Report 1994*, as a complement to the "human development" idea. Again he sought to reorient a central concept, "security," to make it focus on life quality of each and every person. The concept of human security added to the "human development" language by its emphasis on ensuring basic requirements and stability, not just on expansion of the aggregate or average range of attainable favorably valued life paths. Work in terms of "human security" partly occurs as a junior wing of "human development" analysis but has also spread beyond it organizationally and intellectually (UNESCO 2008; Tadjbaksh and Chenoy 2007). The two languages are now often found in parallel professional communities that talk relatively little with each other. Here we treat them as siblings and partners, for "human security" thinking has a potential to enrich the human development approach in ways that are not apparent simply by listing their definitions. "Human security" is a discourse, a way of thinking, that ramifies far beyond a single concept. So too indeed is "human development," which we may see as a less evolved version of the same enterprise (Gasper and Truong 2010; Mine 2008).

Central to being human is that we are embodied persons with various specific requirements. This theme becomes highlighted in human security thinking. Human security thinking focuses on securing the basics—including physical and mental security—for the least advantaged people and on security of basics for all. The Millennium Development Goals programs have been a partial attempt in this direction. The concept of "human security" connects also to people's fears and feelings. It can evoke a sense of real lives and persons, and supports an anthropological-type concern for understanding how individual persons live. Such a perspective can ground human rights and human development thinking better, in attention to the nature of being and well-being (Gasper and Truong 2010). The risks and insecurities are diverse and case- and person-specific, and partly subjective. To "the question: what relieves individuals of fear, what liberates them from duress[, the] answer is obviously culturally contingent, context dependent, fixed in a social field, implicitly linked to a moral environment" (Burgess et al. 2007: 92). Human security work must thus be attentive to perceptions and worries, especially of the least advantaged people but more broadly too.

Attention to risks involves attention to "externalities": interconnections between spheres of life that are conventionally considered as separate, for example, between economic fluctuations on the one hand and phenomena such as health decline, the generation and spread of diseases, environmental changes,and cultural and political reactions on the other. Awareness of these "collateral effects" can build appreciation of a shared human fate: "the recognition of an interconnected world with interconnected threats. The approach of human security broadens the concept of security and emphasizes first and foremost the monitoring and maintaining of human rights everywhere as a basis of security for everyone. [So for example,] security for Europeans can therefore only be achieved by promoting rights-based and universal freedoms for Europeans and non-Europeans alike" (Burgess et al. 2007: 98–99). Unlike in narrow conceptions of "development," which function as formats for attempted generalization and command by rich countries over poor countries, this broad version of human security thinking applies to all regions and to the world as a whole.

Work in Germany by Werthes, Debiel and Bosold (e.g., Debiel and Werthes 2006) and in the Netherlands by Gasper (e.g., 2010b) discusses human security discourse's roles and purposes. The overall role is as a broad meta-discourse that guides work in many more detailed areas. Key specific roles include: (1) the most obvious one, providing certain evaluative criteria, as mentioned above; (2) providing a shared conceptual schema that coordinates endeavors across a wide intellectual community; using these criteria and categories to guide the work of (3) identifying and formulating relevant causal chains and patterns, and of (4) identifying and formulating policy priority problems and actions; and, not least, (5) providing motivation to energize and sharpen these demanding activities. The work in areas of detailed application is extremely diverse. The usefulness of such a conceptual scheme of human security—which is not itself a specific theory and should not be judged by that standard—for motivating and guiding policy-relevant analyses is illustrated in the wide-ranging and creative work summarized by the Commission on Human Security (2003; led by Sadako Ogata and Amartya Sen), in many national human development reports, as summarized by Jolly and Basu Ray (2007), and, for example, in Picciotto et al. (2007) and UNESCO (2008).[3]

UNESCO has used human security as a lead theme to try to guide, coordinate and motivate its vast range of concerns. It commissioned a series of regional reviews of its activities in terms of their relevance to human security. This led to a set of books (e.g., Burgess et al. 2007; Lee 2004; Tadjbaksh et al. 2007), which are synthesized in a recent overview volume (UNESCO 2008). From a survey of resource persons it records this conclusion:

> There is overwhelming agreement that, while the holistic aspect and non-fixed definition of human security is a problem that continues to draw criticism and doubt as to the efficacy

of the concept, it is precisely its breadth and multidimensionality that make it relevant. (UNESCO 2008: 136)

Human security is found valuable as a unifying concept that helps us move beyond archaic nineteenth-century divisions in the organization of knowledge that are built into our academic systems and systems of governance, including in design of the UN system itself (146).

After this outline of a human security perspective, we move to a systematic comparison with the social quality approach.

Situating the Approaches in the Range of Approaches to Quality of Life

Different conceptual and theoretical approaches to quality of life and well-being represent different responses to a series of choices (Gasper 2010a; Phillips 2006). Concerning *focus and scope*: which aspects of *life* are included? The choices made here reflect a further five factors. First, which *values* lie behind a particular interpretation of *well*-being and/or *quality* of life? Second, which *purposes* guide the sort of valuation exercise that is done; is it for purposes of understanding or of evaluating/praising/ condemning or of choosing/acting? Third, by whom and from what *standpoint* is the exercise undertaken: for oneself, for others, for and in groups? Which groups of people are speaking about what (and about whom), and to which audiences? Fourth, which *theoretical framework,* disciplinary tradition and fundamental assumptions are employed? For example, what conception of personhood is adopted? And fifth, which *methods* of observation and/or measurement and which methods of interpretation are employed? All these choices in an approach typically reflect its disciplinary background.

In relation to the aforementioned questions, we observe that quality-of-life approaches range from those that have a primary focus on mental states, through some with a focus on the resources and effective opportunities held by individuals, through others with a focus on societal environmental conditions conducive to good quality of life. Social quality theory is among the approaches that essay a comprehensive coverage, looking at all of these. It gives attention to mental states, including those involved in personal capability, social recognition and personal security, but its main focus has been on what it considers the more objective conditional factors—social inclusion, socio-economic security and so on. In terms of theoretical frameworks, we see a similar range, from more methodologically individualist approaches to more methodologically holist approaches.

Let us consider several of these dimensions of choice in the social quality approach (SQA) and human development/human security (HDS) work. We will not discuss choices of research instrument, for there both streams are flexible and pragmatic.

Comparisons

Focus, Scope and Guiding Values in HDS Work and SQA

Both streams choose a very broad scope. This is more standardized in SQA work and more flexible and wide-ranging in HDS work. The idea of social quality covers at least four major component areas, including social cohesion, social inclusion and social empowerment, not merely socio-economic security. The socio-economic security aspect of SQA concerns life chances and social risks (Beck et al. 2001). These are the same foci as in HDS work, except the latter refers to access to and risks around *all* valued doings and beings, not only those which may be called "socio-economic." SQA does cover some other valued doings and beings, through its attention to social recognition and social membership. It has, however, been a somewhat narrower conception, reflecting its origin in European social policy debates and associated ideas about which matters are within the remit of public policy. In HDS work, the wide-ranging, in principle unrestricted, scope does not mean that its analysis is never-ending but rather that the particular variables that are highlighted will depend on a judgment in the particular case, about which are the threats and interconnections that most demand attention there (see, e.g., Jolly and Basu Ray 2007; UNESCO 2008).

Within social quality work, too, focus within its broad scope will partly reflect ideas about priority values. Lin and Gabe argue that "social quality studies take social integration, citizens' participation and democracy as the key, which is suitable for the cases of European societies" (2007: 347). In China, "familistic groupism" continues as the core component in social cohesion (337); "people have a weak sense of public citizenship, and the normative and institutional contexts … discourage them from developing social democracy in the name of citizenship" (345). Similarly, "as for social empowerment, there is a great distance between … the values and meanings of mass democracy in European and Asian societies" (347).[4] Even in Europe, Calloni (2001) argues that already before its recent enlargements, the European Union was too diverse for the implicitly Northern European / Nordic model in the existing SQA to be valid for all member countries. SQA needed to become more cosmopolitan, she suggested. Achieving this faces no fundamental obstacles, as seen by the ongoing vigorous adaptation of social quality work in East Asia.

Concerning the natural environment, both families of work are humanist in the general sense and have accordingly been relatively weak in attention to environment, although human security work increasingly transcends this. The human development strand, with its emphasis on increasing the range of human choices, has been "problematically ambiguous" on questions of environment (Phillips and Berman 2007: 473). However, the notion of "sustainable human development" has been prominent in United Nations work since the mid-1990s, and the impressive *Human Development Report 2007–08* from the UNDP is on climate change. The human security strand has gone further to include a central concern for environmental sustainability (as in Springer-Verlag's Hexagon book series on Human and Environmental Security and Peace; e.g., Brauch 2007). While no panacea, the human security approach does direct our attention to key issues concerning physical environment and the interlinkages; environmental sustainability will only be possible within governance arrangements that reflect a good understanding of people's felt insecurities. SQA, in contrast, has been preoccupied with social sustainability and gives little attention so far to environmental sustainability. Bouget (2001) and Phillips (2006) pointed out this gap, Phillips and Berman (2007) provided a first response and work is now underway.

A key issue that is perhaps not yet considered by either social quality or human development work concerns the activist strand in capitalist society. Some human security work, with its attention to psychological security and insecurity, does consider this. The unending expansionist drive of capitalism not only stems from its institutional design in which, first, many groups in society gain only if commoditized economic turnover expands and, second, market competitors fear that they will be eaten if they do not first eat others. The institutional design reflects and is added to by deeper factors (Gasper 2009). Not recognized in most classifications of perspectives on quality of life is one of the dominant perceptions in the modern world: an activist stance in which well-being consists not just in maximizing monetized flows but also where the good life is the packed, busy, strenuous life, the exertion to the full of one's human forces in unceasing aspiration, acquisition and contestation. In our era of rapid disappearance of glaciers and the Northern polar cap, research on social quality and human development must look at environmental devastation and dangers and the deeper forces driving them.

Another finding from this comparison of approaches' scope is that—in contrast to its careful exploration of ontology, which we refer to in the next section—SQA's engagement with substantive theory about well-being is as yet limited in some respects, reflecting a mistrust of work on subjective well-being and a distance from the economics-and-philosophy tradition represented by human development theorists like Sen and Nussbaum. SQA has much to gain here from interaction with "the human discourses" and similar work. Bill Jordan (2004, 2008) presents a more elaborate theorizing of the nature and sources of well-being than is used in SQA, undertaken from a philosophical and empirical basis that is closer to SQA than are Sen or Nussbaum.[5]

Theoretical Frameworks—Conceptualizing Being in Society

A strong theme from Phillips's book (2006) surveying theories of quality of life and human well-being is the contrast between individual-centered and society-centered approaches. Human development (HD) and SQA work illustrate this contrast: human development thinking is more individual-centered, SQA more society-centered, and human security thinking lies in between. However, a basis exists for cooperative work.

The human development thinking led by Haq and Sen represents an enrichment of the perspectives of welfare economics. The conception of welfare in mainstream economics has centered on individuals' degree of access to commodities that they prefer. Western economics inherited Descartes's monological picture of subjectivity, with the human subject conceived as "isolated from other subjects and confronting a world of things which it seeks to use and control" (Callinicos 2007: 286, paraphrasing Habermas). Sen transcended, first, the welfare economics focus on commodities by making well-being theory look at the content of people's lives in terms of valued functionings and the ranges of valued options they have, not just at the contents of their wallets and homes (Sen 2009). This notion has wide appeal—it was adopted, for example, by the European Commission, for whom empowerment and development became defined as increasing the range of human choice (European Commission 1996). Sen moves, second, to a richer conception of personhood than the monological subject; he rejects the idea of a single psychic currency of "utility" and gives a central significance to public reasoning (2009).

The formulations remain clearly a variant of liberal individualism: "Durkheim argued that modernity *sanctifies* the individual, as the ultimate basis of value and holiness" (Jordan 2004: 8). This "cult of the human individual—identity, expression and fulfilment" has intensified in the West since Durkheim's day, with increasing preoccupation with "intimate relationships and consumer lifestyles" (ibid.). By the late twentieth century, many rich countries had experienced a decisive shift from a view of social life as rule governed, and as rightly and necessarily so ordered, to a belief in life in society as choice—choices that are and should be made by individuals and "not derived from stable moral or political traditions" (Jordan 2004: 17) but instead by constant review and reconsideration of priorities and directions, including in interpersonal relations.

An approach to human development requires—for purposes of understanding and motivation, not only evaluative accounting—to say more about "human," human action and personhood than just a stress on reasoned valuation and choice. Sen inherited a utilitarian conception of persons and society, in the sense stated by Talcott Parsons (1937): society is seen as a sum of individuals, and individuals are seen as reasoners who make choices, rather than as more fundamentally social actors. His "thinking originates within the liberal tradition of ideas about individuals and society that takes individuals as pre-given independent agents. … Sen does not actually have a *theory* of the individual," according to Davis (2003: 163–164). But a way of life is more than a set of private choices; personality and identity have a psychic and social grounding, and community memberships typically have more than instrumental status. In Nussbaum's richer and more realistic formulation of human development theory, affiliation is treated as a universal good in itself, not just as a handy instrument for giving individuals more options that they value (Nussbaum 2000).

Social quality thinking takes a more social conception: "the individual is totally dependent on the social appreciation [by] his/her social environment" (Beck et al. 2001: 327). Human security work lies in between. But nor does SQA occupy an extreme position in the spectrum: it has explicitly sought a synthesis of individual-centered and society-centered approaches. Thus, its complex definition of social quality (Beck et al. 2001: 6–7) may be simplified to "the conditions necessary for personal well-being," as suggested by Therborn (2001; my paraphrase). These conditions include, first, resources available to individuals, which Therborn suggests subsume the socio-economic security and empowerment aspects (the latter includes individuals' skills and capabilities), and, second, the environments that surround individuals (including norms, institutions, infrastructures), which subsume, he suggested, the social cohesion and inclusion dimensions. In contrast, the mainstream of human development thinking has until recently given little attention to issues of cohesion and inclusion. It has, though, begun to think about the formation of individual identity and the nature of community membership, as in the *Human Development Report 2004* (UNDP 2004).

Sen and the UNDP's human development theory has paid little attention to locating itself in relation to ideas in sociology, a discipline that has traditionally rejected Descartes's stance. In contrast, social quality theory has been preoccupied with doing so. For social quality theory, "the social refers to configurations of interacting people as social beings" (Beck et al. 2001: 312), and the structure of these configurations is critically important: "[it] is not the psychology of individuals which holds the secret of human affairs, but the ensemble of relations of human subjects as social beings" (310). Social quality theory's stance here has similarities to the ideas of Mary Douglas and Pierre Bourdieu. Bourdieu sought to transcend both structuralism, which reduces individuals to the effect of structures, and methodological individualism, which reduces structures to the unintended side effects of individuals' actions (Callinicos 2007; Hodgson 2004). SQA's link to this evolving Durkheimian tradition comes via Habermas, who in turn had drawn on Parsons.

Ananta Giri (2011) criticizes some of these positions in Western social and economic theory. Some of his criticisms are close to those made in other lines of Western theory and to positions taken by SQA and human security theory. First, in contrast to both methodological individualism and socio-centric approaches, we should think in terms of ontological reciprocity of individual and society. Here, Giri is close to the SQA perspective. Second, both "human" and "social" are adjectival terms that refer to ongoing processes of interaction and unfolding. This theme is mirrored in human security (HS) theory, for which "the understanding of the social is not pre-determined but evolves with the monitoring of social change. … the 'social' [is] a multi-layered entity open to transformation by diverse transnational forces, such as transnational families, transnational social activism and new transnational spaces of communication" (Gasper et al. 2008: 27, 28). Third, Giri reminds us that we require a multidimensional conception of the self, as simultaneously consisting of techno/practitioner, the unconscious and the transcendental. The latter two aspects are more attended to in HS thinking than in SQA. Finally, he warns the "human" theorists of the significance of humankind's animal heritage, and he warns "social" theorists that "the social" is by no means automatically normatively favorable. In the modern West, both these strands of thinking about being human in society lack the broad reverence for life that is required as basis for species survival, he fears. Human security thinking, with its concern for environmental embedding and global interconnections, is hospitable, though, to this final point. Social quality thinking is perhaps only beginning to give attention to the elements of violence in "human" and in "social," and to respect for the nonhuman.

Our first two stages of comparison generate the following suggestions: SQA offers a basis in sociological theory to help to ground human security (and human development) work, and the latter provides an agenda of priority criteria and priority threats to help in orientating social quality work. Otherwise, social quality work could face a danger of becoming a factory of routine monitoring of diverse corners of quality of life, serving rather than questioning the "system world."[6] Ulrich Beck's work on "risk society" has extended Habermas's investigation of the invasion by the system world (for example, the impersonal mechanisms of the market) into the lifeworld. The invasion dissolves traditional formations, releases individualization and enlarges risks. Understanding this is central in human security research, whereas human development discourse that talks only of the expansion of choices is in danger of feeding the processes that Beck describes. SQA includes Habermas's concerns centrally, looks at the impact of these invasions and can work in partnership here with human security studies.

Purposes and Standpoint of an Approach

Subordination to the system world is a danger for scientific approaches with large appetites for data, at any rate for funded data collection. Apthorpe (2008) suggests that the work on human development has run into this danger. It has become preoccupied with snapshots of situations rather than attention to institutions and processes. He warns that, for example, a racist situation and racism as an institution— or poverty as a situation of deprivation versus poverty as a religious institution—are very different topics and require quite different forms of conceptualization and research methods. Aspects of situations can be captured by numerical scores, but institutional complexes and social structures cannot be adequately understood in this way. We must consider carefully what to monitor by reflecting on research purposes.

Let us take a longer example, concerning choices of purpose and standpoint for work using the social quality approach. Nijhuis (2007) discusses practices of social policy in Europe (and especially, in his case study, the Netherlands), in which agencies are increasingly sectoralized and "professionalized" so that they operate without much reference to each other or to any coordinating agency, including even local government. They have drifted into their own abstracted worlds of management jargon, "product orientation, accountability, output steering, marketing and advertising," and away from an integrated concern for ordinary people's lives (Nijhuis 2007: 28). He illustrates, in particular, how this undermines or fails to improve people's health. He describes, in contrast, a project with people in a locality of The Hague that, consistent with the social quality approach, treated them as whole people and active agents rather than as sites of particular isolated symptoms or other "customer characteristics." The project very significantly upgraded health, indirectly, by helping people to form new self-images and new contacts that contributed to changing their lifestyle in healthier directions.

Social quality concepts proved useful in this health project "as a conceptual scheme to interpret and clarify what was done" (Nijhuis 2007: 33) and to communicate that to other professionals and policy makers. It "was not introduced by exposing it deductively in its entire social theoretical content and shape" (34). More or less, the same applied in an exercise with managers of the sectoralized, "professionalized" private social service organizations: informal use of social quality concepts gave a language to identify and discuss key issues in their work. But "the proposal to adopt SQ as a common conceptual scheme for the development of a shared vision on urban development in The Hague was strongly rejected by the managers" (36–37). Attempts to introduce social quality theory as an explicit framework to synthesize and organize the work of the numerous different strands of scientific research on urban issues proved equally fruitless. The lesson has been learned for current work with local government councillors, managers and bureaucrats, which proceeds more fruitfully by leaving the full intellectual framework implicit.

Nijhuis distinguishes four possible purposes or roles of the social quality approach, respectively as:

1. a normative political vision;
2. a full scientific approach, providing theory and methodology for description, explanation, measurement and perhaps even prediction: "a comprehensive metatheoretical scheme" (2007: 40);
3. a heuristic conceptual scheme that can serve as a tool of policy influence: "a configuration of concepts and a way of reasoning about urban development ... a language, which can be shared by actors with diverging perspectives. ... It [appears] to carry the great capacity to inspire, to structure, to connect and to guide" (42);
4. use of the heuristic conceptual scheme also as a scientific tool for suggesting relevant lines of research, including relevant categories for organizing observation and measurement.

Phillips (2011) likewise contrasts the options of a total theory and a more loosely articulated perspective. Nijhuis noted that version 2 faced more resistance in urban management circles in the Netherlands and points to the difficulties that any new way of thinking faces: it is hard to absorb by those trained in other "languages" and is seen as a competitor and a threat. In addition, all of the categories that the SQA uses are inevitably somewhat vague—such as empowerment, cohesion, inclusion, lifeworld, system world—and have, or at least had, substantial overlaps (see, e.g., Bouget 2001), so one has to be careful in the associated scientific claims (see also Berman 2008). Any full scientific approach will take many years to develop and require the work of large numbers of people. Yet, even when not yet generating "a scientific theory in the traditional sense" (Nijhuis 2007: 41), SQA's categories and schemata are already clearly useful in increasing aspects of our understanding and in helping to steer our research activity and practical action in better-informed ways. In other words, SQA serves as a heuristic set of maps, both in description/explanation and in processes of planned change. This is similar to the understanding we saw earlier of human security discourse: as a generative methodology and heuristic conceptual scheme rather than as a formal scientific model or evaluation template (see, e.g., Jolly and Basu Ray 2007).

Göran Therborn suggests that social quality work could concentrate on supporting broad social consultation more than on expert working groups to prepare social quality indicators (2001). Arguably however, the preparation and use of indicators can provide a good location for social consultation, depending on how the indicators work is undertaken. Denis Bouget (2001) warned likewise that the variety of distinct purposes in SQA could be in tension: a broad rhetoric with which to point to issues, an interpretive theoretical framework, an explanatory model, a detailed evaluative model, a political program. He advised that the first two might be the more important: a highlighting of areas of concern and a framework for how they interconnect. For these purposes, the SQA diagram of the "architecture of social quality" is central: it lists the posited conditional factors, constitutive factors and normative principles of social quality as three connected pillars.[7] The "quadrant" diagrams—"orthogonal graphs" (Bouget 2001)—using vaguely defined categories are useful as an aide-mémoire, to help recollect agenda items, but do not deserve much more emphasis.[8]

A relevant comparison here is to the influential "Cultural Theory" created by Mary Douglas (1982) and taken further by many associates. Douglas and her co-workers extended ideas from the Durkheimian tradition in a simple and widely applicable but, if subtly used, sophisticated methodology. They too work with quadrant diagrams to identify and understand possible cultural orientations. For some readers the categories have seemed too vague and general, and the diagrams and their dichotomies irritatingly simplistic. Yet Cultural Theory has grown over four decades to become a considerable stream of work (e.g., Rayner and Malone 1998; Verweij and Thompson 2006). By conceiving itself as an heuristic methodology of investigation, not as a photographic mapping of reality, it has proved to be a fruitful way to generate relevant questions, contrasts and insights into complex, fluid, multilayered social realities. It fulfils functions 3 and 4 in Nijhuis's list: a heuristic conceptual scheme that serves both as one scientific tool and as a framework for policy discussions. The combination of simplicity (four main cultural orientations, generated by two orthogonal dimensions) and potential depth has encouraged wide adoption and application in the past twenty years—*after* it became understood as a guiding heuristic rather than as the equivalent of a universally valid X-ray picture of human societies. The quadrant diagrams became reconceived, simply as ways of making relevant contrasts. Thus, within each quadrant one can again subdivide into quadrants, whenever helpful for investigating a particular situation. This is illustrated in Hood's celebrated *The Art of the State* (2000).

Beck et al. imply that SQA might have similar potential: "in each component the same structural determinants exist. In other words, the dialectic between the self-realization of the individual subject and the formation of collective identities determines the essence of each component" (2001: 337). A sister to Hood's book, entitled "The Art of Society," might show SQA as a fruitfully generative methodology for investigation and policy diagnosis-and-design rather than as an attempt to specify a universal DNA of society. Lin and Gabe, for example, present a review of social quality indicators that uses the social quality categories to support a broad investigative and interpretive narrative of social change in China and its risks, including of division and conflict. They use the social quality approach to "[probe] the very foundations of the social system [in China], including both normative and institutional perspectives" (2007: 345).

A Review of Contrasts and Suggestions

We can now summarize possible contrasts and complementarities between the approaches, as a set of hypotheses that can lead to more detailed work. A tabular annex contains a fuller overview and some additional points that arise from a step-by-step comparison. This summary, like the annex and the chapter as a whole, starts from a critique of the human development formulation and a wish to upgrade it, then concentrates on social quality research and human security thinking as sources for doing that, and comes to some conclusions about how they can also support each other.

1. One perspective on respective roles is as follows. Human development thinking provides a survey of issues about human "beings and doings" nationwide and worldwide, as we see in the huge data annexes of the *Human Development Reports*. These annexes, like the whole of HD thinking, need principles based in social theory, such as from SQA, to help identify priorities for the data collection and to better structure their presentation. Human security thinking provides an orientating and motivating overview of major threats and of their interconnections. Social quality theory provides a series of theorized checklists for helping us think about some of the underlying aspects—including the constitution of the human individual in society, the ongoing dialectic of identity formation and self-realization and the nature of some of the threats.

2. The approaches have differences in scope and focus. Social quality work is typically more nation- (and city-) centered, with less focus on natural environment, than is human security work, which is also transnational and global, but this could be a complementarity rather than an incompatibility. They have partly overlapping intended audiences. The approaches could come together in thinking about societal and environmental sustainability, linking global and local themes.

3. They appear similarly potentially compatible in terms of their guiding values and ontology of personhood and society, if we put aside more strongly individualist variants of HD theory. We noted the gap in understanding of the "human" in most work so far in the human development approach, in particular in understanding humans as social beings. In the same way, narrower conceptions of human security considered at length the concept of "security" but not enough the content of "human." But other work on human security (e.g., Burgess et al. 2007; Mushakoji 2003) goes far deeper and can enrich conceptions of personhood and self-development in the human development approach (cf. Giri 2000). Work on "social quality" can complement these efforts. It offers one way to conceptualize some of the issues involved and provides a structured form of thinking about "the social." While it has a risk of itself being in some ways oversimplified, it can—like that in some ways comparable to the Cultural Theory of Douglas and her school—function as a helpful methodology in investigation.

4. This potential role, as a guiding methodology, is less likely to be fulfilled if SQA aspires to be a comprehensive ontology of social life. Phillips (2011) has suggested that if SQA aspires to be a total theory, then it becomes harder for it to have allies, both because it leaves no space for others and because it exposes itself to more criticism. Seen instead as what he calls a loosely articulated perspective, then, it can readily and usefully have partnerships with other loosely articulated perspectives, such as those of human development and human security. Loose articulation does not necessarily represent lower theoretical standards. Within the HDS tradition, Sen adopts an "assertive incompleteness" on many issues—we should not seek more precision and clarity on questions than their nature allows (2009). Many important concepts and values are inherently ambiguous, and we should try to understand and intelligently handle that ambiguity rather than try to eradicate it.

Human security thinking contains suggestions for social quality thinking, which was not originally conceived within a global analytical and ethical framework but emerged from a network of academics and practitioners seeking to influence practice at the levels of municipality, nation and European Union in reaction to neo-liberal trends. The transformation of the EU in recent years by the entry of many new members with an emphatic neo-liberal orientation made that work harder. The project of "social democracy in [one half of] one [sub]continent" proves as elusive as was that of "socialism in one country." For extending its descriptive, explanatory and moral focus in more cosmopolitan directions, SQA will gain much from intensive Europe-Asia interaction and from debate with "the human discourses." It also has much to offer.

Des Gasper is Professor of Human Development, Development Ethics and Public Policy at the International Institute of Social Studies in The Hague, a graduate school within Erasmus University Rotterdam. He teaches and researches on governance and policy discourses, especially in relation to value choices that are involved and to the fields of global environmental change and international migration. His publications include *The Ethics of Development* (2005) and *Transnational Migration and Human Security: The Migration-Development-Security Nexus* (edited with T-D. Truong; 2011).

Annex: A Suggested Comparison of Three Approaches

	Social Quality Approach	Human Development Approach	Human Security Approach
Focus—1	The good society, in a national context (within, originally, the EU regional context)—recently SQA begins to reflect on its European visions of "society," "security" and "state," and to review them in a transnational context.	The good society, in a global context	Risk, disaster, collapse—as parts of the overall texture of real and/or perceived and possible daily existence of real ordinary people—understood in a global context
Focus—2	Apparent lack of much attention yet to ecological sustainability and to global sustainability	Includes sustainability in its definitions and in some of its work	Emphasizes sustainability (including in terms of peace, physical health, mental health, ecology)
Focus—3	Indicators and measurement are a major preferred focus, including with the aim of gaining attention of policy makers.	Contains different streams: – measurers and model builders – institutional analysts and system builders	Focuses on institutional arrangements that reflect the philosophy and methodology mentioned above
Value focus	Welfare, the welfare state—seeks to defend welfare within the nation-state, against impinging forces of globalization	A broader set of values than those measured in markets, constitutive of decent human existence and, further, human flourishing	Human rights, basic rights—prioritization in the face of challenges

	Social Quality Approach	Human Development Approach	Human Security Approach
Intended Audience	Governments (central, local), and intranational and regional agencies (e.g., the European Commission)—this may explain the limited attention to issues of global peace and environment.	National and international agencies seeking coherence in their work—this leads to a typical highlighting of the universal and downgrading of the nationally and socially specific.	National and international agencies seeking coherence in their work— but the situation specificity of actual and perceived threats leads to a strong situational character
Theoretical background: Ontology	Individual and systems as mutually constitutive	Individualist—but aware that the individual exists within social systems	Has many variants—some that are the same in this respect as the human development approach and some that are as the next cell below
... of identity	People are group members, who acquire, generate and innovate identities.	People are individuals who may be faced with identity choices or prioritizations between different elements of identity (Sen 2006).	People are group members whose identities can be sources of conflict and sources of solace in the face of conflicts—with scope for evolution.
... of personhood	How far is the language of sense-making used in SQA?	Persons have emotions and seek meanings.	Persons have emotions, and seek refuges, solace and meanings.
... and of society	Complex notion of "the social": "configurations of interacting people as social beings" who seek to "realize themselves"(Beck et al. 2001: 312, 310). It can help us to think about the evolution of "the social."	Little notion of the social—elements of actual and potential identity are available, floating in the individual's environment, in an unexplained way.	"The understanding of the social is not pre-determined but evolves with the monitoring of social change" (Gasper et al. 2008: 27).
Purposes	Sometimes attempts to be a comprehensive explanatory system; sometimes instead sees itself mainly as a methodology for investigation and evaluation, as do the HD approach and HS approach	Heuristic frame/ methodology for structuring policy-relevant investigation (e.g., Dreze and Sen 1989, 2002; Gasper 2008)	Has a philosophy of interconnectedness but makes no attempt to be comprehensive; instead focuses situation-by-situation on what are adjudged to be the key sources of threat to what are felt as key threatened values in that situation (Jolly and Basu Ray 2007)

Notes

1. Gasper et al. (2008: 25–26) identify as points of similarity between the social quality theory and human development and human security approaches: (1) a focus on the well-being of persons, rather than a primary focus on "the economy"; (2) an explicit normative basis, beyond values as expressed through purchases in markets; (3) multidimensional conception of human well-being, rather than reduction to a "utility" denominator; (4) concern about interconnections that overstep boundaries and threaten sustainability; (5) dissatisfaction with nineteenth-century disciplinary divisions; (6) a perception that every entity is a nexus of relations and that entities are mutually constitutive.
2. I do not adopt the narrow interpretation of the term "quality of life," which equates "quality of life" work to a data-dominated, under-theorized and/or individualist stream in Northern sociology. I treat "quality of life" work as much broader (as in, e.g., Nussbaum and Sen 1993; Phillips 2006) and see social quality theory as a particular, complex approach to quality of life.
3. See also the *Thailand Human Development Report 2009.*
4. The European Foundation on Social Quality puts high weight on the values in all four of its domains. Chan (2007: 270) warns that in Hong Kong people put much more weight on socio-economic security than the other three and even doubts "whether an entity called 'society' do [*sic*] exist in [Hong Kong]" (271), given the prevalent "everyone for himself" mentality (272). By "everyone" and "himself," Chan presumably means family units.
5. Jordan (2008) presents "the idea of *shared* social value—goods and people derive their worth from a set of *collective* meanings, standards and practices" (115), including ritual values given through cultures and institutions. He proposes that we can analyze "the sources of well-being in social relations in terms of *intimacy, respect* and *belonging*" (136), for well-being relates to "esteem, regard and empathy … [which] stem from and reside in relationships, not individuals or their material possessions" (128). Economic growth generates only economic value and is often antagonistic to social value. In Jordan's terms, SQA treats social value—value generated in culturally structured interaction between persons—as well as economic value ("welfare" in Jordan's usage), which is the market measure of the types of value that can be managed by markets.
6. Social quality theory takes from Habermas and Parsons the idea that societies centrally contain an interplay of lifeworlds and system worlds. It contrasts "the essentially communicative understanding of actors rooted in a shared lifeworld (social integration)" with "the functional interdependence of sub-systems operating according to logics which we cannot fully control (system integration)" (Callinicos 2007: 288–289).
7. "Constitutive" may be a more suitable term than "constitutional," given the latter's legal connotations.
8. SQA writings have spoken of the "social quality quadrant" to refer to these Cartesian maps. However, a "quadrant" means one of the four spaces in such a map, and a better term for the SQA cross-figures would be "quadrants diagram." It functions as a generator and reminder of concepts and their relevance, and of fields for each of which a variety of concepts are relevant, not just one. The space of interaction of the system world and of individual life trajectories, for example, is a space where we look at issues of social responsiveness and social inclusion—but also at much else. Beck et al. (2001: 324) acknowledge that the quadrants diagrams should be read as simplified heuristic devices, not as sufficient representations.

References

Apthorpe, R. 1997. "Human Development Reporting and Social Anthropology." *Social Anthropology* 5(1): 21–34.

Apthorpe, R. 2008. "The 'Human' and the 'Social.'" Paper prepared for the Human Development and Capability Association Conference, September 2008 in Delhi.

Beck, U. 1992. *Risk Society*. London and Delhi: Sage.

Beck, W., L. van der Maesen and A. Walker. 2001. "Theorizing Social Quality: The Concept's Validity." pp. 319–352 in *Social Quality: A Vision for Europe,* eds. W. Beck, L. van der Maesen and A. Walker. The Hague: Kluwer Law International.

Berman, Y. 2008. "An Empirical Analysis of the Interrelationship between Components of the Social Quality Theoretical Construct." *Social Indicators Research* 86(3): 525–538.

Bouget, D. 2001. "Identification of the 'Problematique.'" pp. 47–67 in *Social Quality*, Beck et al.

Brauch, H.G. et al., eds. 2007. *Globalisation and Environmental Challenges: Reconceptualising Security in the 21st Century*. Berlin: Springer-Verlag.

Burgess, J.P. et al. 2007. *Promoting Human Security: Ethical, Normative and Educational Frameworks in Western Europe*. Paris: UNESCO.

Callinicos, A. 2007. *Social Theory: A Historical Introduction*. 2nd ed. Cambridge: Polity Press.

Calloni, M. 2001. "Gender Relations and Daily Life: Towards a Cross-cultural Approach." pp. 69–86 in *Social Quality*, Beck et al.

Chan, R. 2007. "Social Quality in Hong Kong: Who Cares? Which Quality?" pp. 237–276 in *Second Asian Conference on Social Quality and Sustainable Welfare Societies*. Taipei: National Taiwan University.

Commission on Human Security. 2003. *Human Security Now*. New York: Commission on Human Security.

Davis, J.B. 2003. *The Theory of the Individual in Economics: Identity and Value*. London: Routledge.

Debiel, T. and S. Werthes, eds. 2006. *Human Security on Foreign Policy Agendas: Changes, Concepts, and Cases*. INEF Report 80/2006. Duisburg: University of Duisburg-Essen.

Douglas, M. 1982. *In the Active Voice*. London: Routledge & Kegan Paul.

Douglas, M. and S. Ney. 1998. *Missing Persons: A Critique of the Social Sciences*. Berkeley: University of California Press.

Dreze, J. and A. Sen. 1989. *Hunger and Public Action*. Oxford: Clarendon.

Dreze, J. and A. Sen. 2002. *India: Development and Participation*. Delhi: Oxford University Press.

European Commission. 1996. "Human and Social Development (HSD)." Working Paper from the Commission of 9 October 1996. Brussels: European Commission (DG-V).

Gasper, D. 2008. "From 'Hume's Law' to Policy Analysis for Human Development: Sen after Dewey, Myrdal, Streeten, Stretton and Haq. *Review of Political Economy* 20(2): 233–256.

Gasper, D. 2009. "Capitalism and Human Flourishing? The Strange Story of the Bias to Activity and the Downgrading of Work." pp. 13–41 in *Global Social Economy*, ed. J.B. Davis. London: Routledge.

Gasper, D. 2010a. "Understanding the Diversity of Conceptions of Well-Being and Quality of Life." *Journal of Socio-Economics* 39(3): 351–360.

Gasper, D. 2010b. "The Idea of Human Security." pp. 23–46 in *Climate Change, Ethics, and Human Security*, eds. K. O'Brien, A.L. St. Clair and B. Kristoffersen. Cambridge: Cambridge University Press.

Gasper, D., L. van der Maesen, T.D. Truong, and A. Walker. 2008. "Human Security and Social Quality: Contrasts and Complementarities." Working Paper no. 462. The Hague: Institute of Social Studies.

Gasper, D. and T.D. Truong. 2010. "Development Ethics through the Lenses of Caring, Gender and Human Security." pp. 58–95 in *Capabilities, Power, and Institutions: Toward a More Critical Development Ethics*, eds. S. Esquith and F. Gifford. University Park, PA: Penn State University Press.

Giri, A. 2000. "Rethinking Human Well-Being: A Dialogue with Amartya Sen." *Journal of International Development* 12(7): 1003–1018.

Giri, A. 2011. "Rethinking the Human and the Social." *International Journal of Social Quality* 1(1).

Habermas, J. 1987. *The Theory of Communicative Action*. Cambridge: Polity Press.

Hodgson, G. 2004. "Can Economics Start from the Individual Alone?" pp. 57–67 in *A Guide to What's Wrong with Economics*, ed. E. Fullbrook. London: Anthem.

Hood, C. 2000. *The Art of the State*. Oxford: Oxford University Press.

Jolly, R. and D. Basu Ray. 2007. "Human Security—National Perspectives and Global Agendas: Insights from National Human Development Reports." *Journal of International Development* 19(4): 457–472.

Jordan, B. 2004. *Sex, Money and Power: The Transformation of Collective Life*. Cambridge: Polity Press.

Jordan, B. 2008. *Welfare and Well-Being: Social Value in Public Policy*. Bristol: Policy Press.

Lee, S.W. 2004. *Promoting Human Security: Ethical, Normative and Educational Frameworks in East Asia*. Paris: UNESCO.

Lin, K. and K. Gabe. 2007. "Social Quality in Mainland China: A Reflection on Social Change and Development in the Process of Economic Reconstruction." pp. 332–351 in *Second Asian Conference on Social Quality and Sustainable Welfare Societies*. Taipei: National Taiwan University.

Mine, Y. 2008. "Human Security: A Conceptual Exploration." Paper prepared for the Human Development and Capability Association Conference, September 2008 in Delhi.

Mushakoji, K. 2003. *Ningen-Anzennhoshou-Ron Josetsu (Introduction to Human Security)*. Tokyo: Kokusai Shoin.

Nijhuis, H. 2007. "The Significance of the Theory of Social Quality (SQ) in Processes of Urban Development." pp 24–46 in *Second Asian Conference on Social Quality and Sustainable Welfare Societies*. Taipei: National Taiwan University.

Nussbaum, M. 2000. *Women and Human Development*. Cambridge: Cambridge University Press.

Nussbaum, M. and A. Sen, eds. 1993. *The Quality of Life*. Oxford: Clarendon.

Parsons, T. 1937. *The Structure of Social Action*. New York: Free Press.

Phillips, D. 2006. *Quality of Life: Concept, Policy and Practice*. London: Routledge.

Phillips, D. 2011. "The Individual and the Social: A Comparative Study of Approaches to Quality of Life." *International Journal of Social Quality* 1(1): 71–89.

Phillips, D. and Y. Berman. 2007. "Social Cohesion and the Sustainable Welfare Society." pp. 446–480 in *Second Asian Conference on Social Quality and Sustainable Welfare Societies*. Taipei: National Taiwan University.

Picciotto, R., F. Olonisakin and M. Clarke. 2007. *Global Development and Human Security*. Piscataway, NJ: Transaction Publishers.

Rayner, S. and E. Malone, eds. 1998. *Human Choice and Climate Change*. Vols. 1–4. Columbus, OH: Battelle Press.

Sen, A. 2006. *Identity and Violence*. London: Penguin.

Sen, A. 2009. *The Idea of Justice*. London: Penguin.

Tadjbakhsh, S. and A. Chenoy, eds. 2007. *Human Security: Concepts and Implications*. Abingdon: Routledge.

Therborn, G. 2001. "On the Politics and Policy of Social Quality." pp. 19–30 in *Social Quality*, Beck et al.

UNDP (United Nations Development Programme). 2004. *Human Development Report 2004: Cultural Liberty in Today's Diverse World*. New York: UNDP.

UNESCO. 2008. *Human Security: Approaches and Challenges*. Paris: UNESCO.

Verweij, M. and M. Thompson, eds. 2006. *Clumsy Solutions for a Complex World: Governance, Politics and Plural Perceptions*. Basingstoke: Palgrave Macmillan.

CHAPTER 7
Social Quality in Britain
A Welfare State?

Sue Hacking

Introduction

This chapter introduces the four components of social quality from the British perspective. The main issue that this chapter highlights is the difference between British and European social understandings of inclusion and social policy.

First, a brief note about the geography of the United Kingdom, without which it is difficult to appreciate its cultural and social diversity. The union of the countries of England, Scotland, Northern Ireland and Wales has a large and very diverse population. Each country has a rich unique social and cultural history as well as varied traditions, geography and cultural life, even within regional boundaries. In England, a common term, the "North–South divide," refers to the difference in wealth and sophistication of the South of England from the rest of the country. Greater London has a dense urban cosmopolitan population, a fast-moving modern corporate and economic life tuned to international markets, a significantly different lifestyle and culture from most of the UK. The Midlands and North of England, largely in the last stages of a rapidly fading industrial economy, have a poorer population with different attitudes, economy and lifestyle from the South. In the principalities of Wales, Northern Ireland and, to some extent, Scotland (outside the major cities of Glasgow and Edinburgh), which are more rural, average incomes are lower and there are fewer ethnic minorities. In addition, because of the devolution of government, legal systems, educational systems and other public services differ between countries, as do the means of measurement, complicating compilation of standard information. Standardized national statistics are now widely available but differ considerably from those produced for international comparisons.

Key to the understanding of social attitudes in Britain is an understanding of the reconstruction of the political Left over the past thirty years. Before the 1980s, social and economic politics of the Left had remained rooted in class-oriented, Keynesian collectivist ideals. The Thatcher government of the 1980s brought significant social change in attitudes to a whole generation and introduced a possessive individualism that Britain has not shaken off. The British Left absorbed both German and French influences, but the move away from a direct redistribution of inequality model began with Labour's Policy Review of the 1980s. Since 1997, UK politics have been heavily influenced by globalism, moving further away from European capitalism toward North American/Australasian market-orientated individualism. The shift in the political Left is apparent in that skills training and work are now linked with economic success; it is the transfer of opportunity or participation rather than a paternalistic distribution of benefits that counterbalances social cost. This distinguishes Britain from the collectivist and interventionist social democracies of her neighbors in Europe (although the influence of globalization continues to penetrate Europe).

Over the past twenty years, a number of social and institutional reforms in public services have been introduced, for example, in the areas of quality control, evaluation of services and consultation with service users, which has lately become very important. Much of the evidence base for service reform, particularly that for social and mental health in young people, comes from research done in the United States. The UK government has introduced numbers of national programs for early intervention and prevention of antisocial behavior in youth as well as those aimed at increasing social capital in deprived areas. However, the UK is well behind the US in developing an evidence base for the evaluation of outcomes (Carr 2004). The transfer of social programs to Britain is problematic, partly because of cultural differences in community management and services but also because Britain has a long list of pre-existing and concurrent social reform programs with overlapping territories, objectives and funding policies (France et al. 2005). A major emphasis of social reform interventions in recent years has been on the acculturation, suppression and control of antisocial youth (Pitts 2001; Davies 2005). The construction of a problematic youth culture and its punitive control was recognized at European policy level twenty years ago (EU Commission 1994) and is still being addressed by policy analysts (see, e.g., Pitts 2003, 2005).

In Britain, social quality has become embedded in the politics of economic security and social exclusion. Development around social cohesion is just emerging on the UK policy front as a response to the "failure" of multiculturalism and is again conceptualized as a facet of social inclusion. All this tends to polarize UK social politics toward a focus for social action on poverty through the reduction, or empowerment, of excluded groups, conceptualized as reclamation of economically or morally participative citizens. In 1997, a social exclusion unit was set up with the remit to implement local initiatives to target socially excluded groups, and the inclusion agenda has never really evolved. Social exclusion in Britain has become the marker against which success or failure of the welfare system is judged, rather than the distribution of wealth and income across society as social transfers.

So, development of theory around the subject matter of the four components as equal sectors of social quality could help to progress the British agenda closer toward Europe to relate the individual and the community to the formation of collective identity.

Socio-economic Security

Of the four components, socio-economic security is the best evidenced one for the UK, particularly in relation to poverty and social disadvantage. British socio-economic security is less concerned with the transfer of social benefits to compensate an inequality in distribution of wealth than with social protection for those who come into the lowest and most deprived income bracket. Market economy politics tends to create an employers' market, and income distribution becomes polarized, particularly in the north, where the drift of skills to the south of the country follows the availability of jobs and higher wages. Out of the fifteen original member states of Europe, Britain appears to have the second highest proportion of people with an equivalized income below the risk-of-poverty threshold (19 percent in 2000 earned 60 percent below median income [Eurostat 2000; see Table 7.1]), and this has remained fairly stable since 1997, when the minimum wage was introduced as a social governance to prevent exploitation of the poorest and least educated members of society.

There is no governance on top earnings outside the public sector and little collective action or solidarity. Inequality statistics often do not include young people between the ages of sixteen and eighteen, who are technically part of the working population but are unable to claim social transfers, or the minimum wage. Employers may recruit young people for government-funded training placements, which offer an allowance well below subsistence. Young people not in education, training or employment may find themselves without any source of income at all. Of the working population, 15 percent are students (Labour Force Survey 2003), and 35 percent of young people between eighteen and twenty-one participate in higher education (DFES 2001–2002). Students in Britain now incur large debts due to deferred student loans and university fees, on entry to the labor market.

Comparisons between Britain and countries with different health and social packages may be difficult, because benefits in kind are not included. In Britain, primary and secondary health care, subsidized prescriptions, education to the age of eighteen and a range of social and environmental benefits are provided universally without cost to the whole population and paid for out of income and local taxes. For example, all children in education receive medical prescriptions and eye and dental treatment without charge. In kind benefits for people already receiving social transfers include free prescription charges, dental and ophthalmic treatment, free milk for children, free school meals, subsidized or free clothing for children, subsidized or free child care, rental and community charges remission and free local education classes. The period for entitlement to non-means-tested unemployment benefit is six months, but means-tested social security benefit carries on indefinitely, regardless of contributions towards tax and national insurance.

In the UK, 19 percent of households are at risk of poverty (Table 7.1); where social transfers are the main income source, the figure rises to 38 percent, the third highest in Europe (apart from Ireland and Portugal) and markedly higher than the European Union average of 28 percent.

Table 7.2 shows that social transfer in Britain has less effect on poverty than most of Europe. As in the rest of Europe, the effects are still skewed toward males, but in Britain, females are considerably disadvantaged relative to males, and above the EU

Table 7.1. At-Risk-of-Poverty Rate before and after Social Transfers

	EU-15	B	DK	D	EL	E	F	IRL	I	L	NL	A	P	FIN	S	UK
Total	15	13	11	11	20	18	16	20	18	12	10	12	21	11	11	19
Work	10	6	6	5	15	13	10	9	16	9	8	6	15	5	6	9
Social transfers	28	31	31	23	33	32	28	57	22	21	17	29	40	27	20	38

Source: Eurostat 2000. The share of persons with an equivalized disposable income below the risk-of-poverty threshold, which is set at 60 percent of the national median equivalized disposable income.

Table 7.2. At-Risk-of-Poverty Rates before and after Social Transfers (Including Pensions)

	Total		Males		Females	
	before	after	before	after	before	after
Belgium	40	13	36	12	44	15
Denmark	32	11	29	10	35	13
Germany	39	11	35	10	43	11
Greece	39	20	37	19	41	20
Spain	37	18	35	17	39	19
France	41	16	39	15	43	16
Ireland	37	20	35	19	38	21
Italy	42	18	40	18	44	19
Luxembourg	39	12	37	12	41	12
Netherlands	36	10	33	10	39	10
Austria	37	12	33	9	41	14
Portugal	38	21	36	19	40	22
Finland	32	11	29	9	35	13
Sweden	43	11	41	10	45	11
UK	41	19	37	16	44	21
EU-15	40	15	37	14	42	16

Source: Eurostat 2000, free data, social cohesion

average. This could be explained by gender disproportion in hours worked (89 percent of males to 56 percent females work more than thirty-one hours per week [Eurostat 2000]). Men still largely financially support the family, and women do most of the caring. After social transfers, income for the poorest, relative to 60 percent of the equivalized mean, still lay below Hungary, Sweden, Finland, the Netherlands, Germany and France and was below the average for Europe (15 percent).

Britain, however, enjoys a relatively comfortable lifestyle, given that around half the average household income is spent on basic necessities, lower at all levels of income than most European nations (Table 7.3).

Table 7.3. Percent of Average Weekly Household Income Spent on Basic Necessities

	Food	Clothing	Housing	Health	Total
Total for Britain[a]	16	6	16	16	54
By income level[b]					
1st quintile	15	5	32.4	0.8	53.4
2nd quintile	13	5.5	32	1	51.2
3rd quintile	11.3	5.7	29	1.1	47
4th quintile	10.2	5.6	28	1.1	44.8
5th quintile	7.6	5.5	25.3	1.3	39.7

[a] Expenditure and food survey, ONS 1999–2002; [b] Proportion of income spent on food (UK), Eurostat 1999.

Over the past fifteen years, the government has introduced healthy eating initiatives in response to concerns about the low nutrient value of the diet of poorer people, particularly their children. In Table 7.3, which shows household spending differentiated by income level, it is clear that those in the lowest income strata must spend a considerably higher proportion on food. In Britain, contribution to health care is funded universally from taxes; therefore, comparisons of relative spending are difficult.

Over the past decade there has been increasing concern about the decrease in quality health care in the National Health Service (NHS), and all major public hospitals have long waiting lists for operations. Dissatisfaction is still widespread, even after the introduction of sweeping changes in governance, management and roles of hospital staff, increasing efficiency, cost cutting and consultation with patients. Over the past ten to fifteen years, much of the poorer population has had no access to dental treatment because of the shortage of NHS dentists. Private medical and dental insurance is becoming more popular among the middle classes.

Housing and environment are particularly important to British people, and the national focus on house purchase has particular cultural and political implications. One of the most popular policies of the last Conservative government in Britain, still not repealed, was the introduction of the "Right to Buy" social housing for tenants in occupation. In 2001, 69 percent of homes in Britain were owner occupied, with least in Scotland (62 percent) and most in Ireland (73 percent) and Wales (72 percent) (ONS 2001); this compares with the EU average of 63 percent (Eurostat 2000). Most privately owned homes in Britain are occupied by a single household (one family), but single ownership is becoming more common as marriage occurs later. Home ownership is a source of status and respectability in the UK community, but it is not usually accomplished through outright purchase. The vast majority of "homeowners" spend most of their lives in debt to a bank or building society, even those in modest circumstances. Britain's social housing compares well with the rest of Europe: in the UK people below the poverty line occupied 2.4 rooms per person, compared with the EU mean of 1.9 (Eurostat 2000).

At the other end of the housing spectrum, from a social quality perspective, information about the powerless in society is even more informative than that about the enfranchised, and this is difficult to find. The government claims to have reduced rough sleepers by 70 percent (Social Exclusion Unit 2004), but Shelter and other organizations dispute this. In 2002 a quarter of a million single people, mostly male, were estimated to be living in inadequate accommodation at any one time in Britain, and approximately a thousand of these people a night were thought to be sleeping rough (ONS 2002), fluctuating with climate and education cycles.

Britain appears as the country with the highest risk in Western Europe for killings, violence and burglary (United Nations 2000). Crime reached a high in 1995, when more than 40 percent of the population reported to have been a victim of some sort of crime, but has fallen in recent years, as it has all over Europe, and is recently at a level of 26 percent of the population. Total crime in 2000 was 86 per 1,000 people compared with an average over the EU of 56 (Table 7.4). Crime, however, is very difficult to compare between countries, due to different reporting and policing policies, and thus may be unhelpful as an indicator for social quality of individuals.

Table 7.4. Crime in Europe: Total Crimes (Per Capita)—Top Twenty Countries

Country	Total crimes per 1,000 population
Finland	102.15
Denmark	93.64
United Kingdom	86.04
Netherlands	80.84
Germany	76.02
Norway	72.60
France	62.67
Hungary	44.80
Estonia	41.03
Czech Republic	38.19
Italy	38.03
Switzerland	37.02
Portugal	35.96
Slovenia	34.93
Poland	32.80
Spain	22.95
Lithuania	22.92
Latvia	21.37
Ireland	20.71
Bulgaria	19.75
Weighted average	56.47

Source: Seventh UN Survey of Crime Trends and Operations of Criminal Justice Systems, covering the period 1998 to 2000 (UN Office on Drugs and Crime, Centre for International Crime Prevention)

For environment and community, social quality might be perceived better in terms of neighborhood problems than crime rate: in Britain in 2001, people from lower income groups mentioned local order problems as much as crime as an area problem (although this might not reflect occurrence). Of poorer households, 40 percent reported frequent crime in their area and 28 percent drug dealing, twice the level of more affluent households (English House Condition Survey 2001).

To sum up, according to social measures of income sufficiency, relative to most of Europe, Britain has greater risk of poverty, more inequality in income distribution and more social problems. However, some economic comparative measures may not be sensitive to a range of social and health benefits given in kind. Britain seems to perform well in the areas of housing and environment generally, although on all these measures social quality increases incrementally with income. However, this dimension captures only part of the social framework. Poverty of circumstance—for example, homelessness, being a single mother or belonging to a particular minority or excluded group—limits access to the institutions of society through barriers other than obvious or legal ones, and equity of access may be compromised for a variety of other reasons. Thus, poverty has come to be identified with exclusion, and underrepresentation of excluded groups.

British Understandings of Social Inclusion

It is important to recognize here that concepts in social policy depend on the culture to which they are introduced. Britain did not originally recognize or sign up to major social reform elements of the Maastricht Treaty of 1991, reflecting substantial differences in social policy. Prime Minister Blair acknowledged, in 1996, major divergences in understanding of social exclusion/inclusion between Britain and most of Europe in the relative roles of community and in social, political and civil life.

The notion of a binary understanding of inclusion and exclusion is simplistic, and a trap the British seem to have fallen into is to keep redrawing the boundaries of the criteria of exclusion/inclusion and the differentiation and identification of level and type of exclusion rather than promoting inclusion as a policy goal. The Social Exclusion Unit, established in Britain in 1997, focused on the definition of indicators of the state of isolation, powerlessness and discrimination for vulnerable groups. In 1998, its definition of social disadvantage was still orientated on the state of exclusion:

> What can happen when people or areas suffer from a combination of linked problems such as unemployment, poor skills, low incomes, poor housing, high crime, bad health and family breakdown? (Social Exclusion Unit 1998)

Social policy in Britain has been greatly influenced by "risk and protection" theory imported from the United States, aimed at identifying and rehabilitating antisocial individuals. The social agenda also includes "prevention," to identify potential in problem circumstances reflected in current policy toward the moralistic identification of dangerous groups. The concurrent focus on the reclamation into the labor force of "workless" or "at risk" excluded individuals of working age, tends to stigmatize such groups, particularly young people (Levitas 1999). The EU condemned this "hierarchy of moral credibility" in designating particular groups as deserving or undeserving in 1991, citing particularly the emphasis on youth as incurring state disapproval and the elderly as being more worthy (Room et al. 199). Thus, exclusion politics is all about identifying and adjusting the state of poverty—the removal of barriers and what rights and entitlements constitute equal citizenship.

In contrast, the European Commission saw social exclusion as an outcome of poverty: "It is clear that contemporary economic and social conditions tend to exclude some groups from the cycle of opportunities" (European Commission 1994). Generally, across the EU, an understanding of social inclusion has evolved to construct the process of isolation, powerlessness and discrimination for vulnerable groups, and de-emphasizes the state of poverty as the main cause and focus of intervention.

In 1999 the British government set up units for neighborhood renewal, rough sleepers, teenage pregnancy and children and young people in designated areas of poverty and disadvantage. However, in 2004 the Social Exclusion Report admitted that identified unskilled or unqualified adults, people with chronic illness or disabilities and poor ethnic minority communities were helped little by these measures, and it is only recently that social policy for inclusion has moved more toward whole community participation and consultation.

So, having explained a little of the understanding of social inclusion and exclusion, and because many indicators are already covered under the social economic domain, we focus here on a small section, including those indicators concentrating on the social domains and the rights of citizens, and equity in employment for the whole community, that are especially relevant to Britain.

To Europeans, inclusion is indivisible from solidarity. The politics of difference, identity and social justice place issues of citizenship at the heart of an inclusive democracy and there is no contradiction between democratic citizenship and differentiated citizenship where people can hold multiple loyalties. Social inclusion goes beyond formal equality and into substantive equality.

British social policy in reconstructing equality as offering equity of opportunity does offer inclusion, particularly in educational reform and tax concessions, intended to narrow the gap between the excluded and mainstream society, but not by social transfer of money. Citizenship is thus vitally important here because the locus of economic political and administrative power is also the locus of citizenship.

The local institutions that support a sense of structure and national pride are more focused on regional or cultural loyalty, particularly in the principalities. For example, 48 percent of English people describe their nationality as British, only 27 percent of Scottish and 35 percent of Welsh (ONS Living in Britain 2001).

Falling birthrates, increasing minority populations living for the most part in poverty, together with an increasing percentage of older people with more money and power than ever before, has resulted in a political shift to target an older electorate, marginalizing and disempowering the young. The General Household Survey reports 30 percent of younger people (sixteen- to nineteen-year-olds) as socially isolated from their communities, compared with 14 percent of those over forty (ONS 2001). The Young People's Social Attitudes Survey reported political interest among young people was low in 1994 and even lower in 1998. Only 33 percent of younger people (aged eighteen to twenty-four) believed they should vote, compared to 80 percent of elderly people (aged sixty-five and over), and the social attitudes held by the young are more likely to prevail over time. Younger people and ethnic minorities have less sense of national inclusion and of influence on the structure of society and wider political issues; consequently, they vote less and feel less responsible for the continuance of community values.

Britain has had legislation for equity in employment since 1976; the imbalance in equity of employment for women remains but has improved steadily. In 2002 the gender gap narrowed to its lowest value since records began, when women's average hourly pay was 82 percent of men's (Figure 7.1).

Although there is a large imbalance, Britain has many more women managers and senior staff (32 percent) than most European countries and ranks in the top quartile of twenty-three countries (Eurostat 2000). In 2002 women comprised 55 percent of non-manual civil service staff, 28 percent of local councillors and 18 percent of members of Parliament (Equal Opportunities Commission 2002).

At the level of decision making in management and higher socio-economic employment, superficially, there seems a representative equity of participation for ethnic minorities. The 2002 Labour Force Survey (ONS) records 8.4 percent white

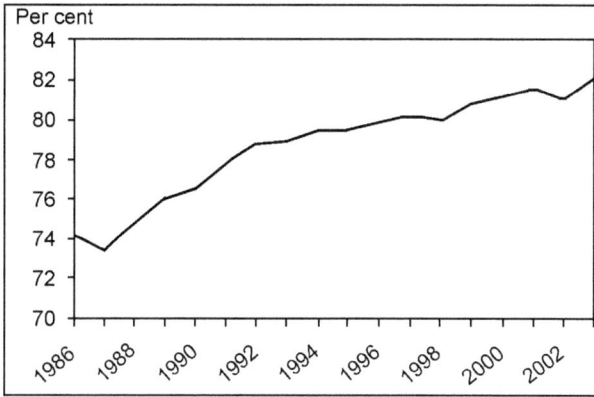

Figure 7.1. Hourly Earnings, Sex Differential, Great Britain (ONS 2002–2003)

British in managerial positions and 9.3 percent in other ethnic groups. However, the least likely to be employed in management were Pakistani, Black Caribbean and Bangladeshi at 3 to 4 percent and the most likely were White Other groups (15 percent). There are certain problems with the interpretation of social inclusion as integration into the workforce for particular groups. Paid employment is only one among a range of multiple forms of inclusion and presents other problems, for instance, where poor-quality employment damages an individual's health or where employment is temporary. In Britain, the benefits system is difficult to join and leave. Consequently, unless people enter a job with some prospect of continuance, they may suffer a period of waiting without income. Access to employment therefore does not guarantee a greater average income. In 2000, parents most vulnerable to severe poverty were those who followed the government's advice to escape poverty by taking work whenever it was available (Gordon et al. 2000). It is also interesting to note that fewer British people (78 percent) than any other EU nation claim that work is important to their quality of life (European Values Study 2000).

When we look to the future, savings for retirement are dropping, while the Turner Commission (2004) has described the British pension system as one of the least generous in Europe (when compared with GDP) and the most complicated. Other EU governments spend much more on pension provision than the UK—Germany 11.8 percent of GDP, France 12 percent, Finland 11 percent—and the EU average is 10.4 percent (Pensions Commission 2004). In the aftermath of publicity about the failure of many private pension schemes to provide guarantees or even deliver on promises, the government is considering a universal contributory compulsory scheme to provide pensions for people in employment at 25 percent of average income, thus subsidizing only the very poorest through social transfers. It seems to follow that if community responsibility for social cohesion continues to erode, the youth that will support such pensions will probably be fairly unsympathetic to increases in tax, so it is likely that a large percentage of older people will be subject to means testing all their lives.

A debate as to whether inclusion is equal and opposite to exclusion is not appropriate here. However, inclusion does imply a positive focus on the mechanisms of institution and equity of access to public and private institutions for the whole community, while exclusion concentrates the focus on particular groups and attitudes or cultural values preventing that access, that do not apply to the general community. "You can lead a horse to water, but you can't make it drink," is the maxim on which this discussion seems to pivot. In Britain, legislation for inclusion comprehensively exists. There is equity in law as far as possible for disabled people, marginalized groups and ethnic minorities, in employment, education, legal and civil assistance and access to local and national policy through mediating institutions that represent the interests of minorities. However, in a speech to the Fabian Society in 2002, Deputy Prime Minister John Prescott pointed out that poorer services still discriminate against communities in poverty, and social attitudes toward difference and the mechanisms to include people who are hard to reach are still being developed.

Social Cohesion

Despite Labour's embrace of the market economy, much social and economic policy in Britain is still about communitarian inclusion rather than the politics of self, but the definition of "community" has changed from class to nation (Byers 1999), and policy shift in welfare from community to individual, from paternalism and collectivist institutional welfare to consumerism, individual and moral responsibility and choice. The new communitarianism is about rebuilding social cohesion and morality undermined by individualism. Britain's neighborhoods are becoming less socially cohesive: in 1984, 40 percent of respondents to the British Crime Survey saw their neighborhood as one where residents "help each other out." However, in 2000, only 35 percent did so, demonstrating that neighbors help each other less, have less interest in politics and local issues and trust each other less (ONS 2003). Although legislation, working practices and the institutions to provide community resources exist, fewer British people belong to neighborhood groups than in most EU countries. All these factors are demonstrated to correlate in damaging the social fabric and health of communities (Kawachi and Kennedy 1997). These traits are more common among younger people (ONS General Household Survey 2001), so as the population ages, neighborhood cohesion is predicted to drop.

Eighteen years ago the polarization of income distribution was seen as the key determinant of the widening gap in social cohesion in both Britain and in the United States. Since then, in the past fifteen years, social interventions have focused on deprivation, poor achievement, low aspirations and promoting the understanding of cultural diversity. Community leaders were elected to provide a surrogate voice for ethnic minority groups with the agenda of celebration of multiculturalism as a path to social inclusion. The current discourse on lack of social cohesion in poorer communities in Britain, however, centers on the failure of multiculturalism to address social exclusion.

Comment on British minorities refers to migrant populations, not the indigenous Welsh, Irish and Gaelic communities that maintain a separate identity through preservation of their language and culture (although they would probably qualify under the Council of Europe Parliamentary Recommendation). The recent perceived loss of control of borders in recent years to asylum seekers and refugees has fueled media hysteria and tension in provincial areas already hit by deprivation, where large numbers of economic migrants were posted without the allocation of corresponding support and resources. Scotland, Wales and Northern Ireland in particular have a very low proportion of other ethnic minorities, and traditional suspicions of "foreigners," which designation often includes the English.

Events since 11 September 2001 have seen the end of multiculturalist policies, and the adoption of racial profiling in policing has become acceptable as part of antiterrorist operations. Furthermore, the government multicultural agenda has not been compatible with anti-immigrant media attention. Tolerance of migrants in Britain is low because of perceived lack of control of immigration, and the media attention that has been focused on illegal workers and migrants in deprived areas competing for resources. The British National Party (BNP) has gained ground in local elections in some regions, although there is little danger of widespread support. The government has denied the BNP a political platform, for fear of an increase in support for them and of racial violence. Inconsistently, however, Islamic fundamentalists such as al-Muhajiroun retain their platform, yet the reasons for allowing this are the same—to diffuse racial tension and support. This has placed further pressure on British Muslims' allegiances.

Until recently, South Asian culture was perceived as deferential, having similar values to traditional British ones, supporting education, self-employment and hard work. Asians were the minority most predicted to succeed in Britain, but it has not happened: the majority of Bangladeshi and Pakistani communities remain in poverty. Increasingly, young Asians are adopting antisocial activity usually associated with white and African-Caribbean youths (Anthony 2004). The 2001 Community Cohesion Report (Cantle 2001) cited the polarization of parallel cultural lives in towns and cities to be the most apparent factor impacting on social cohesion, and the direct outcome as racism. Like social exclusion, social cohesion is thought to depend upon social networks, identity and discourse rather than disadvantage. A new National Community Cohesion Task Force will set out core values, put limits on multiculturalism, establish pathways for people of ethnic minority backgrounds to gain "a greater acceptance of the principal national institutions," English language skills and introduce a new policing measure, the ID card, not yet implemented.

As home secretary in 2004, David Blunkett suggested that immigrants take an "oath of allegiance" to Britain and adopt British customs, putting the emphasis on a British identity. Media debate has speculated on the clarification of the rights and responsibilities of a British citizen, and what a British identity is, but many aspects remain unclear. The general non-minority population are wary of overt demonstrations of patriotism (such as display of the flag) as this is associated with extreme groups. Regional identity is more dominant for the majority of the population, especially in the principalities (ONS Living in Britain 2001). However, the principalities are not areas with large ethnic minorities.

There are complex reactions to European nationality within Britain, including resistance to what is seen as federalist conformity of culture across the EU, fear of change, language difficulties and distance. Only 47 percent of British people, the lowest in Europe (European Values Study 2000) feel pride in European citizenship. The British media does not generally support a European identity and projects a critical view of examples from the European courts and edicts from Brussels that commonly reflect a large, unwieldy bureaucracy, insensitive to local culture. Typically, in Britain, references to "Europe" do not include Britain, even in official government literature.

To summarize, for the majority British population, social networks, community cultural and social values are deteriorating and most people have a sense of confusion about what it means to be British, coupled with little confidence in the control of migration by the government.

Social Empowerment

The Right to Buy (social housing) scheme introduced by the Thatcher government of 1979 was the beginning of what David Davis, MP, has called "a policy of empowerment" (Davis 2002) that had a massive impact on the poor: it allowed them status and control over their environment as homeowners. The Blair government extended this opening of the institutional structures of the more affluent to the poorer classes, and individual empowerment has increased for the poor and particularly for women. Poorer families have greater access to university education than ever before (11 percent in 1992 to 19 percent in 2002 [DFES 2001–2002]), and it is this participation that has the potential for the most effect on income. In 2001, both men and women graduating from university at the age of twenty-one earned 50 percent more than their contemporaries who left school at sixteen (Labour Force Survey). Major reforms in social policy to empower excluded groups have increased social community institutions, such as preschool education, neighborhood centers, legal and social representation and the funding and processes of social reform and centrality of social agencies for the poor. New laws for flexible working and initiatives for retraining workers, workfare schemes and youth employment schemes have increased participation in work for much of the low-paid workforce.

Government initiatives for "joined up solutions" to social exclusion, through partnerships between local authorities, health and social care agencies since 1997, have intensively addressed deprived communities that are seen to have a fragmented social culture and little collective agency. Residents are involved in collective decision making. Processes for community consultation are intended to generate interaction and social capital, in an attempt to promote an environment where meritocracy can flourish and the individual is responsible for his or her own advancement, while at the same time encouraging communitarian responsibility and support.

Laws regarding freedom of information exist in more than thirty countries, and most EU states now have such legislation (Frankel 2001). The British government has had a culture of secrecy, embodied since the 1911 Official Secrets Act, and although a number of statutes and statutory instruments conferred upon citizens a right of access to records held about them, the government resisted a compulsory and comprehensive legislation until the Freedom of Information Act 2000, which introduced legislation that applied over the whole public sector. The White Paper, "Your Right to Know: The Government's Proposals for a Freedom of Information Act" of 1997, proposed the first model freedom of information covering the whole public and private sector in UK history and was a major fundamental policy underpinning Labour's new manifesto (Cornford 2001). From 2005, private individuals now have the right in law to access public information. Recent years have seen the explosion of consultation initiatives, mostly directed at younger people as part of an inclusive government agenda to promote better and wider consultation through the use of Internet resources and e-government. Internet use has risen sharply, particularly as more than 80 percent of young people make some use of the Internet (ONS 2003), possibly reflecting the provision of free access in libraries and schools. The "Big Conversation" of 2004 was the largest consultation exercise ever undertaken, a process where the electorate could take its views and discussion points to high-level government through individual face-to-face meetings and Internet resources. The exercise has been criticized as highly managed, unrealistic in any expectation for regulated systematic feedback (HMSO 2002) and the purpose and outcomes seem unclear, apart from promoting the idea of democratic inclusion and "open government."

In all these initiatives, the end product is not empowerment for the community but rather that the mechanism of opportunity itself should be recognized. Individuals may thus access paths to development, but empowerment of the community is restricted by control of the institutions through which it is developed. It could be argued that the collective agency enables the community as individuals to take advantage of opportunities for development. The process of individual empowerment may even reduce the emphasis on collective representation of views through mediators such as the national press and popular media.

Britain has seen the systematic destabilization of collective empowerment over the past thirty years. Empowerment through union membership is the lowest in Europe, particularly for the poor. Union density is very low and coverage by collective bargaining, compared internationally, compared with the rest of Europe at around 30 percent (Brook 2001) equates the UK with Japan and Korea, rather than the EU. This probably reflects the current British political emphasis on a market economy, which tends to marginalize relations with the workforce and increase inequalities and unemployment in the pursuit of economic growth—thus linking the UK with such capitalist nations as the US.

Most of the EU countries appear around the top of Figure 7.2, at around 80 percent coverage, although the density of trades unions varies. In 2001, 23 percent of union memberships were better-educated public service workers. Additionally, many of the traditional recourses to collective action are now disenfranchised or weakened. Unions must often sign up to no-strike agreements; pickets or protest marches are now illegal, and solidarity between trades, where one trade supports another's collective action, is now illegal.

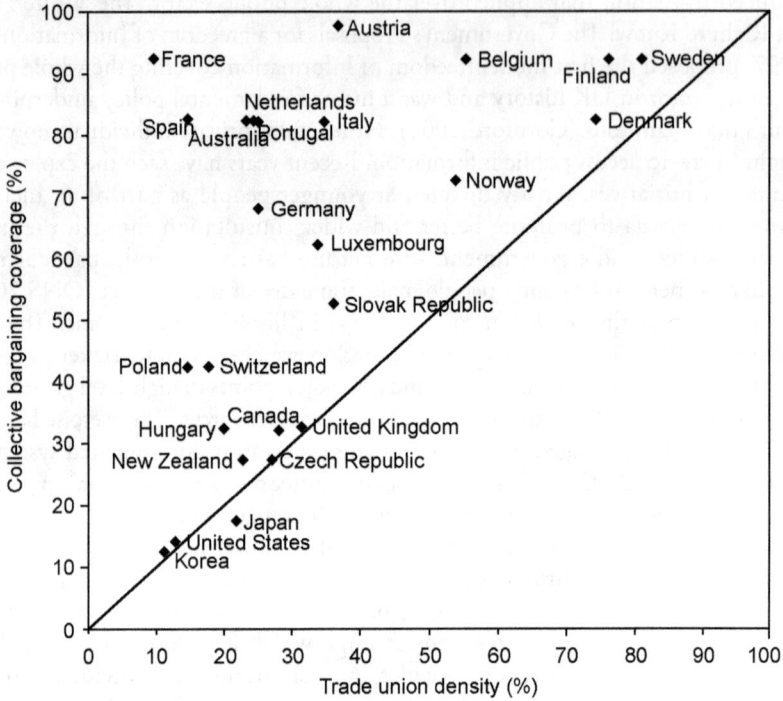

Figure 7.2.: Trades Union Membership (2001 Labour Force Survey)

Conclusion

In terms of socio-economic security, Britain appears to be able to offer the institutions of social need and security relatively well in comparison with most of Europe. People in difficult circumstances can live securely within most communities with the basic means of support covered, and processes exist to include hard-to-reach and vulnerable groups.

Social empowerment has not been a stated policy of the British government, and there is a danger that the replacement of collective support with a global, individualistic Western culture in British young people will reduce community cohesion. British society also reaps the products of the change in social values generated by the Thatcher government of the 1980s described by Deveney (2000) as "a society that promoted greed above responsibility to others." It is obvious that youth culture is concerned with commodification, in the importance assigned to possessions: mobile phones, designer clothes, cars and gadgets, particularly in areas of deprivation, where the increasing importance of rhetoric, image and outward accoutrements reinforce notions of respect through buying power. Increasing problems, among youth, of alcohol abuse, drugs and antisocial behavior have been largely met by more punitive measures than ever before. Nacro (2003) reported an increase in custody for children of 90 percent between 1992 and 2001, while the Audit Commission (2004) reported no increase in incidence of youth crime over a five-year period. The Labour government on coming to power in 1997 pledged to "fast track the punishment of persistent young offenders," and this agenda has remained a policy objective despite the findings of the 2003 Crime and Justice Survey (Wood 2003) that most young people grow out of criminal behavior without any contact with police or court. Bernard Davies (2005) describes the culture of fear of youth and fear for youth that has resulted in a loss of confidence in the morality, authority and structural processes of government in general. Davies goes on to criticize resultant UK policy that curtails and restricts the rights of children and have even prompted criticisms from the European Commissioner for Human Rights (Gil-Robles 2004: 36).

In terms of inclusion of minorities and vulnerable groups, the processes of support exist, but there is evidence that collective support from the community is needed to increase awareness and participation of minorities, disabled people and excluded groups. Blunkett's proposals to introduce allegiance pledges and language tests for immigrants in the wake of the summer riots of 2001 and the Cantle Report of the same year, signaled the death of the multiculturalist "celebration of difference," which had dominated race relations thinking in Britain for two decades, and a change to integrative policy. The Cantle Report findings of polarization of parallel societies in cities with large ethnic minority populations do not indicate good integration, but that has not been the aim of previous social politics. It is too early yet to tell whether social interventions to reduce deprivation and enhance inclusion of minority communities have made any difference. It seems likely that the new National Community Cohesion Task Force has problems ahead if policies to enforce integration emerge. Minority communities are well known to have cohesive internal relations, unlike some indigenous white communities. Increasingly, moral panic about asylum seekers, refugees and economic migrants is replacing multiculturalism as a pivotal issue (CARF 2002). The new focus on integration is now seen as the solution to the perceived lack of cohesion between ethnic minority communities and the majority culture. The tolerance of minority culture and diversity that characterized multiculturalist policy is now seen as increasing separatism and emphasis on cultural heritage possibly damaging to national identity.

In terms of integration into Europe, Hutton (1995), among many others, has criticized the model New Labour economy for perpetuating the competitive individualism of the United States and global influences over the more stable capitalism of northern Europe. Meanwhile, Britain has further to go to integrate its own diverse communities under one flag. Despite the value shift in the 1980s toward individualism and materialism, Britain does not share a global value system with America. Technically, Labour promotes collectivism, and community in Britain remains an active component of society. The transfer of US social policy does not take into account the enduring influence of collective responsibility in British policy, undermined but still present. European policy guidelines go some way toward addressing these issues but they are not clear cut; British policy on social reform appears to be simultaneously attempting to introduce meritocracy and individual responsibility as well as a social democratic model of collective responsibility and community action in partnership with social agency. The US has nothing like Britain's intervention overload, and against the backdrop of massive social change in many domains, overlapping programs with different aims, changes of policy and direction, as well as the introduction of new initiatives under different funding streams, it is impossible to find stable areas of comparison and disentangle the effect of any one program.

Meanwhile, the British government seems to have established a position of more centralized authority, fragmenting local systems even more. Efforts to change this have been made through centralizing local agencies in partnership agreements, thus effectively limiting the collective empowerment of communities through social agencies and introducing power relations (Carr 2004). Simultaneously, the Blair government was successful in undermining the power base of the House of Lords, the Civil Service and the major media to criticize and obstruct. Additionally, its consultation exercises effectively directly challenged existing press representation of the people through direct appeal to the individual electorate through Internet resources, but may, as McGavock (2000) has noted, represented a discrete community of younger people with unrepresentative technical mobility.

For social quality, the four components framework (ENIQ) offers a useful comparative structure to balance UK domains against a standardized European collective representation of what defines and shapes social values in each country. The development of social welfare in Britain cannot progress independently: it must have a reference group. Social and cultural expectations relative to a reference group are key to how personal and community happiness and aspirations are conceived individually. The best reference group is obviously one from a nation similar in culture, outlook, economy base, population and social structure. Therefore, benchmarking of these very simple characteristics is primary to comparison. Use of social quality indicators on a national scale to benchmark progress with Europe is important for Britain to understand and appreciate the differences in European goals, needs and wants and to synthesize a common goal for Europe, if not a common language. If British people are expected to have an active interest and to participate in European policy and convergence, the first step is to have an understanding of the divergences in culture, what is expected for a quality life and the commonalities between countries. This will reduce the fear, very commonly expressed in the media, of a bland superculture Europe, where everything is the same.

Sue Hacking most recently served as a Senior Research Fellow in the School of Health at the University of Central Lancashire and comes from a research background developing quantitative measures for artwork. She moved into evaluating social interventions for children and families in the 1990s and has maintained an interest in social inclusion theory. She has recently worked across the Midlands region to assess the needs of children with life limiting conditions and their families.

Statistical Sources

Housing

Owner occupation: Department for Transport, Local Government and the Regions, National Assembly for Wales, Scottish Executive and Department for Social Development, Northern Ireland (2001), Office for National Statistics (ONS).

Housing, proportion of owner occupation: Eurostat (2000), NewCronos database, Theme 3, Housing.

Housing, persons per room: Eurostat (2000), NewCronos database, Theme 3, Housing.

Effectively homeless people: Various sources aggregated by ONS (2002).

Residents' views of neighborhood problems: English House Condition Survey (2001).

Nuisance and neighborhood problems: DETR 1999–2000 Survey of English Regions; Living in Britain (2001), ONS; General Household Survey (2000–2001), ONS.

Young People

Young People's Social Attitudes Survey (1994–1998), ONS.

Social isolation of young people: General Household Survey (2000–2001), ONS (proportion who spoke to neighbors more than once per week: 86 percent aged over 40, compared with 30 percent aged 16 to 19).

Political interest of young people: Young People's Social Attitudes Survey (1994–1998), ONS.

Internet Access—*Households and Individuals by age (16–24)* (2003), ONS, data from the Expenditure and Food Survey and Family Expenditure Survey.

Participation in education by social class: Department for Education and Skills (1991–2002).

Students as a proportion of the working-age population: Labour Force Survey, spring quarter (2003).

Participation by young people in higher education: Age Participation Index (API), Great Britain, Department for Education and Skills (DFES) 2001–2002.

Equity and Equality

Women's and men's hourly pay: Hourly earnings, sex differential, New Earnings Survey (2002–2003), ONS.

Working hours: Eurostat (2000), New Cronos database, Theme 3, Income and Living Conditions.

Women in managerial positions by country: Eurostat News Release STAT/02/121 8 October 2002.

Women in managerial positions in the UK: Annual Local Labour Force Survey (2001–2002), DETR, ONS; House of Commons weekly information bulletin 12 January 2002, issued as part of fact sheet, 2002 Equal Opportunities Commission.

Proportional effect on earnings of a degree level qualification: by sex and degree subject, 1993–2001, Labour Force Survey.

Trades union membership: An analysis of data from the 2001 LFS by Keith Brook, Employment Relations Directorate, Department of Trade and Industry (http://webarchive.nationalarchives.gov.uk/20070603164510/http://www.dti.gov.uk/er/emar/artic_02.pdf).

Poverty and Disadvantage

At risk of poverty: by main source of household income—Eurostat (2000), NewCronos database, Theme 3, Income and Living Conditions.

At-risk-of-poverty rate before and after social transfers (including pensions): Eurostat (2000), NewCronos database, Theme 3, Income and Living Conditions.

Expenditure and Food Survey, UK (1999–2002), ONS and Northern Ireland Statistics and Research Agency.

Proportion of household expenditure in four basic consumption functions by income quintile: Eurostat (1999), NewCronos database, Theme 3, Household Budget Survey.

Crime

Community spirit in neighborhoods: England and Wales, 1984–2000, ONS (2003), sources taken from British Social Attitudes Survey and British Crime Survey, National Centre for Social Research; Seventh UN Survey of Crime Trends and Operations of Criminal Justice Systems, covering the period 1998–2000, UN Office on Drugs and Crime, Centre for International Crime Prevention.

Quality of Life

Annual Local Labour Force Survey (2001–2002), ONS; European Values Study: A Third Wave (question 1), Proportion of the population for whom work, family, friends, leisure time, politics is important to quality of life (2000): GB (78 percent) lowest out of 15 member states.

Proportion having membership of a community group: Eurobarometer 2000 European Values Study: A Third Wave (question 5).

Trust of foreign nationals: General Household Survey (2000–2001), ONS.

Identity

National identity: Living in Britain (2001), ONS: [People living in England were more likely to describe themselves as British (48 percent) than those in Scotland (27 percent) or Wales (35 percent); 50 percent of people described themselves as English, Scottish, Welsh or Irish; 31 percent described themselves as British only, with 13 percent choosing British and either English, Scottish, Welsh or Irish].

National pride/pride in being European: Standard Eurobarometer 60: full report 2000.

References

Anthony, A. 2004. "Multiculturalism Is Dead: Hurrah?" *Guardian*, 8 April.

Audit Commission. 2004. *Youth Justice 2004: A Review of the Reformed Youth Justice System*. Audit Commission.

Blair, A. 1996. *New Britain: My Vision for a Young Country*. London: Fourth Estate.

Byers, S. 1999. "Government for the Many, Not the Few." Labour Party Conference Speech. UK Politics, BBC Online.

Cantle, T. 2001. *Community Cohesion: A Report of the Independent Review Team*. London: Home Office.

Campaign against Racism and Fascism (CARF). 2002. "Community Cohesion … Blunkett's New Race Doctrine." *CARF Newsletter* 66.

Carr, S. 2004. *Has Service User Participation Made a Difference to Social Care Services?* London: Social Care Institute for Excellence.

Cornford, T. 2001. "The Freedom of Information Act 2000: Genuine or Sham?" *Web Journal of Current Legal Issues* 3.

Davies, B. 2005. "Threatening Youth Revisited: Youth Policies under New Labor." *The Encyclopaedia of Informal Education* (www.infed.org/archives/bernard_davies/revisiting_threatening_youth.htm).

Davis, D. 2002. "Full Text of Speech to Conservative Party Conference." *Guardian*, 8 October.

Deveney, C. 2000. "Iain Banks: Underachiever, and Proud of It." *Scotland on Sunday*, Spectrum Supplement: 16–19.

European Community Observatory on National Policies to Combat Social Exclusion. 1991. *First Annual Report*. Brussels: European Commission and the Centre for Research in European Social and Employment Policy.

European Commission. 1994. "European Social Policy: A Way Forward for the Union." White Paper, COM (94) 333 final. Luxembourg: Office for Official Publications of the EC.

France, A., I. Crow, S. Hacking and M. Hart. 2004. *Does Communities That Care Work?: An Evaluation of a Community Based Risk Prevention Programme in Three Neighbourhoods*. London: Joseph Rowntree Foundation.

Frankel, M. 2001. "Freedom of Information: Some International Characteristics." Paper presented at the "Transparency in Europe" seminar for government officials from EU member states organized by the Dutch Ministry of the Interior and Kingdom Affairs, February in The Hague (www.cfoi.org.uk/pdf/amsterdam.pdf).

Gil-Robles, A. 2004. "Report by Mr. Alvares Gil-Robles, Commissioner for Human Rights, on His Visit to the United Kingdom 4–12 November 2004." Geneva: Office of the Commissioner for Human Rights.

Gordon, D. et al. 2000. *Poverty and Social Exclusion in Britain*. London: Joseph Rowntree Foundation.

Hutton, W. 1995. *The State We're In: Why Britain Is in Crisis and How to Overcome It*. London: Jonathan Cape.

Kawachi, I. and B. Kennedy. 1997. "Socioeconomic Determinants of Health: Health and Social Cohesion: Why Care about Income Inequality?" *British Medical Journal* 314: 1,037.

Levitas, R. 1999. "Defining and Measuring Social Exclusion: A Critical Overview of Current Proposals." *Radical Statistics* 71.

McGavock, K. 2000. "Risking Disconnection? Mobility, Place and Education Today." Paper presented at the European Conference on Educational Research, 20–23 September in Edinburgh.

Network of Academic Corporate Relations Officers (Nacro). 2003. *A Failure of Justice: Reducing Child Imprisonment*. London: Nacro.

Office Deputy Prime Minister. 2002. "In the Service of Democracy." Consultation Paper, July.

Pitts, J. 2001. *The Politics of Youth Crime*. Lyme Regis: Russell House.

Pitts, J. 2003. The *New Politics of Youth Crime: Discipline or Solidarity?* Lyme Regis: Russell House.

Pitts, J. 2005. "The Criminal Victimisation of Children and Young People." In *The Russell House Companion to Youth Justice*, ed. T. Bateman and J. Pitts. Lyme Regis: Russell House.

Prescott, J. 2002. "Mainstreaming Social Justice for the 21st Century." Conference of the Fabian Society and the New Policy Institute, Building Partnerships for Social Inclusion, 15 January in London.

Room, G. et al. 1992. *Observatory on National Policies to Combat Social Exclusion: Second Annual Report of the European Community*. Brussels: European Commission.

Social Exclusion Unit. 1998. *Bringing Britain Together: A National Strategy for Neighbourhood Renewal*. London: Her Majesty's Stationery Office (HMSO).

Social Exclusion Unit. 2004. *Breaking the Cycle of Social Exclusion*. London: HMSO.

Turner, A. 2004. *Pensions: Challenges and Choices – The First Report of the Pensions Commission*. London: The Stationery Office (TSO).

Wood, M. 2005. *The Victimisation of Young People: Findings from the Crime and Justice Survey, 2003*. Home Office Findings 246. London: Home Office.

CHAPTER 8
Social Quality in Sweden

Göran Therborn and Sonia Therborn

Introduction

"Social quality" is not a common term in Sweden, and its sister notion "quality of life" is used mainly with respect to the conditions of particular individuals and rarely, if ever, in social analysis. Swedish social statistics and social studies focus on "levels of living" or "living conditions." The perceived subjectivity connotations of "quality" in this context have not been attractive. On the other hand, Swedish social research and policy evaluation have de facto been very much concerned with measuring what may properly be called qualitative dimensions of living conditions and correspondingly less interested in, for example, the possession of consumer goods.

The Swedish Level of Living surveys, conducted since 1968, focus on individual disposal of resources, in a medical, social and economic sense. The social quality concept—centered on social and economic participation—was developed in the late 1990s and is now being gauged empirically in the European Union. The project's founding book (Beck et al. 1997) defined social quality as "the extent to which people are able to participate in the social and economic life of their communities under conditions which enhance their well-being and individual potential." The latter is a more communitarian approach than the egalitarian individualism adopted in Sweden and draws upon social philosophical reactions to the anti-egalitarian individualism of the Anglo-Saxon world of the 1980s. While the Level of Living surveys concentrate on the individual and his or her resources, the social quality approach is interested in community variables, such as cohesion, inclusion and empowerment. However, there is a large overlap for research.

The summarized sub-domains in the left-hand column (Table 8.1) indicate topics not clearly included in living surveys. On the other hand, there are several aspects of the living components that are not included in the ninety-five indicators of social quality, for instance on individual income and health situation. The methodology is

Table 8.1. Components of Social Quality and Level of Living

Social Quality	Level of Living Surveys
Socio-economic security	Health and access to medical service
	Employment and working conditions
	Economic resources and consumer protection
	Knowledge and possibilities of education
	Housing and community services
	Security of life and property
Social cohesion	Political resources
Trust, values, identity	Family and social relations
Social inclusion	[Aspects of all the above]
Citizenship rights	Leisure and culture
Social empowerment	[Some aspects of the above]
Information access	
Openness of institutions	
Public space	

also different. The Living Surveys gather their data from designed national surveys, whereas the above social quality research is based mainly on data already in the public domain, whether from statistical registration or from other surveys, and it draws upon international as well as on national sources.

Socio-economic Security

The Swedish language has two words corresponding to the English "security." In the context of social policy and social conditions, *trygghet* is the most common word. It has a strong positive value charge and is also used with reference to psychological and emotional conditions. *Trygghet* is a central concept of Swedish social policy and of the Swedish welfare state. The other word, *säkerhet*, is less emotionally charged, although it also denotes something positive. It corresponds to the English word "safety," as well as to "national security" and international "security policy." Espionage and counter-espionage are in Sweden handled by an organization known as *Säkerhetspolisen* (Security

Table 8.2. Household Expenditure in 2003 (Percent of the Group Total)

	Single parents	All households
Housing	35	28
Food (incl. non-alcoholic drinks)	17	18
Clothing	6	5
Health	2	2
Transport	11	14
Leisure and culture	16	18

Source: SCB 2003a

Police). Security in the first sense of *trygghet* is a main goal of Swedish social policy, that is, "general welfare" purpose, referring to principles of income compensation for all major income groups as well as for all kinds of income-reducing events.

Income Sufficiency

Swedish household budgets are usually presented in terms of the demographic composition of households rather than in terms of income deciles. A hint of the expenditure situation of a vulnerable large social group may be captured by looking at single parents.

Even single parents have, on average, a considerable share of discretionary income and the expenditure structure is rather similar across household demography. Child day care costs only 1 percent of their income. Housing costs are the main variable. Cohabiting couples need only to devote a quarter of their income to housing.

The risk of falling into (relative) poverty is smaller in Sweden than in the non-Nordic EU. Only 9 percent of the population did this in 1999, as compared to 15 percent in the EU-15. By contrast with most other European countries, there is no gender difference (European Commission 2003: Appendix I and II). The risk is highest (25 percent) among young people aged sixteen to twenty-four, who tend to live on their own after finishing secondary school. Of single parents, 19 percent fell into relative poverty in 1998 compared with an EU average of 35 percent.

Another measure of income (in)security is the proportion of people running into an acute economic crisis. Swedish statistics defines this as not being able to buy food or pay rent without having to ask for social assistance or having to borrow from relatives or friends. In the mid-1990s, this happened to about a tenth of the total population aged sixteen to eighty-four each year; in 2000, to 8 percent. It happened to a third of single mothers (in 1998 and 1999, 45 percent) and to a fifth of single fathers. Economic crises mostly befall people in the age group sixteen to forty-four, and in particular the subgroup twenty-five to thirty-four, among whom one in five ran into a personal economic crisis in 1996 and 1997 (SCB 2002b: Table EK.5).

The Swedish social security net is vast and intricate. One person in five aged twenty to sixty-four is full-year provided for by public social support. The figure (19.6 percent) refers to 2003 and is somewhat lower than the peak at the early 1990s depression, 22.7 percent in 1994, but significantly higher than the precrisis level of 15 percent in 1990.

Table 8.3. The Structure of Public Income Support before Old Age Retirement in 2003

	Percentage of population aged 20–64 full-year equivalents
Early retirement	7.7
Sick pay	4.9
Unemployment allowance	3.6
Employment promotion	1.7
Social assistance	1.6

Source: SCB 2004a: 220

Table 8.4. Market Income Distribution and Disposable Income Distribution

Fifth wave of Luxembourg Income Study surveys, 1998–2002 (Gini index)

	Market income	Disposable income
Sweden	0.44	0.26
Germany	0.44	0.26
Finland	0.37	0.25
Canada	0.41	0.31
UK	0.46	0.35
US	0.46	0.38

Source: Luxembourg Income Study 2004

The system of income redistribution sustaining this vast income security is naturally very large. The redistributive flows make up 85 percent of disposable household income, and they make a great difference in the pattern of distribution.

The Swedish distribution of market income is surprisingly similar to that of the United States and was in the more than two decades of the Luxemburg project usually more unequal than the core of Western Europe. However, the redistributive outcome is much more equal, although the latest wave shows Sweden on a par with Germany, after a Swedish increase from 0.22 to 0.26. If individual public consumption—of education, health and social care, public transport—is also taken into account, the Swedish Gini coefficient is estimated to 0.20 (OECD 2002: Table A2).

Housing Security

Housing costs weigh heavily on Swedish household budgets. For all households, rented dwellings cost 26 percent of household income in 2000; after housing allowances, condominiums 21 percent; and a one-family house 20 percent, with a slightly decreasing tendency since the end of the 1990s (SCB 2004b: Table 1.11). According to the latest census—1990—41 percent of dwellings were owner occupied and 15 percent were condominiums. Tenants with firsthand contracts with the owner enjoy considerable legal protection. They cannot be dismissed at will, nor can their rent be unilaterally raised beyond clear limits. About 40 percent of dwellings were held by these legally protected contracts, whereas 4 percent were inhabited by less secure, secondhand contracts and 1 percent lacked information of ownership or tenancy (SCB 2004b: Table 10.1). Tenancy contracts are usually undetermined in time and require three months' notice.

Housing Conditions

The social quality of neighborhoods, or, as they are called in Sweden, "dwelling areas" (*bostadsområden*) is another matter, with social problems at least superficially similar to French, German or Dutch problem suburbs. Considerable efforts at raising their quality have been made in the past twenty to thirty years, but social problems also increased in the 1990s, with substantial refugee (and family reunion) immigration and a more closed labor market. Ensuing frustrations and alienation lead to vandalism and violence and are damaging several suburbs.

Reported crimes rose continuously after the Second World War to a peak in 1990. Since the early 1990s, the level has stabilized, with about the same value in 2002 as in the mid-1980s. Traffic offenses excluded, they amount to 130 per 10,000 inhabitants, compared to 25 in 1950 (including traffic offenses) (SCB 2004e: Table 556, Figure 548). Security of life and property was added to the Level of Living studies in the 1980s. Their results show that about 7 percent of the total population aged sixteen to eighty-four had been victims of violence or threats of violence from 2000 to 2001. In the 1990s this figure rose from about 5 percent in the 1980s. Young men, aged sixteen to twenty-four, run the biggest risk (20 percent), followed by young women (17 percent) (SCB 2003b: chap. 17).

Health Care

Health care in Sweden is primarily organized and provided by the provinces, financed by provincial taxes and governed by their elected assemblies, although under considerable national supervision, including financial. Sweden is an internationally outstanding health care cost cutter. In spite of population aging—Sweden has the highest world proportion of people above eighty (4.5 percent)—health care costs as a percentage of GDP are lower in 2000 than they were in 1980, 7.9 percent and 9.5 percent, respectively. In PPP dollars per capita as well as in GDP proportion, Swedish health expenditure is slightly below the EU-15 average (OECD 1990: 10; 1993: 69).

Public sickness insurance covers all Swedish residents from the age of sixteen. Children under sixteen are covered by school health and child health systems. The insurance covers health care costs and, for those in the labor force, sickness allowance, which is 80 percent of earnings (for most employees) from 1 January 2005. However, there is always a patient fee, which varies among the provinces but is no longer symbolic, around €20 (with an annual ceiling, a high cost protection). Patients' co-payments amounted to 2 percent of public health care expenditure in 1999 (Hjorstberg and Ghatnekar 2001).

Employment Security and Working Conditions

Labor contracts are governed by an Employment Security Act of 1982. A normal labor contract must be without time limits and employees are well protected against individual firings, even for minor misconduct. The workplace trades union has been given a crucial say in any termination or change of the employment contract, including the individual order of collective dismissals for scarcity of work. In this way, the law provides for local flexibility to the extent that the employer can reach an agreement with the union. The minimum length of notice is one month for employees under twenty-five, then two months, and from forty-five years of age or ten years of employment, six months.

According to national employment statistics, in 2002, 15 percent of employees had a temporary job contract. The normal Swedish working week is forty hours. However, 10 percent of male employees and 34 percent of females work fewer than thirty-five hours a week. The large time budget survey of 2000 and 2001 found that men worked on the average a good thirty-eight hours and women twenty-five hours (SCB 2001a: 1).

Swedish employees are often de facto absent from work. In any average week in 2000, 15 percent of employed men and 24 percent of women were absent for the whole week, but these figures also include holidays. Paid sick leave takes a good 4 percent of total normal working time and parental leave another 2 percent (SCB 2004a). Absenteeism peaked in 1990, when 40 percent of employed women with children under (the school age of) seven were absent. (SCB 2002a: 52).

Social Cohesion

In general historical terms, Sweden is a cohesive nation. There has been an old realm of unbroken medieval continuity. Lutheranism unified the nation religiously, although a large plethora of dissenting movements developed in the second half of the nineteenth century. After the regional power dreams were shattered in 1809, the country became ethnically and linguistically homogenous, with only tiny peripheral minorities. Modern politics has been characterized by institutionalized conflict, with competing ideological left and right party blocs and powerful, well-organized "counterparts"—not "partners"—on the labor market, but all playing by rules. The only violent capital-labor clashes took place in 1931, in forest industry port areas in the north. There, strikebreakers were still used and the army was called in to protect them. Seven strikers were killed in the most serious clash.

Trust

Swedes have little reason to feel "betrayed by history"—a powerful source of social mistrust in the Mediterranean region, analyzed by C. Giordano (1992). The peasants preserved their personal freedom, and their ancient institutions of local self-government were fitted into the monarchical state. The fifty years of Absolutism, ending in 1718, had an anti-aristocratic, proto-populist bent, at least in its first half. The largest part of the population was never excluded or alienated from the state. The relative modesty of the monarchy and even of the nobility corresponded with the poverty of the people.

Consequently, Swedes today tend to be trusting: together with the other Scandinavians, the most trusting in the world. In both World Values Survey waves (1990 and 2000), 66 percent feel that most people can be trusted. There was then slightly more trust than in 1981 (Rothstein 2002: 320.) While age plays no role in the level of trust, income and education does with people of low income and low education having less trust in people. Nevertheless, a good half of them has (Inglehart et al. 2004: question A165).

With regard to their confidence in institutions, Swedes are less outstanding. About half, or just under, have confidence in the survey list of public institutions, from parliament and the armed forces to churches, labor unions and major companies. Questions about political parties and—in the 2000 wave—about government, were not asked. In 2000, Swedes had most institutional confidence in the health care system and the police (three-quarters) followed by the educational and the justice systems (barely two-thirds). The Eurobarometer of February and March 2004 gives similar results but adds a clearly greater trust in the national government and, even more, in the national parliament than on the average of the EU-15. In Sweden, the trusters and non-trusters were 48 percent versus 47 percent for the government, compared with the EU average of 30 to 61 percent. Parliament was trusted by 58 percent and not trusted by 37 percent in Sweden, corresponding to 35 to 54 percent in the EU as a whole (European Commission 2004: first results, Table 5a).

Nine out of ten Swedes, like most people in the world, regard family as very important. Friendship is more important than in other European countries, and so are leisure and politics. The importance of work is rather average and religion less. Considerably fewer Swedes (44 percent) than the world average (82 percent) or the average of France, Germany and Great Britain (64 percent) think that parents are due unconditional respect (Inglehart et al. 2004: Tables A1–6, 25).

Altruism and Tolerance

In terms of attitudes, Swedes appear relatively tolerant. In the World Values Survey of 2000, only 3 percent expressed reservations against having immigrants as neighbors, and 9 percent against Muslim neighbors (Inglehart et al. 2004: questions A128–129). Just 6 percent would be worried by homosexual neighbors. Worrying neighbors were, as in other countries, drug addicts, people with a criminal record and alcoholics.

A Eurobarometer survey found Swedes most frequently "actively tolerant" (33 percent as compared to an EU average of 21 percent) and less frequently "intolerant" (9 percent), than the average (14 percent). The Spanish came out as least actively tolerant and most often passively tolerant. These indices include views on non-civic behavior, such as fraudulent claims to public benefits, tax and fare cheating, car theft ("joyriding"), littering and drunken driving, which were distinguished from other issues of tolerance.

Social Contract

In 2000, Swedes were the least likely to blame people in need for their poverty; in fact only 7 percent did so, compared with the 50 percent that blamed social injustice instead (Inglehart et al. 2004: Tables E190–191). Election after election, the majority of Swedes have reconfirmed their commitment to high taxation as a necessary price for social services. Most recently, this happened in the parliamentary election of 2002, which not only re-elected the Social Democratic government—dependent on the support of the Left and of the Environment parties—but also gave a strong setback to the right-wing moderates, who put forward far-reaching tax reduction proposals. In the governing political elite it seems that taxation has now reached its ceiling and tax cuts have now entered the Social Democratic agenda. The level is much higher than in the rest of the EU and of the OECD. In 2001, taxes and social security contributions comprise around 54 percent of the Swedish GDP compared with the EU average of just under 41 percent.

Networks

Swedes are a people of joiners, with strong traditions of associational membership. Some, previously large, organizations have declined, religious denominations, temperance associations, in the past decades also political parties and their youth and women's wings. Trades unions have maintained themselves extraordinarily well, albeit not without losses, and sports clubs and passive membership of support-cause organizations, like Amnesty International or Greenpeace, has increased. By the end of 2002, trade unions organized about 80 percent of Swedish employees.

Ninety-five per cent spend time with friends at least once or twice a month (Inglehart et al. 2004: question A58). However, in national surveys, one in five say that they lack a close friend (Fritzell and Lundberg 2000: 41, Table 2.2.)

Identities

Together with the Danes, Portuguese and Irish, Swedes were the only Europeans whose feelings of national pride had increased in 1990. However, the level remained below the Western European average (41 percent for Swedes; 45 percent for Western Europeans. In the 2000 wave of the Value Surveys, there were still 41 percent proud—about the same as in France and Italy but much higher than in Germany or the Netherlands.

Against a background of successful neutrality—which kept Sweden out of the two world wars—postwar full employment and a system of social security and equality, which has been second to none since the 1960s, the limited European enthusiasm of the Swedish population is quite understandable. Swedes are divided almost equally among those who think positively about the EU (37 percent in spring 2004) and negatively (33 percent) and neither positive nor negative (29 percent). Nearly 60 percent held that Sweden had not benefited from EU membership, while 27 percent found benefits from membership. However, with their propensity for trust, Swedes are as frequent in their trust of the Commission as the average European (European Commission 2004).

Social Inclusion

Citizenship Rights

Swedish citizenship is historically based on the principle of *ius sanguinis* (right of descent), but also on residence. Minimum residence length requirements are rather low (two years for Nordic citizens, five years for others), children who at twenty-one have lived for ten years in Sweden only have to give notice of their desire for citizenship, whereas for adults, a non-criminal record is important. Sweden was a pioneer in giving non-citizen, long-term residents the right to vote in municipal elections. In 2002, 220,000 non-citizens were entitled to vote—just 3 percent of the electorate. However, participation is rather low and in the end there were only 25,000 more votes in the municipal than in the simultaneous parliamentary elections.

In 2001, women's gross wages as percentage of men's were 84 percent in the private sector and 90 percent in the municipalities. Controlled for occupation, branch, education and age, female wages made 92 percent of the male wage on the whole labor market, 90 percent in the private sector, 92 percent among state employees, 93 percent among the provincial employees (the bulk of health care) and 99 percent among municipal employees (Gustafsson et al. 2003: A4). These national data from Statistics Sweden are geared to an identification of gender discrimination. However, if gendered occupational choice is allowed to count, Swedish women fare less well, because of a rather gender-segregated labor market and many women in low-paid social service jobs. Eurostat data for average hourly earnings in 2001 point to a larger gender gap in that sense than on average in the EU, an 18 percent gap in Sweden compared to a 16 percent in the EU.

Ombudsman is a Swedish word and concept that spread around the world in the last decades of the twentieth century. It goes back to the Constitution of 1809, instituting two parliamentary administrative offices for receipt and investigation of complaints about the public administration and about the military. The ombudsman in this sense has the right start investigations on own initiative and to bring cases to court, but the main function is one of public criticism of officialdom and its practice. The ombudsman is a representative of the people, usually with a legal training but not a politician. In recent times there has been a proliferation of ombudsmen in Sweden, preoccupied with not only the state apparatus but also the functioning of society at large. In addition to the main parliamentary ombudsman office, there are now a number of Ombudsmen (see Table 8.5). The Parliamentary Judiciary Ombudsman deals with four to five thousand cases a year. The cases of the new offices vary considerably.

Women's representation is an officially recognized issue, with gender distribution rules throughout the public sector, commitment of all political parties to some definition of a "balanced" electoral representation and public pressure also on private business. Data supply is accordingly ample.

Service Access

Every resident adult is covered by health insurance, and all children by child and school health care. But as adult medical consultation and care are no longer free (consulting a

Table 8.5. Cases by the New Public Ombudsmen in 2002

Consumer Ombudsman	8,922
Disability Ombudsman	1,955
Ombudsman against Ethic Discrimination	1,551
Children's Ombudsman	1,218
Equal Opportunities Ombudsman	862
Ombudsman against Discrimination because of Sexual Orientation	446

Source: SCB 2004e: Table 575

Table 8.6. The Proportion of Women in Various Public Bodies in 2003–2004

	Percent
Cabinet	50
Parliament	45
Board members of state authorities	
Central	47
Regional	50
Provincial executives	47
Municipal executives	36
Trade union executives	
LO (manual workers)	27
TCO (white collar)	55
SACO (professional)	56
Corporations listed on the stock exchange	
Board members	15
CEOs	1

Source: SCB 2004d: 84ff

public doctor costs €20 to €25), with an annual ceiling, there is an actual shortage. In 1999, 2 percent of men and 4 percent of women over the age of twenty said they could not afford medical care. The proportion is highest among women aged twenty to twenty-four (5 percent) and lowest among elderly men (1 percent) (SCB 2001a: Table 8).

Local social workers have estimated the number of homeless people in Stockholm at 3,000 (interview with Erik Finne at the Social Services of Stockholm). On a national scale, there are an estimated 10,000 homeless (Welfare Committee 2000: 246–247).

Nine years of schooling are compulsory. After that, about 90 percent of the cohort are qualified for secondary education. Nowadays, two thirds of a cohort get a tertiary education (SCB 2002e: 102). Women make up 61 percent of tertiary education undergraduates and 63 percent of first degree-takers from 2001 to 2002. They were 49 percent of beginning postgraduate students and 43 percent of the PhDs, a year later 45 percent (SCB 2004f).

All towns have local transport, which is heavily subsidized. In the countryside there is also an extensive public bus service, organized by the provinces. Elderly and disabled people have the right to personal transport services for a modest fee. To our knowledge, there is no clear Swedish definition of "access to public transport." Statistics Sweden uses distance to a bus stop as a criterion (250 meters or more) with the nearest bus service running less frequently than every half hour. In those respects, about 40 percent of the population had limited access to public transport in the mid-1990s and 17 percent had no car. However, the proportion having neither a car nor a bus stop within 250 meters was only 4 percent (for the sixteen to seventy-four population) (SCB 1997: 262–263).

Social Networks

About 40 percent of the population have no contact with their neighbors but a third relate to neighbors every week. Of the population aged sixteen to eighty-four, 5 percent lack a close friend (Fritzell and Lundberg 2000: 112), and in the European Values Study 95 percent say they spend time with friends at least once a month. About half of the population spends leisure time with colleagues. Since the 1970s, the networks of friendship have become denser. Almost 60 percent are with friends—who are not close relatives, work colleagues or neighbors—at least every week, an increase of 12 percent between the mid-1970s and the late 1980s, after which there has been a certain stabilization. Only 2 percent of the population aged sixteen to eighty-four lack social relations outside their own household and are in that sense isolated.

Social Empowerment

The large popular movements, especially the religious dissenters who strove for temperance and labor, rose in Sweden in the second half of the nineteenth century and were to set their imprint on the twentieth-century development. They were very much concerned with what today's public discourse calls "social empowerment": to enhance their members' ability to cope with their lives and with social challenges. A core institution of this "empowerment" was the study circle, for collective self-study, a tradition that is still being financially supported. The latter are often, but not always, linked to religious or political currents, and include also political youth organizations. Currently, about 2.8 million people annually participate in study circles, according to official statistics (SCB 2002d: Table 596). The topics are wide ranging, from Swedish for immigrants, civic and political topics, to art and hobbies. But they are not vocational.

Knowledge Base

A good part of the Swedish labor force is overeducated in relation to their jobs, 37 percent in 2000. From 1974 to 2000, average education of the labor force increased from 1.6 to 3.8 years after compulsory school, whereas average employer demand has augmented from 1.8 to 3.6 years. About a quarter of all jobs require no particular qualification (LeGrand et al. 2004).

Knowledge from experience is often treated on par with study merits. Income differentiation by educational level is rather modest. In 2002 a male employee with at least three years of tertiary education had 34 percent higher gross wages than one with only two years of secondary school. Among women the differential was higher, 52 percent (SCB 2002c: Table 2a). Nevertheless, there is an increase of the educational differential in spite of the oversupply of education mentioned above.

Sweden has a somewhat greater social "fluidity" of relative social mobility odds, compared to most countries, although the differences are small. In particular, children of unskilled workers have had better chances in Sweden (Eriksson and Goldthorpe 1992; SCB 1997: chap. 27). Education is a major channel of social mobility but also a mechanism of social selection and reproduction. Sweden is one of the few countries where there has been a long-term decline of social bias in the educational system, but equalization flattened out after 1970. International differences are surprisingly small, and Sweden seems to have about the same overall social bias in education as Britain and the United States, with their many private upper-class schools, but somewhat less than the public elitism of France and Germany. (SCB 1997: chap. 28).

Labor Market

About 67 to 70 percent of the total labor force was unionized in early 2003 (SCB 2004a; 2004e: 335), a trend that is slowly declining. There is virtually no difference between the public sector and the private industrial sector, but private services have a lower rate of unionization. Swedish trades union membership is sustained by the fact that most unemployment insurance is administered by the unions, although overwhelmingly publicly financed, and also by the strong, legally backed, workplace presence of the unions. The Co-Determination Act and the Employment Security Act make all workplace reorganization and employment contract changes subject to employer–trades union negotiations. Of old, the labor market counterparts have a strong autonomy from the state. Collective bargaining covers almost the whole labor market and takes place between the organizations of employers and employees only. The state is not seldom providing "mediators," but no arbitrators and no fiat.

Sweden became known in OECD policy circles in the 1960s for its "active labor market policies"—that is, of policies providing work or retraining for the unemployed. Such back-to-work schemes have recently been scaled down, but they are still significant. Discounting special schemes for the disabled, they covered 2.7 percent of the labor force in 2002.

Openness of Institutions

The Swedish political system has traditionally had an emphasis on "representative democracy," centered in parliament, in party and trade union congresses and executives. While trades union executives still keep control of labor market conflict, political parties are now holding consultative primaries, and referenda have become important. The latter are not constitutionally binding but are generally respected by the political elite. From 1980 to the mid-2000s, Sweden held three important referenda: in 1980 on nuclear energy, in 1994 on EU membership and in 2003 on the Euro. At the municipal level, referenda have to be put on the agenda, but not necessarily held, if 5 percent of the municipal voters so demand. Most municipal referenda held have been on division/secession.

Public planning decisions, urban plans and non-urban road plans must by law be submitted to public scrutiny and debate before they can be passed. Municipalities sometimes invite public initiatives and opinions, on whatever issue.

The Swedish public bureaucracy is—like the other Nordic countries—uniquely accessible to civic questioning. All its files, except on private matters and judicial cases, are in principle accessible to anybody requesting them. The office has a legal obligation to provide them upon request with in- and outgoing correspondence, receipts, minutes and so on. Investigative journalism is much facilitated. From our personal experience, we know that interviewing public bureaucrats, including by university students as part of their education, is much easier in Sweden than, for example, in the Netherlands.

The openness of the economic system is primarily provided by the rights and power of trades unions. It is not possible to run a significant anti-union enterprise in Sweden. In the 1970s, the Stockholm plant was the first ever unionized IBM plant in the world. In the 1990s the anti-union retail chain Toys "R" Us was forced by a strike to choose whether to negotiate or to quit the country. It chose to quit. (Ryanair has so far been able to circumvent the Swedish unions by having its Swedish employees officially employed in England.)

Public Space

Sweden nurtures an old concept of nature as public space. Fields, forests, meadows, mountains and waters are in principle accessible to everybody (*allemansrätt*, literally "the right of everybody"). Even on private property you can do your walking, flower picking, swimming, camping and so on.

Civic organizations of all kinds, including political parties, receive considerable economic public support, nationally and locally. This support is particularly important for the parties (with their youth organizations), for associations of immigrants and for adult education organizations. A special wage support program subsidizes the employment of handicapped or unemployed people and organizations of "public utility" can thereby get 90 percent of their wages from the public purse. In this way, sports organizations employ about eight to nine thousand people and other associations three to five thousand (*Dagens Nyheter* 2004: 8). A recent voucher system supports a number of private schools, including religious ones.

Personal Relationships

A noteworthy change in personal relationships occurred at the end of the 1960s. The Swedish language never developed a generalized polite second-person pronoun, like the German *Sie*, the French *vous* or the universalistic English *you*. Instead, in polite language you had to use clumsy third-person circumventions, using titles if known, otherwise some neuter third-person circumlocution. In the telephone book, people with the same surname were listed according to their titles or occupation. Then, in just a couple of years, everybody was empowered to say *du*, using the intimate, informal second-person pronoun, to everybody including the prime minister, the archbishop, the teacher and the boss (but not the royal family). The phone book now lists persons with the same surname by their first names, in alphabetical order.

Conclusion

It may be concluded, hopefully without nationalist bias, that social quality in Sweden is relatively high. This is also borne out by the United Nations Development Programme reports, which place Sweden at the top of their Human Development

Index, in 2004 as second after Norway. Nor is the position contested by liberal American economists (see, e.g., Sachs 2004). It is noteworthy that it goes together with a top ranking of "world competitiveness" by the World Economic Forum, putting Sweden third among 102 countries of the world in 2003, after Finland and the United States. The national Level of Living and Living Conditions surveys bring out a basic trend of social quality amelioration since 1968, when the series started.

As already hinted at, the Swedish position is not unique but rather part of a somewhat broader Nordic spectrum, which has developed through the five countries learning from each other as well as from parallel trajectories. The Nordic nations share an egalitarian tradition, from a forceful preindustrial peasantry and a tradition of limited patriarchy. Their Lutheran churches provided early universal literacy and then became wide open to industrial secularization. From the late nineteenth century, they grew rapidly economically, on the basis of commodity exports in mounting demand, but of commodities conducive to fruitful industrial linkages domestically. All this provided the fertile soil for the twentieth century labor and women's movements. The smallness of the countries, but also their capacity of rapidly and smoothly overcoming historical conflicts and frictions among themselves, put domestic reform and development at the top of the political agenda, unhampered by imperial or irredentist ambitions or concerns.

The new challenges of the past decades have been weathered rather well by the Swedes and their institutions. Deindustrialization after 1965 did not lead to mass unemployment, and most of the effects of the deep (financially induced) crisis of the early 1990s have been overcome. The wave of large immigration has caused friction and tension but less xenophobia than in most countries of Europe. New political priorities—of gender equality, of environment protection, of equal sexual rights—have been well received by the political system.

However, there are also some clouds above the rose garden. Tendencies of social polarization are operating, although their outcome is still limited. Economic inequality has increased substantially, from a Gini index of disposable income of 0.20 in 1980 to 0.28 in 1999, that is, up to a western European average.[1] The large wave of immigrants, of the late 1980s to the early 1990s, did not make it very well due to the slack labor market, and there is now a substantial pool of ethnic unemployment. The very successful cost containment of health care is now beginning to hit the quality of the service. But politicians, if not yet citizens, seem to be converging on the idea that taxation has reached its limit. Meanwhile, the population is aging further: the big cohorts of the 1940s are nearing retirement. And the working population is to a large extent either on their stress threshold or harboring a strong leisure preference. Here, in the triangle of need, taxes and care, work dilemmas and conflicts are building up. And externally, increased competitive pressures are mounting, from eastern Europe and from East Asia, threatening countries of currently high social quality, either by eroding their economic base or by inspiring their leaders to lower the standards.

An upward equalization of the social quality of the enlarged union should be a prime goal of the European Union, much more important to its citizens than, for example, a common foreign and security policy.

Göran Therborn is Professor Emeritus of Sociology at the University of Cambridge (United Kingdom) and Affiliated Professor at Linnaeus University (Sweden.) Before Cambridge, he was Co-Director of the Swedish Collegium for Advanced Study in Uppsala. He has worked on several fields of empirical and theoretical social science and has taught in several countries in Europe, the Americas and Asia. Among his recent books are *Between Sex and Power: Family in the World 1900–2000* (2004), *Les sociétés d'Europe du XXe au XXIe siècle* (2009), *Power and Powerlessness: Capital Cities in Africa* (edited with S. Bekker; 2011), *The World: A Beginner's Guide* (2011) and *The Killing Fields of Inequality* (2013). He is currently writing a global study of *Cities of Power*.

Sonia Therborn is a clinical psychologist, now retired, specialized in the psychology of children and the elderly. She has also worked together with Göran Therborn on projects about social quality, families in the world and cities of power.

Note

1. That is a comparable measure over time. In 1996 the methodology was changed, for the better—by not assuming a priori that all people above the age of eighteen lived on their own—and, according to the new measure, the 1999 value was 0.26, up from 0.24 in 1996.

References

Beck, W., L. van der Maesen and A. Walker, eds. 1997. *The Social Quality of Europe*. The Hague: Kluwer Law International.

Dagens Nyheter. 2004. 24 September.

Eriksson, R. and J. Goldthorpe. 1992. *The Constant Flux*. Oxford: Clarendon Press.

Eurobarometer 61, 2004.

European Commission. *The Social Situation of the European Union in 2003*.

Fritzell, J. and O. Lundberg. 2000. *Välfärd, ofärd och ojämlikhet*. Stockholm: SOU.

Giordano, C. 1992. *Die Betrogenen der Geschichte*. Frankfurt: Campus.

Gustafsson, C.H. et al. 2003. "Hopplösa fel om löneskillnader." *Dagens Nyheter*, 15 January.

Hjorstberg, C. and O. Ghatnekar. 2001. *Health Care Systems in Transition: Sweden*. Copenhagen: European Observatory on Health Systems and Policies.

Inglehart, R. et al., eds. 2004. *Human Values and Beliefs: A Cross-Cultural Sourcebook Based on the 1999–2002 Value Surveys*. Mexico: Siglo XXI.

LeGrand, C. et al. 2004. "Arbetslivet halkar efter: de enkla jobben försvinner inte." *Sociologisk forskning* 1.

Luxemburg Income Study. 2004. Results kindly communicated by Dr. Thomas Cossack, Wissenschaftszentrum Berlin.

OECD. 1990. *Health Care Systems in Transition*.

OECD. 1993. *Society at a Glance*.

OECD. 2002. *Economic Surveys 2001–2002: Sweden*.

Rothstein, B. 2002. "Sweden." In *Democracies in Flux: The Evolution of Social Capital in Contemporary Society*, ed R. Putnam. Oxford: Oxford University Press.

Sachs, J. 2004. "The Best Countries in the World." *Newsweek*, 26 July.

SCB (Statistics Sweden). 1997. *Levnadsförhållanden Rapport 91*. Stockholm.

SCB. 2001a. *Tidsanvändningsundersökningen 2000–2001*.

SCB. 2001b. *Hälso- och sjukvårdsstatistisk* Årsbok.

SCB. 2002a. *Arbetskraftsprognos*.

SCB. 2002b. *Levnadsförhållanden*.

SCB. 2002c. *Lönestatistisk* Årsbok.

SCB. 2002d. *Statistisk* Årsbok.

SCB. 2002e. *Svensk utbildning i internationell statistik*.

SCB. 2003a. *Hushållens utgifter*.

SCB. 2003b. *Levnadsförhållanden Rapport 100*.

SCB. 2004a. AKU (Labour Force Surveys).

SCB. 2004b. *Bostads-och byggnadsstatistisk* Årsbok.

SCB. 2004c. Press Information, p. 220.

SCB. 2004d. *På tal om kvinnor och män*.

SCB. 2004e. *Statistisk* Årsbok.

SCB. 2004f. *Utbildning och forskning*.

Welfare Committee. 2000. *Välfärd vid vägskäl*. Stockholm: SOU 3, pp. 246–247.

CHAPTER 9

Visions of the Sustainable Welfare Society
Extending Social Quality into an Asian/Developmental Context

Yoshinori Hiroi

Conceptual Frameworks of the Sustainable Welfare Society

Definition and Implications

The ideal of the "sustainable welfare society" is described as a society where a high level of social quality within social structures and distributional justice is achieved in a sustainable manner, given finite natural resources and environments (Beck 2001; Gasper et al. 2008). This concept has certain policy implications, which seem to be particularly important for researchers discussing social policy issues in Asian countries, as distinct from the European ones (Goodman et al. 1998; Kwon 2005).

   Indeed, the notion of the sustainable welfare society suggests valuing the integration of social policy and environmental policy into a uniform one by combining the terms "sustainability" and "welfare." At present, many Asian countries have experienced speedy economic development that has inevitably increased their consumption of natural resources, as in the examples of China and India (Walker 2007; Walker and Wong 2005). This growth makes the issue of environmental sustainability a critical one for our discussion of social policy issues. Thus, we need to incorporate an element of environmental sustainability into the discourse of social policy debate in the context of Asian countries.[1]

Welfare, Environment and Economy

Depending on the contexts in which they are used, the concepts of "welfare" and "environment" contain a rich variety of meanings. To make a conceptual comparison, "welfare" mainly concerns the distribution of wealth and the condition of its equity (or equal distributional justice), whereas "environment" mainly concerns the total volume of wealth, and its sustainability.[2] Thus, in some ways, these two concepts can be closely related to each other, and therefore the integration of these policies is essential for sustainable welfare societies. Within this relationship, if we consider "economy" as dealing with the production of wealth and the efficiency of resource allocations, we thus have a triangular structure of the three elements as presented in Table 9.1 below.[3]

Table 9.1. Issues and Objectives of Welfare, Environment and Economy

	function or issues	objective
Welfare	distribution of wealth	equity (or equal justice)
Environment	total volume of wealth	sustainability
Economy	production of wealth	efficiency

If we explore the relationship of these three elements, the following conceptualization might possibly show a conceptual framework with which to understand human society. As shown in Figure 9.1, human society can be analyzed on three levels: first, individuals; second, community; and third, nature. In other words, "individuals" are seen in the context of market or economy, while "nature" corresponds to the environments within which human beings act. In modern times, the "individual" expanded rapidly with the development of the market economy and became alienated from communities and nature. As a result, in the relationship between the market economy and communities, there is a decline of community power but an increase of inequality. The distorted relationship between market economy and nature took the shape of environmental destructions and the unsustainable consumption of natural resources.

Accordingly, the issues of welfare concern the relationship of (A) and (B), and the environmental issues concern the relationship of (A) and (C). Accordingly, the issues of both welfare and environment are, to some extent, only part of the problems in human society. In this context, the integration of welfare policy and environmental policy is essential.

Figure 9.1. Relationships among Environment, Welfare and Economy

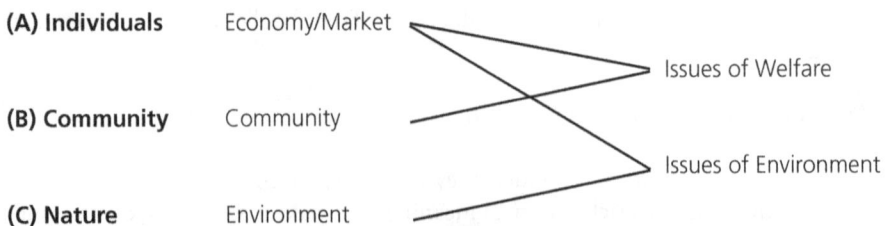

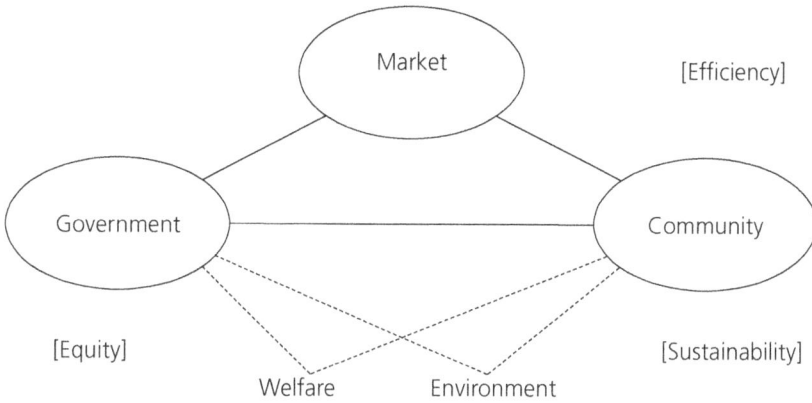

Figure 9.2. Market-Government-Community Nexus and Welfare and Environment

Thus, we should inquire further about the relationship between the roles of government, market and community. This forms part of the discourse in the realm of comparative welfare states.[4] If we have the policy areas of environment in perspective, the tentative configuration can be shown as in Figure 9.2. Here both "welfare" and "environment" refer to "government" as well as "community." We must also note that the concept of "sustainability" is allied with "community" because community includes elements of sustainability or duration including intergenerational succession.

Even so, we still should be aware of the several meanings and/or contexts that the term "sustainability" implies. For instance, the term "sustainability" sometimes denotes financial sustainability of some institutions or systems, as in the example of the "sustainability of pension system." However, the term "sustainability" became highlighted in the area of environmental policies as well as in the area of "sustainable development policies." Thus, we should distinguish between the different dimensions of "sustainability" from short-term to long-term.

Figure 9.3 below is a revised and extended version of Figure 9.2. In this figure, three dimensions of "sustainability" are distinguished. They include:

1. sustainability (in a short-term): concerning with market and government;
2. sustainability (in a long-term): concerning with community;
3. sustainability (in a far long-term): concerning nature.

Thus, when we discuss the notion of the sustainable welfare society, we should not only consider the factors in the first dimension but also the factors in the second and third dimensions since the sustainability of natural systems is fundamental for the existence of human society.

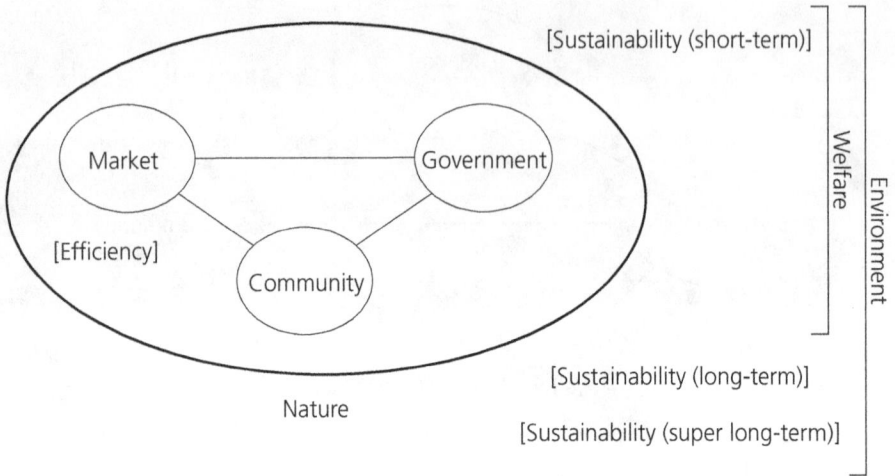

Figure 9.3. The Nexus of Market–Government–Community in Relation to Welfare and Environment

Failure in a Shift from Industrial Policy to Social Policy? The Dynamic Relationship of Welfare, Environment and Economy in the Process of Economic Development in Postwar Japan

Using the analytic framework sketched in the previous section, we can further examine the Japanese experience with a focus on the dynamic relationship of welfare, environment and economy. In the late nineteenth century, Japan became the first industrialized Asian country and went through a rapid process of economic and social transformations. The Japanese experience of social policy and the formation of social protection systems thus provides many interesting points of observation, which seem different from those of Western countries (McGillivray and Clarke 2006; Institute for International Cooperation 2004). For instance, when Japan tried to achieve universal coverage of social insurance programs between the 1940s and 1960s, around 40 to 60 percent of the total population was engaged in agriculture, unlike many Western countries but similar to many developing countries. Another case concerns the dynamic relationship of economic policy, social (or welfare) policy and environmental policy in the process of development. As a "latecomer" in industrialization, Japan (and many other Asian countries) took social policy as a "dependent" policy area, often "embedded" in economic policy or industrial policy, particularly at the earlier stages of development. Here I will briefly review the postwar Japanese experience of public policy regarding income redistribution and examine the dynamic relationship of economic, social and environmental policies.

Stage 1: Policy Initiatives for "Equality of Opportunities" in the Postwar Era

The postwar Japanese policy developments in income redistribution can tentatively be divided into four stages. The first stage is the period right after the end of the Second

World War under the occupation of the United States of America. This stage is characterized by strong policy initiatives for "equality of opportunities." Two policy developments were significant in this context: first, radical redistribution of land by the agricultural land reform and second, a mandatory educational system of junior high schools.

The land redistribution initiated by the occupation force was aimed at the dissolution of feudal land ownership. Indeed, by 1946, the Special Law for the Creation of Landed Farmers was enacted, and a lot of agricultural land was mandatorily bought by the government and sold to the peasants. As a result, the ratio of land owners to the total number of farmers increased from 31 percent in 1945 to 62 percent in 1950. The introduction of a mandatory education system has also had a very strong effect on land redistribution because it provided people with equal opportunities at an early stage of life. In a social sense, this system served as a basis for later economic development as it cultivated a labor force capable of engaging in economic activities.

Figure 9.4 shows the relationship between the egalitarian effect of land distribution and economic growth in the twentieth century. In this graph, the egalitarian effect of land distribution is measured by using the Gini coefficient. The positive correlation between two sets of factors is evident. This experience can also be observed from Korea, Thailand and Taiwan. The issues of land ownership and distribution, although not the central issue in the discussion of welfare states, are important when we examine the social policies of developing countries in Asia. Some of these policies concern assets rather than income, so the study of social policy development should not only pay attention to income redistribution but to assets as well.

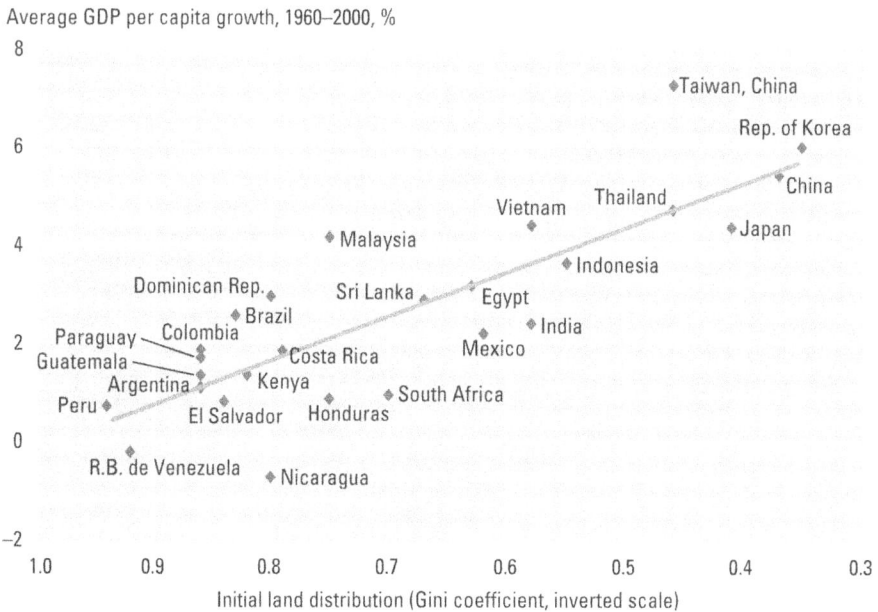

Figure 9.4. The Egalitarian Effect of Land Distribution and Economic Growth
Source: World Bank 2005

Stage 2: "Redistribution for Production" in the Period of High Economic Growth (1950s to 1960s)

The notion of "redistribution for production" may sound odd to most European social policy scholars, but this is the most important aspect of Japanese redistribution policy in the postwar period. In European welfare states, production is the process occurring in the sphere of market operations, whereas income redistribution happens in the field of social protection (and related mechanisms, e.g., progressive taxation). However, in postwar Japan, policies made in the production sphere played a major role in enhancing the effect of income redistribution, whereas the policies of social protection have a relatively weak function of income redistribution.

To address these policies specifically, we can refer to the following policies, which are often categorized as "industrial policies in the broad sense": first, subsidies to farmers (i.e., the income distribution between the urban and the rural population); second, tax redistribution between the central and local governments; third, subsidies to small and medium enterprises and to the factories of declining industries.

To make a general assessment, the subsidies to farmers was a very important policy measure because in this period, the process of industrialization coincided with a huge population transferred from rural areas to urban areas. This turned the income gap between farmers and the urban residents into a major political issue. The redistributive mechanism of tax revenues from the national government to local governments was an important means of resolving the issue of social protection in the poor regions. There were still other significant income redistribution mechanisms, which helped the workers in various industrial sectors. As the element of income redistribution in these policies was mingled with the industrial policies made by the government, their

Table 9.2. Government Expenditure in Japan by Policy Area (billion yen)

	Social protection (by tax)	Tax transfer from central to local governments	Public projects
1958	122	224	190
1960	193	328	304
1965	546	716	726
1970	1152	1772	1441
1975	4136	3308	3487
1980	8170	6952	6896
1985	9902	9690	6891
1990	11480	15931	6956
1995	14543	12302	12795
2000	17636	14915	11910
2005	20824	15923	8015

Source: Ministry of Finance, Japan 2006: 432

implementation blurred the contrast between the issues of "resource allocation" and "income redistribution."

Thus, Japan achieved a wide coverage of social insurance in 1961 in the fields of health care and pensions, and this contributed to the work of the strong redistributive mechanism formulated by the setting up of a number of "industrial policies" beyond the policies of social protection. This results in a change in the composition of government expenditures, as Table 9.2 shows. In the table, the expenditures resulting from tax transfer from central to local governments and from public projects were bigger than those spent on social protection schemes until the 1970s. These mechanisms played major roles in realizing an equal distribution of income.

Stage 3: Public Projects and the Beginning of Social Protection Policies for the Elderly (1970s to 1990s)

From the 1970s onward, Japan entered a period of low-rated economic growth. In terms of redistribution policy, this period is characterized by the following developments: first, the growth of public projects as a mechanism of income redistribution and second, social policies for protecting the elderly. In this period, the state spent money on public projects that impacted income redistribution. Figure 9.5 shows the relationship between the increased public projects per capita and the raised per capita income level in various prefectures of Japan. This relation was weakly identified during 1955 and 1960, but, in the 1990s, the data show that in the regions where the level of per capita income was low, the volume invested into public projects was high. This means that in this period, public projects, beside their primary aim of providing necessary infrastructure, played a part in income redistribution in the low income regions.

In this period, the idea of "redistribution for production" was still maintained, but these "production-oriented" sets of policies, which had been effective in the past, gradually became obstacles for the development of social policies, particularly in regard to social provision for the working population. Besides, using public projects

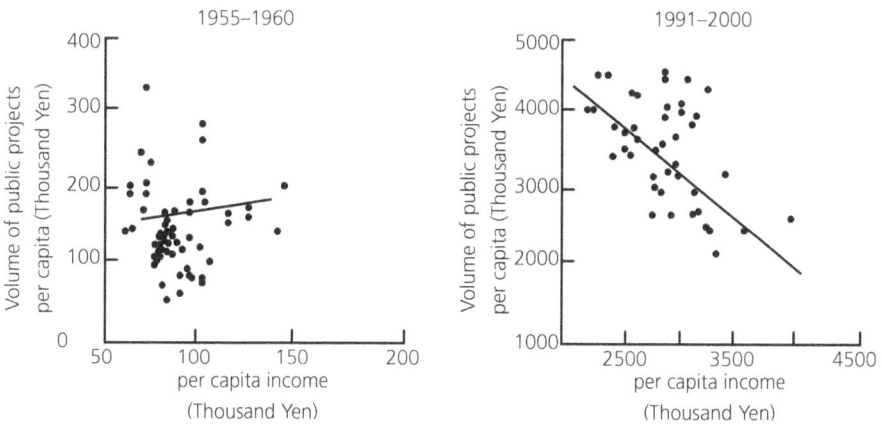

Figure 9.5. Public Projects and Per Capita Income at Different Prefectures of Japan
Source: Daiwa Research Institute 2005: 21

as a redistributive mechanism would have the side effect of discouraging a transfer of labor from old industries to the newly emerging ones. Projects such as building local infrastructure of roads and dams might lower the unemployment rate in the short term, but they might cause environmental destruction in the long run.

Meanwhile, this period is also characterized by the beginning of redistribution through social protection for the elderly. As the size of the group of elderly persons who were retired from the labor force increased, the mechanism of "redistribution for production" could no longer work effectively, as many of them were out of the labor market. Given a quickly ageing society (the ratio of people over 65 rose from 7.1 percent in 1970 to 17.3 percent in 2000), some kind of social protection system became inevitable. Therefore, a number of social policies were produced in the area of pensions, health care and long-term care.

Stage 4: Pro-Market Reforms and the Outcomes (2001 and Afterward)

With regard to Japanese redistribution policy, the last stage of evolution coincided with the so-called Koizumi Reforms of 2001. This reform was characterized by a strong pro-market or neo-liberal policy initiative. Through the reforms, the idea of "redistribution for production" and other government interventions in the market, which had characterized redistribution policy in postwar Japan, was abandoned or minimized. These reforms had a positive effect in dissolving vested interests and reducing the inefficiency of government interventions, but it had a negative effect of increasing income inequality. Taking the Gini coefficient in household income (after the redistribution by tax and social protection schemes) as an example, this figure increased from 0.3606 in 1996 to 0.3873 in 2005 (Ministry of Health, Labour and Welfare 2005: 26), which was among the highest in developed countries.

After the Democratic Party of Japan won the general election in August 2009, the process of Japanese social policy development was re-dynamized. This event was regarded as a historic victory and a turning point of Japanese political history, which ended the one-party rule (by the Liberal Democratic Party) that had lasted for more than fifty years. Many promises made in the election by the members of the Democratic Party have had to be abandoned. In the social policy area, new decisions on increased and extended family allowances for children, reforms of the health care system for the elderly, reorganization of the pension system and so on are likely to be taken, although how strong the actual policy initiatives of the new government will be still is an unsolved question. A set of factors that will inevitably influence the process of policy making in Japan includes an ageing society (the ratio of people over 65 years was 22.1 percent of the total population in 2008) and changes to the economy and society.

From a Development-Oriented Approach toward a Social Quality Approach: The Policy Implications

Based on a review made on the changes in Japanese public policies from a redistribution perspective, we can make the following evaluations. First, in the postwar era, the most effective and perhaps most successful sets of policies in terms of redistribution were very strong policy initiatives for an "equality of opportunities," which later provided a basis for economic development. Second, "redistribution for production" worked relatively successfully in the early stages of Japanese economic growth, but it became a burden after 1970 and curbed the development of social protection as such. The recent pro-market reforms, intended to eliminate the negative aspects of government interventions, have led to increasing income inequality.

These policy developments may be described as "a failure in a shift from industrial policy to welfare policy." In the period of high economic growth, the government interventions into the production sphere were successful both in terms of efficiency and redistribution, but these later became a burden since the pro-market reforms combined with the underdevelopment of social policies, worsening the situations of income equality. This discourse of development may be observed also from many more later industrialized countries.

In addition, in the late 1960s and early 1970s, the environment problems were recognized as policy issues, and some policy responses were initiated by various enhanced laws and regulations and the creation of an Environment Agency in 1971. Environmental protections were enacted by government ministries in charge of each industrial sector (the Ministry of International Trade and Industry, the Ministry of Transport, the Ministry of Public Works, etc.). Even so, in comparison with the goal of economic growth, the issue of environmental protection was treated as a policy area of secondary importance. In the context of growing public concerns about environmental issues, the new development initiatives will be taken by the central and local governments. However, much remains to be done. Thus, in the discussion of welfare, environment and the economy, we need to promote the social quality approach (see Table 9.3).

In Table 9.3, four policy areas—industrial policy, welfare or social policy, land policy and environmental policy—are placed in perspective. In Japan, public policies in the early stage of industrialization are likely to be "development (or production)-oriented," in which social policy and/or environmental policy are either embedded in economic policies (such as industrial policy and land policy) or marginalized. As the economy grew, there was a need for transition in policy orientations from the "development-oriented" to "social quality-oriented": this transition was not made easily and often failed. Accordingly, attention should be paid to studies showing the dynamic relationship between the factors of welfare, environment, economy and policy making, which are significant in the realization of sustainable welfare societies. Policy models for assisting such transitions should be based on comparative research.

Table 9.3. Orientations of Social Analyses

The process of economic development ⟶

	Development-oriented	Social quality-oriented
Dimensions Regarding Human/Labor	Industrial policy	Welfare (or social) policy
Dimensions Regarding Place/Space	Land Policy (agricultural policy, urban Policy)	Environmental policy

Agenda for Promoting Sustainable Welfare Societies

In Asia, many countries have been going through the process of rapid economic development and industrialization. Although there are huge variations among these countries in the degree of industrialization, urbanization and population structure, as well as in cultural and ecological aspects, we may still assume that there is some sort of common agenda for the ambitions of Asia and Europe to realize sustainable welfare societies.

In regard to the environmental sustainability, the situation in Asia, at first glance, seems very serious as some gigantic countries, including China and India, are now accelerating resource consumptions as the result of their economic development. However, if we look at the trend of population from a longer perspective, the situation is less pessimistic because the population in East Asia will reach its peak in the 2030s (about 2.1 billion people according to the UN population forecast). The aged population and increased consumption of food, energy and other natural resources per capita will increase the necessity for policy makers to produce the policies for realizing sustainable welfare societies in Asia, from local to national and regional levels, making it the most urgent agenda.

With regard to welfare and income distribution, the relationship between economic development (GNI per capita) and income inequality (Gini coefficient) in Asian countries can be summarized by Figure 9.6. These data may illustrate a pattern of Kuznets's hypothesis of the inverted U-shaped curve (although the precise context should be further explored).

As for income inequality, various coping measures should be taken in these countries, not only for social policies but also for industrial policies. As discussed in

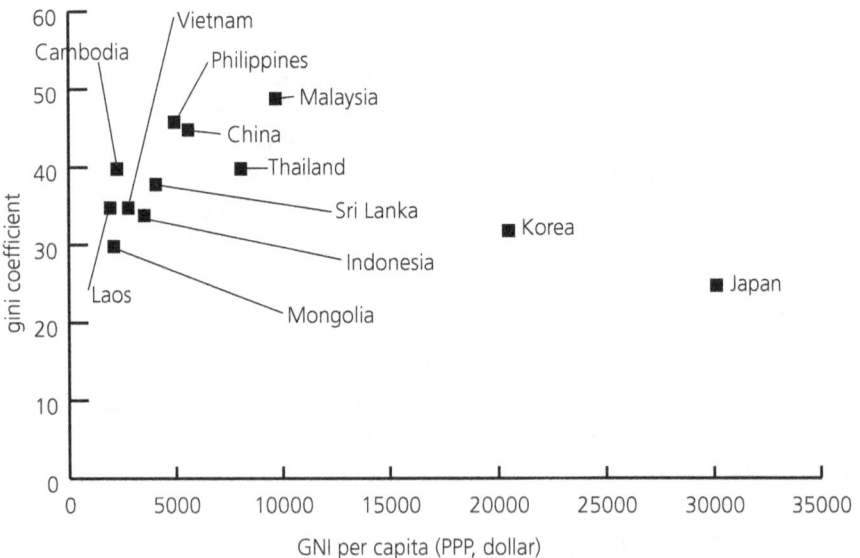

Figure 9.6. Economic Development and Income Inequality in Asian Countries
Source: World Bank 2006: 292

The process of economic development ⟶

Pre-industrial society | Industrialization | Post-industrial society

Government

'Traditional Community'

'New Community' ex. NPO, civil society

Market

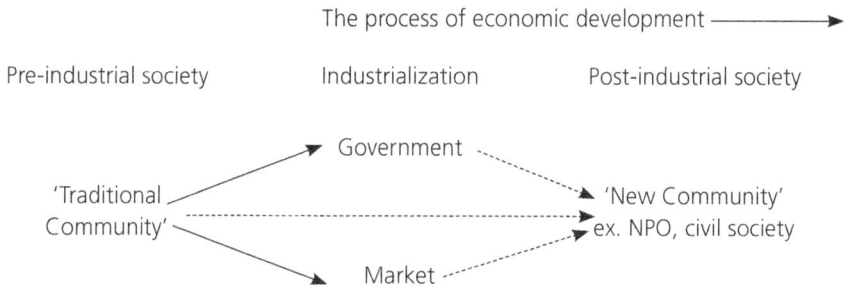

Figure 9.7. The Relationship of Community, Government and Market

the previous section, this requires integration of industrial policies and social policies and an appropriate transformation of policy orientations from developmental to social quality. It is crucial to theorize such policy models through comparative research in Asian and European countries. We should also note that in Asia, the major agents in delivering welfare are not only the states or governments but also the community organizations and civil society agents.

Unlike European countries, where the state is a "welfare state," Asian states, at least up to the present day, play a relatively small role in providing welfare, but the local community acts as a basic welfare provider. Thus, we need to be very cautious about conclusions drawn from any "(East) Asian model" of welfare or from a "Confucian model," but there is a possibility that these Asian countries have some commonalities in the process of industrialization and post-industrialization, as well as in their governments, markets and communities, and that these features may differ from the European ones. Also, they may have a common interest in reaching the goal of "sustainable welfare societies," but the paths of development in Asia and Europe will differ.

Accordingly, we may view welfare development in Asia at the supranational level and implement various kinds of policies to progress the development process in this region. These policy measures can include first, international cooperation in the area of social protection in Asia; second, establishing an "Asian Welfare Network"; and third, a commitment to study and operate "welfare states" at the supranational level. Thus, some projects can be set up: for instance, the Japan International Cooperation Agency's project started in 2006,[5] which aimed to increase the effective operation of old-age pensions in the rural areas of China. Other forms of international cooperation in social protection should also be enacted. Third, communication and networking should be facilitated for researchers, local civic groups and helpers in the areas of welfare or social policies, including comparative research. Last, but not least, community policies should be created for East Asia, as well as other forms of cooperation, to be enacted among member states, including a redistributive mechanism at the supranational level in Asia.

Yoshinori Hiroi, after graduating from the University of Tokyo, was a government official at the Ministry of Health and Welfare between 1986 and 1996. He became Associate Professor at Chiba University in 1996 and currently teaches social and public policy. In 2001 and 2002 he was a visiting scholar in the Department of Political Science at the Massachusetts Institute of Technology. His many Japanese publications include *Social Security of Japan* (1999), *Sustainable Welfare Society* (2006) and *Rethinking on Community* (2009). He received the Japan Economist Award in 1999 and the Osaragi Award in Social Sciences in 2009.

Notes

1. In a European context there are discussions of "green social policy" (e.g., Fitzpatrick and Cahill 2002), and the concept of sustainable welfare society expressed here has many common policy concerns, although the latter may pay more attention to the process of economic development.
2. For instance, the welfare state discussions are mainly concerned with the effect of distributional justice and the economic outputs of human activities, while the focus of environmental discourses is used to locate the issue of sustainability in human economic activities with the finite natural resources and the maintenance of a functioning ecosystem. In welfare discussion, the term "sustainability" can refer to the sustainability of human society including intergenerational relationships and the financial sustainability of state social protection systems.
3. There is a similar discussion in the area of ecological economics (see Daly 1996; Daly and Farley 2004).
4. For instance, see Esping-Andersen (1999).
5. See www.jica.go.jp.

References

Beck, W., L. van der Maesen, F. Thomése and A. Walker, eds. 2001. *Social Quality: A Vision for Europe*. The Hague: Kluwer International.
Daiwa Institute of Research. 2005. Economic Planning Agency of the Japanese Government, Prime Minister's Cabinet Office. *Nihon Keizai Shinbun*, 1 March 1, p. 21.
Daly, H.E. 1996. *Beyond Growth*. Boston: Beacon Press.
Daly, H.E. and J. Farley. 2004. *Ecological Economics*. Washington, DC: Island Press.
Esping-Andersen, G. 1999. *Social Foundations of Post-Industrial Economies*. Oxford: Oxford University Press.
Fitzpatrick, T. and M. Cahill. 2002. *Environment and Welfare: Towards a Green Social Policy*. Bakingstoke: Palgrave Macmillan.
Gasper, D., L. van der Maesen, T.D. Truong and A. Walker. 2008. *Human Security and Social Quality: Contrasts and Complementarities*. Working Paper no. 462. The Hague: Institute of Social Studies.
Goodman, R., G. White and H.J Kwon. 1998. *The East Asian Welfare Model: Welfare Orientalism and the State*. London: Routledge.
Gough, I. and J.A. McGregor, eds. 2007. *Wellbeing in Developing Countries: From Theory to Research*. Cambridge: Cambridge University Press.
Institute for International Cooperation. 2004. *Development of Japan's Social Security System*. Tokyo: Japan International Cooperation Agency.
Kwon, J., ed. 2005. *Transforming the Developmental Welfare State in Asia*. New York: United Nations Research Institute for Social Development.

McGillivray, M. and M. Clarke, eds. 2006. *Understanding Human Well-Being*. Tokyo: United Nations University Press.

Ministry of Finance, Japan. 2006. *One Hundred Years of Japan by Figures*. Yano-Tsundeta Kinen-kai, p. 432.

Ministry of Health, Labour and Welfare. 2005. *Survey on the Redistribution of Income*. Tokyo: MHLW.

OECD. 2005. *Extending Opportunities: How Active Social Policy Can Benefit Us All*. Paris: OECD.

Walker, A. 2007. "Society Quality and Sustainable Welfare Regimes." pp. 1–4 in *The Second Asian Conference on Social Quality and Sustainable Welfare Societies*. Taipei: National Taiwan University.

Walker, A. and C.K. Wong, eds. 2005. *East Asian Welfare Regimes in Transition: From Confucianism to Globalisation*. Bristol: Policy Press.

World Bank. 2005. *World Development Report 2006: Equity and Development*. Oxford: Oxford University Press.

CHAPTER 10
Risks of Society Stability and Precarity of Employment
A Look at Russia

Vyacheslav Bobkov, Olesya Veredyuk and Ulvi Aliyev

—◄○► ———— ◄○► ———— ◄○►—

Introduction: Stability and Instability of Development

When analyzing the stability of a system, we shall consider its ability to maintain control when the quality characteristics change. The loss of stability paves the way for new fluctuations, defining a hierarchy of system instability. In the theory of non-equilibrium systems, chaos is a term to characterize a high degree of instability (Haken 1985). Thus, the stability of societies can be characterized by their ability to develop without social revolutions, which lead to the loss of control and forcibly eliminate prevailing antagonistic contradictions between government and social classes and social groups opposing them.

Sustainable social development requires prevailing common interests resulting from prevailing overall goals of development of the social classes and social groups. The main criterion of the stability of societies is their ability to serve for the development and implementation of abilities of progressive social groups, which represent a bulk of the population of a country. The more selfish, private interests prevail in a society, the higher the degree of instability of such society. The society is shaken and, in the end, broken by the antagonistic contradictions. A criterial basis for estimating social sustainability can be elaborated on the theory of social quality.

The concept of social quality, developed by Western European researchers, is based on the measurement of the quality of the social content of everyday life. It defines the contours of the space in which people have the opportunity to participate in the economic, social and other spheres of society, which enhance their well-being and greater disclosure of personal potential (Beck et al. 2001). Such an approach usually focuses on individuals of social groups as actors operating in the emerging social conditions.

Here "the social" is understood as the result of the dialectical relationship between the formation of the individual in a society and self-realization of individuals, and between the global and biographical processes (Abbott and Wallace 2010). Social quality is defined as the degree to which people are able to participate in their communities' life on the conditions that promote the growth and well-being of their individual abilities (Walker 2005). Achieving a decent social quality requires a fulfillment of the following conditions:

- Access to social and economic protection;
- The opportunity to realize the phenomenon of social inclusion;
- The ability of people to live in a community characterized by social cohesion;
- The possibilities for activity for everyone and for achievement of personal fulfillment through collective participation.

In these conceptual contexts, Russian researchers have been actively involved in social quality research and have used this concept to analyze the Russian circumstance (Shestakova 2010). Russian social history of the third quarter of the twentieth and early twenty-first centuries, and especially in the past twenty years, is an example of a violent destruction of the socialist public system in its state-monopoly form and an attempt to build Russian state-monopoly capitalism (Bobkov 2012). Russian (and USSR) state-monopoly socialism of the twentieth century was an unstable society with a lower social quality in comparison with a people-humanistic socialism, which has not been formed yet in any country.

Even more, the instability of social development is now manifested in the society with state-monopoly capitalism, which is based on a lower social quality of a capitalist society as compared to the socialist society. This basic instability is magnified by its state-monopoly form. Material self-interest, the monetary absolutization of human being, and a socio-atomic model of society, as well as the achievement of personal freedom at the expense of justice and solidarity, environmental destruction, asymmetric distribution of economic power in favor of large business and the bureaucracy, and globalization based on the world's subordination to capitalocracy domination—all these are the sources of instability of state-monopoly capitalism, especially in its oligarchic and plutocratic forms.

All this can be clearly seen during twenty years of capitalist reforms in Russia and has been followed by significant deterioration of the social and economic status of a mass of the society. In this study, state-monopoly capitalism, state-monopoly socialism and people-humanistic socialism are discussed as the alternative bases of social quality development, which are presented in Table 10.1.

Table 10.1. Criterial Bases of Social Quality Development under Different Types of Society

	State-monopoly capitalism	State-monopoly socialism	People-humanistic socialism
1.	The primacy of the material and financial progress. Consumer society. Material self-interest, due to the lack of spirituality.	Material constraints in consumption due to the nationalization of the economy and ideological monopoly.	The leading role of spiritual progress compared with the material. Self-limitation of humanity in material over consumption and in material pleasures.
2.	Monetary absolutization of a person. The cult of money and power on the basis of money. The primacy of personal enrichment. Manipulation of mind on the monetary base.	Recognition of the value of knowledge, work and creativity as the basis of life. Intellectual confrontation of commodity and non-commodity basis of socialism. Ensuring the right to work. Routine nature of prevailing forms of labor. Manipulation of mind on an ideological basis. Weak material incentives.	Absolutization and implementation of values, knowledge, work and creativity as the basis of life. Ensuring the right to creative work and the implementation of abilities and their decent material and moral incentives.
3.	Social-atomic model of society. Individualistic, selfish human nature. Egocentrism. Individualistic concept of quality of life. The growing inequities in the distribution of quality of life, social stratification due to global capitalization of the world and appropriation of its main resources by the countries of the "golden billion."	Social-collectivist model of society dominated by state control of forms of economic and social life on the basis of egalitarian distribution of limited goods. Formation of an unstable society of low and lower-middle welfare of people.	Social-collectivist model of society dominated by forms of direct democracy and self-government in the local economic and territory entities. Implementation of the social nature of an individual. Social responsibility and social cohesion. Solidarity as the main direction of public policies. Social state. Building sustainable societies of middle and high welfare and harmony. Public obstruction of unfair distribution of profits and excessive inequality.

4.	Anti-state treatment of individual freedom and self-realization. Personal freedom through justice and solidarity.	Freedom, understood as the perceived need of implementing state-monopolistic ideology. Force restrictions on dissent. The unification of the rules of public life by strict government rationing. Justice, understood as the right of the state to use the abilities of people followed by equal distribution of the results of their work.	Ensuring the free will of the individual through the direct democracy (referenda, popular vote, participation in local and regional levels). Person dignity, freedom to realize potential. Collective way of realization of individual freedom.
5.	Environmental destruction (*antiekologichnost'*) caused by the pursuit of maximum profits of corporations, particularly from the export of capital. Humanity's ecological disaster.	*Antiekologichnost'* of production due to old technologies, public policy, declaring the domination of people over nature and low consumer culture of the population.	Socio-natural harmonization and security of humankind. Preserving the diversity of the biosphere and its homeostatic mechanisms, of the earth.
6.	Reassessment of the role of market forces in the economy due to the domination of the monopolies and the underestimation of the role of the state and society. Asymmetric distribution of economic power in favor of big business and the bureaucracy.	Reassessment of the role of the monopoly state. The identification of the state and public ownership of the means of production in the economy. The desire to plan everything "to nail" from a single center.	The society of managed socio-natural evolution. The market is regulated by the local government and the people-humanistic state. The development of key industries is under public control. Development of cooperation, economic democratization, the development of all forms of ownership.
7.	Dominance of cosmopolitan ideals. Diminution of the role of the nation-state, national and religious affiliation. Globalization based on the subordination of world to the domination of *capitalocracy*. Military punishment of disobedient nations and countries.	Creating the national state closed to the outside world. Restrictions on freedom of conscience. The ambition for a world domination based on an ideological export of revolution and a competition in the arms race.	Priority to the values of the national state and patriotism. Freedom of religion, the comprehensive development of indigenous cultures. Global peace based on the cooperation of states, the unacceptability of war and violence in dealing with international problems.

Classification by V. Bobkov

Current Social Situation of Society

Capitalism, which has been formed in Russia after twenty years of transformation, can be characterized as oligarchic and plutocratic. The basis for this is the non-economic appropriation of state property, lucratively inclined exploitation of Russian natural resources, legislation and "own understandings," reflecting the interests of the oligarchy.

The growth of Russian capitalism had passed through two phases of its transformation: from 1992 until 2000 and from 2000 up to now. The first stage can be characterized by the destruction of the foundations of socialist economy: (a) the substitution of economic planning for natural market regulators of the circulation sphere (free pricing), (b) privatization of state property practically without compensation, (c) the deliberate weakening of the economic role of the state and (d) the destruction of the USSR. The first stage in the formation of Russian capitalism has led to a sharp economic downturn, the enrichment of a narrow layer of large private owners and the impoverishment of the majority of the population and sharp economic stratification.

The second stage is characterized by the creation of a market-capitalist economy based on a liberal-capitalist model with a weak state, acting in the interests of the oligarchy and plutocracy. The standard of living has increased in all segments of the population, but inequality has continued to rise. Thus, rapid and sustained increase of economic inequality is one of the most distinctive traits of Russian capitalism.

On the whole, more than twenty years of capitalist reforms have led to a decrease in living standards for more than 40 percent of the population in Russia. The contradictions between labor and capital and between the majority of the population and the financial oligarchy have been sharpened. The population has been significantly reduced; people's (especially children's) health has deteriorated. Thus, in the eighteen years between 1992 and 2010, the difference between the number of births and deaths in Russia equaled more than 13.1 million people. There was a significant increase in the mortality of men of working age. Due to the influx of migrants into Russia, the overall population has decreased by about 4.5 million people (Human Development Report 2011). From 1991 to 2008, the morbidity rate of children under the age of fourteen increased by 1.5 times, and of adolescent children (15–17 years) by 2 times. The growth of this indicator is partly explained by better diagnostics but is mostly explained, according to experts, by real deterioration of health (Kislicina 2011). Also, decomposition of education and science by state elites has become grounds for a false sense of life and manipulations of the mind for large segments of the population. The influence of capitalist reforms in general on all aspects of life for the majority of Russians is devastating.

In the evaluation of the current situation, the most important are the following social risks and challenges. First, there are threats to the moral mode of society. For our people, who have rich traditions, history, unique geography and psychological features, there is devaluation of certain basic moral values such as kindness, justice and honesty, conscientiousness, chastity, repentance, loyalty, philanthropy, self-sacrifice and self-restriction in favor of others; at the same time, there is the spread of negative phenomena in the spiritual life such as anger and aggression, lies, dishonesty and cynicism, self-interest, corruption, hypocrisy, selfishness and greed. Spiritual independence is oppressed by the dictatorship of vulgarity, fashion and group self-interest. Labor morality, compassion and solidarity are not the driving forces in our society.

One can observe a domination of the financial oligarchy and its serving plutocracy. Corruption and privilege among Russian officials and business are widespread, followed by the merging of commercial and power interests. For many legal authorities, power, in effect, has become a kind of business. On the other hand, power is concentrated among those with much money (as seen in the financial disclosure of members of the government, administration of the president and members of the Federal Assembly of the Russian Federation for 2012). "Oligarchs" are actively lobbying their interests through their representatives in government institutions. Many members of the ruling and business elites do not care about their people and country and instead are motivated by profit, personal gain in everything that "comes to hand" and indifference to the ordinary people.

In such an environment, selfish motives to use the national wealth for personal gain are widespread; the conditions for sustainable development and spiritual and material foundations of life for future generations are undermined. "Oligarchic" and near-power groups have excessive wealth and seek to direct the country's development in the direction of their private interests. High are the risks of further mergence of power, crime and big business. Overt and covert "owners" of life have severely divided society into two poles: the powerless majority and the all-powerful, self-interested minority. Government and business are often used not for the public good. All this causes rejection from the side of the overwhelming majority of the population and distrust of government and business.

Second, there are extraordinary losses of human potential in peacetime. There is a huge contradiction between the needs of spiritual, cultural and innovative development of the country and the loss of much of the physical and, in particular, intellectual and spiritual abilities of people. "Disease" of a family becomes a disease for the country. There is an extremely low birth rate and a high mortality rate, and life expectancy has dramatically decreased. In 1990 life expectancy was sixty-nine years; in 1993 it dropped to sixty-four, and only in 2011 did it reach the pre-reform level (ROSSTAT 2012). Some positive changes in the last few years, for example, the suspension of depopulation in 2011–2012, do not change the fundamental negative assessment of the demographic situation. The population has serious problems with health. All this brings high social risks and threats to people and to the Russian state.

There was a loss of the value of knowledge and labor in Russia. Intellectual work and knowledge are not in demand. Industry science is largely destroyed. Academic science has come under increasing pressure from those who want immediate results— "short" money. Scholars, teachers, doctors, engineers, artists and many other professional groups of intellectuals are not motivated, but rather they put in the humiliating position of low moral and financial remuneration for their work. One can observe that professionals are forced to play a secondary role in society. Belonging to the "elite" is formed by the short distance to power and property, and not by intelligence, potential and contribution to the development of the country. Wages and income of most qualified employees bear no resemblance to the economic and social significance of their work.

Third, there exists absolute income poverty and housing poverty, excessive and unfair economic and social inequality, and high regional and settlement (between city and countryside) differentiation in quality and standard of living for the masses. Millions of Russian citizens are forced to think about their daily survival. They have lost an effective motivation to work, based on less possibility of earning an honest living to provide a decent quality of life for themselves and their families. Misery and poverty and the consequent inability to change radically their lives result in disunity and discontent of the people. They have, in fact, been sidelined from the development of the country and will not be able to get themselves out of this marginal status. On the other hand, and generally accepted in Russia, there are often unfairly and unjustly inherited wealth and real power.

Fourth, there is a high degree of social stress, social exclusion in society and a mass of difficult life situations in families due to the lack of work and high unemployment in the medium and small cities and rural areas; "irrelevance" of many young people to their country; unprecedented levels of child homelessness; widespread drug abuse and alcoholism, prostitution and crime, terrorism and extremism; and cynicism and indifference. Under the conditions of human misery and loss of health and life, there is a growth of huge capital bigwigs "in law" and "in the shadows."

Fifth, there is a disruption of ecological balance between nature and society. It can be seen in the global environmental crisis, which has become characteristic of the first phase of a global ecological disaster as a result of the anti-ecological market-capitalist forms of economic consumption of natural resources (Subetto 2008). Global environmental problems are evidence of the spiritual crisis of modern civilization, its inner emptiness and lack of great spiritual purpose.

Sixth, there is weakness of civil society, including high social apathy among the population, fragmentation and disunity of people left alone with their numerous problems. People have a high degree of distrust, not only in business and government but also in each other (Russian Academy of Sciences 2012). The downside of this process is the absolute uncontrolled power of the bureaucracy and its limitation of civil liberties.

The Current Economic Situation of Society

The capitalist transformation was based on cutting labor costs by employers in traditional forms of employment. A sharp depreciation of wage labor in the early 1990s, throwing real wages of the majority of employees over the official poverty line (Bobkov 2012), has not subsequently undergone a fundamental revision. The state limited its role by establishing an extremely low (less than the subsistence minimum for working age population) official minimum wage, mandatory for all branches of economy and by the introducing such pay systems in the public sector, which barely allowed workers to make ends meet. Business—except mineral-resource and financial sectors, which employ a small portion of the total number of workers—was also guided by the low price of labor. As a result, many employees dropped below the minimum subsistence income level for the working-age population, and among others, workers with low and below-average wages are in the majority.

In order to estimate the distribution of employees on wages, the following social standards were suggested:

- *First social standard*—wage (income) corresponds with budget of subsistence minimum of working-age population (BSMw);
- *Second*—wage (income) corresponds with socially acceptable (replacement) consumer budget. It equals 3 BSMw;
- *Third*—wage (income) matches consumer budget of middle class. It equals 7 BSMw;
- *Fourth*—wage (income) meets consumer budget of high income. It equals 11 BSMw.

To build such a system of different levels of consumer budgets, a number of methodological approaches were used to model the satisfaction of socially acceptable minimal needs for the physical, intellectual, cultural and social development of the person and the family. A comparison of shares of employees after grouping them in terms of real wages, corresponding to different social standards of consumption, is given in Table 10.2.

It was in 1986, with the launching of the restructuring (*perestroyka*), that mechanisms worsening the financial situation of working people were introduced.

From the comparison of the distribution of hired workers by the level of real average monthly wages in 1986 and 2010, given in Table 10.2, we can see that the proportion of hired workers with incomes below the subsistence minimum level of working-age population (BSMw), that is, receiving lower wages, grew during twenty years from 3.1 percent to 12.5 percent, or about 3.9 times. Such level of wages for the lonely person, and especially for a worker supporting a family, usually determines the average per capita income below the absolute poverty line (below the average per capita subsistence minimum, BSMav).

The group of workers whose size of real wage was below the socially acceptable consumption budget of the working-age population (about 3 BSMw) has decreased by 1.3 times over these years. In the USSR, that was about 60 percent of the total number

Table 10.2. Grouping of Employees in Terms of Real Wages, Corresponding to Different Social Standards of Consumption (on Average for a Month, in Percentage of Total Number of Employees)

	1986	2010
Less than 1 BSMw	3.1	12.5
From 1 BSMw to 3 BSMw	59.1	46.4
From 3 BSMw to 7 BSMw	35.5	31.2
From 7 BSMw to 11 BSMw	2.1	6.7
More than 11 BSMw	0.2	3.2

Estimations are based on ROSSTAT (2011b: 31).

of workers, and now it is about half of their number. Those employees should be classified as workers with low wages, the purchasing power of which (in the case of a complete family with two workers and children) also determines the per capita income below BSMav and absolute poverty of corresponding households in practice. The group of workers with real wages below the average level (more than 3 BSMw but less than 7 BSMw) has decreased but only slightly—by 1.1 times, reaching 31.2 percent.

The share of middle-income workers, from 7 BSMw to 11 BSMw, has increased by about 3 times, from 2.1 percent to 6.7 percent. However, their share of total employees is currently very low: 1.9 times lower than that of workers with the lowest wages. Moreover, the share of high-wage workers has increased by 16 times, from 0.2 percent to 3.2 percent. The growth rate of this group of workers seems impressive, but the representativeness of this group of workers is very low, even lower than the average-paid group, and mainly covers those employed in mineral-resource and fuel and energy sectors, as well as in financial sectors.

Consumer pressure on wages has significantly increased in today's Russia. In the USSR, access to the most pressing social needs in education, health, institutions of childcare, housing and other public services was provided by public consumption funds, that is, free to the public. In today's Russia, these services are mostly paid by households primarily from salaries and other sources of cash income, and only a small share (much smaller than it was in time of the USSR) is paid by the state from compulsory social insurance and the state budget. As a consequence of these changes, there was a twofold increase in inequality of wage distribution among workers (ROSSTAT 2011b: 31): in 1990, the composition of the funds coefficient was 7.8 (ROSSTAT 1997: 111), and in 2010, it equaled 14.4 times (ROSSTAT 2011c: 128). The Gini coefficient (the concentration index of total wages) has grown significantly from 0.317 (ROSSTAT 1997: 111) to 0.413 (ROSSTAT 2011c: 128).

Because of the instability of employment, "gray" (informal) schemes of payments and the resulting large scale of shadow incomes, the state statistics agency (ROSSTAT) in its accounts should increase the estimated aggregate value of total and average wage in Russia by about two times. It will be shown that this greatly reduces the positive impact on the standard of living of households, reduces the share of employees with low and lower-middle levels of income, and increases the share of employees with average and high levels of income. The results are represented in Table 10.3. The estimations for 1990 and 2010 in Table 10.3 were made by experts of the All-Russian Centre of Living Standard using ROSSTAT (2011b: 31).

In 1990, there were hardly any representatives of the group in the most need in Soviet Russia. The share of households with low incomes was slightly more than 30 percent of the population. Twenty-five years ago, the majority of Russia's population, about 60 percent, belonged to the group with the average level of income, while the share of groups with the middle and high levels of income was 6.7 percent and 0.7 percent, respectively. After twenty years the structure of society based on consumption level dramatically changed: the segment of people in the most need grew by about 90 times and reached 17.4 percent. The share of households with low income increased by 1.7 times and amounted to 53.6 percent. By 2010, the two lowest groups by level of income accounted for almost three-quarters of the population. The middle income

Table 10.3. Grouping of the Population of Russia on Income Used for Consumption, Compared with Consumer Budgets of Different Levels of Material Income (Average per Month, Percentage of Total Population)

	Share of the population (in %)		Changes in 2010 (in percentage point, p.p.)
	1990	**2010**	**p.p.**
Those in most need (less than consumer baskets of subsistence minimum, CB)	0.2	17.4	17.2
Low-income group (from 1 CB to 3 CB)	31.7	53.6	21.9
Group with income less than average (from 3 CB to 7 CB)	60.8	24.6	−36.2
Group with middle income (from 7 CB to 11 CB)	6.7	3.4	−3.3
Group with high income (more than 11 CB)	0.7	1.0	0.3

Estimations are based on ROSSTAT (2011b: 31).

group was reduced by almost half to equal 3.4 percent of the population. The share of the high-income group in Russia remained low at approximately 1.0 percent.

In 1990 the equal distribution of income prevailed—more than 90 percent of the population had incomes below the average level of material well-being, from 1 consumer basket (CB) to 7 CB (consumer basket is a minimum set of food and non-food goods and services essential for a person's health and ability to live; Federal Law of the Russian Federation 1997). Over twenty years of capitalist transformation, more than two-thirds of the population found themselves among the most vulnerable, with low-income level at current consumption. Along with the changes in the proportion of groups with different levels of material wealth, there was a dramatic increase in social and economic inequality. This is demonstrated by the rise in a funds' coefficient (showing the ratio between the average incomes of the 10 percent group with the highest income and 10 percent group with the lowest income): for cash income, it increased from 4.5 (ROSSTAT 1996: 9) to 16.5 (ROSSTAT 2011c: 126) times; for the income used for consumption, it increased from 4.6 to 13.2 times (estimations made by the experts of the All-Russian Centre of Living Standard based on ROSSTAT [2011a: 16]). The Gini coefficient has risen by income from 0.260 (ROSSTAT 1996: 80) to 0.421 (ROSSTAT 2011c: 126), and by the income used for consumption from

0.227 to 0.398 (estimations made by the experts of the All-Russian Centre of Living Standard based on ROSSTAT [1996: 80; 2011c: 126]).

Again, the situation of the socio-economic inequality in terms of current consumption in different groups of the population can be estimated by a coefficient of the ratio of average income spent on consumption, in groups with consumption above 11 CB and below 1 CB (called the Bvn coefficient). The Bvn coefficient was 14.4 in 1990 and 20.8 in 2010 (estimations made by the experts of the All-Russian Centre of Living Standard based on ROSSTAT [2011a: 16]). In relation to 1990, the size of the coefficient rather symbolically characterized the socio-economic inequality. At that time there was not a separate group for people in the most need. Thus, in a capitalist economy of Russia, there is a huge gap between the consumption of the group of people that is most in need and the consumption of the high-income group.

All of the above-mentioned coefficients of socio-economic inequality indicate its excessive level in Russia: in some regions where private companies in the circulation sphere, especially in the financial sector, are widely represented (Moscow, St. Petersburg, etc.) and where there are private corporate monopoly productions of mineral and raw resources (Tyumen, Vologodskaya regions, etc.), the average magnitude of the socio-economic inequality has reached forty and more times. Thus, the general conclusion is that during twenty years of capitalist reforms in Russia, the proportion of the population with low current consumption and socio-economic differentiation have dramatically increased. The latter is much higher than the normal level, which is determined by the size of gross domestic product, is excessive, prevents economic and demographic growth and is a source of high social tensions in Russia. This final result of the twenty years after the fall of the USSR, being expanded to the annual dynamic of the series of the population with different levels of material wealth, would have revealed an even more dramatic picture, indicating that in the 1990s up to 40 to 50 percent of the population fell below the poverty line (see Bobkov 2012).

Employment as an Important Characteristic of the Stability of Society

A distinctive characteristic of modern Russian capitalism is the transition from full-time employment to its unstable form with dramatic features sometimes. Fluctuations between these forms of employment characterize the economy transition from a stable system with full-time employment to the perturbed system with employment instability.

Work (employment) is the material basis of human development. How is this component taken into account in the existing indicators of sustainability? Twenty-three out of the thirty-three best-known international indexes include the component associated with the use of the labor force and unemployment, as well as the income of the population (authors calculations). Eight of them consider these components simultaneously (namely, in the General Index of the United Nations Institute for Social Development [GID], American Demographics Index of Well-Being [ADIWB], Index of Social Health [ISH], Consumer Confidence Index [CCI], Index of Human

Suffering [HIS], Quality Grade of Life, Johnston's Quality of Life Index [JQOLI] and Gender Empowerment Measure [GEM] [Bobylev et al. 2011: 51–55]).

The approach of the Commission on Sustainable Development of the UN, based on the construction of a system of indicators (and not on the integral one), includes employment in the group of indicators of economic development in the form of such indicators as the level of employment (including vulnerable employment), labor productivity, costs per unit of labor and the proportion of female employment in non-agricultural sector (United Nations 2007). In the *Millennium Development Goals Report*, achievements of full and productive employment and decent work for all, including women and young people, are the targets of one of the eight main goals— eradicate extreme poverty and hunger. Relevant indicators include employment-to-population ratio, proportion of own-account and contributing family workers in total employment and proportion of employed people living on less than $1.25 a day (United Nations 2012). Sustainable development of the economy requires sustainable employment. In this sense, sustainability of employment is seen as a desirable vector of labor relations. In the Soviet Union, the economically active population was provided the right and the duty to work; employment in the national economy was guaranteed. In the Soviet Union, the phenomena of employment instability and unemployment were absent. It appeared only with the beginning of capitalist transformation (Bobkov et al. 2011b: 13–14). In the literature, among the most fully analyzed (and widely spread in Russia) are such forms of formal employment instability as the following: (1) employment on fixed-term contract; (2) part-time employment; (3) employment based on leasing (outstaffing) contracts between employee and employment agency; and (4) employment based on contracts with the condition to work outside of the place of employer.

Informal unstable employment has a huge scale in Russia. Informal employment usually refers to employment in personal farming for own consumption and/or for the sale of products and services in order to obtain cash income; non-registered individual paid services and small retail trade; and non-registered production like cooperatives, among others. According to various sources, informal forms of employment before reforms varied in the Russian economy from 20 to 25 percent of total employment (Kapelyushnikov 2004). The expansion of employment in the informal sector has a negative impact on economic perspectives of the development of the country by reducing tax revenues in the state budget. At the same time, an informally employed worker cannot even count on a relatively small pension, insurance and other social guarantees and benefits.

In the Russian model of the capitalist transformation, the following forms of employment instability (usually described as ugly forms) are represented: (1) hiring of individual entrepreneurs who are unable to carry out their own business; (2) hiring without legal registration of relations or with registration but violating the labor rights of workers—such workers can be called "invisible workers"; and (3) the recruitment of employees by intermediaries, created for the benefit of financial funds manager. In total, there are more than 20 million workers both in formal and informal forms of employment instability in Russia now. The huge scale of employment instability, when the employment relationship between employers and employees is built on a fixed-term contract, does not reflect its formal content or is not contracted at all, and workers have their labor and social rights violated.

A significant part of unstable employment is labor migration. This is due to the fact that from the very beginning, an immigrant worker must stop labor relations in the region of residence (due to low wages, poor working conditions, the inability to find a job, etc.) and search for an opportunity to establish new labor relations at a new location in the country or abroad. Unemployment can be considered an extreme form of employment instability, when labor relations are temporarily terminated, and the sources of income for material things are extremely limited. With regard to unemployment in Russia, the level was 5.7 percent of the economically active population in 2012 (Ministry of Economic Development of the Russian Federation 2013). According to the Forecast of Long-Term Socio-economic Development of the Russian Federation for the period up to 2030, Russia will experience a steady decline in population of working age and, as a consequence, reduction in the number of economically active population (from 72.6 million in 2012 to 66.1 to 68.4 million in 2030). This will also decrease the number of employees from 68.3 million in 2012 to 63 to 65.6 million in 2030. The unemployment rate in this case will change from 5.9 percent of the economically active population in 2012 to 4.1 to 4.7 percent in 2030 (Ministry of Economic Development of the Russian Federation 2012).

In a situation of employment instability, people hardly have good life perspectives; in other words, the possibility of long-term planning is limited. Obviously, such a situation has a negative impact not only on the life quality of an individual but also on the stability of society as a whole. Such effects can be seen in a reduction in consumer demand for products that require prolonged financial payments, an insufficient investment in human capital (education, health), a reduced ability to accumulate work experience, a limitation of credit (including mortgage) availability and so forth.

While the phenomenon of unemployment has been actively studied and relevant statistics are widely presented, the phenomenon of employment instability has not yet found a proper research interest (especially by economists) and comprehensive reflection in socio-economic statistics. So, in the next part of the chapter, we will concentrate on characteristics of instability (precarity) of employment as a feature of modern labor relations and will try to give some evaluations of this phenomenon in the labor market in Russia.

Instability (Precarity) of Employment as a Labor Market Problem

The term "precarity" is used to characterize instability. It is interesting to note that, according to one version, this term was widely used in political debates in France at the end of the 1970s. To refer to a social phenomenon of poverty, they used the term *précarité*, which was later used to describe employment (Hepp 2012: 342). In the context of labor relations, the term can refer to the highest degree of their forced insecurity and instability. However, while the study of the phenomenon of employment instability is a common occurrence in Europe, especially by sociologists from Germany, France and Italy, we have not paid enough attention to this problem in Russia.

Existing approaches to the definition of the term "precarity" have a common understanding, according to which precarity is treated as the disappearance (up to a total loss) of a sense of confidence with respect to the individual social, family and other abilities and rights. In general, precarity is described as a sense of existential insecurity deriving from an employment situation. The latter is characterized by contractual temporariness, which is associated with an irregular participation in the labor market and with a lack of a stable income, suitable to plan one's life over a medium to long period (Hepp 2012: 315). In this respect, unemployment can be considered the highest degree of precarity. We should also note that informal employment is also part of the phenomenon of instability of employment. Thus, "general precarity" has employment as its base. The following factors of precarity employment can be considered: (a) the terms of labor contract (or the absence of legal registration); (b) lower and unstable payments; and (c) bad working conditions.

The precarity of employment can be defined as a condition in which there is an increase in the level of uncertainty and risk in the labor market, and employment no longer serves as a source of medium- and long-term planning and improvement in the quality of life for economically active population. When precarity of employment takes place, risks associated with the employment relations are forcedly redistributed from an employer to an employee. Among such risks are reduction in size and frequency of wage income, worsening of working conditions, lowering of the level of social protection, uncertainty of duration of employment relations and so on.

Risk factor		Factor characteristics
Type of labor contract	⇒	Legally registered fixed-term labor contract or the absence of legally registered labor contract
Form of employment	⇒	*Nonstandard employment*, including the legal and organizational methods and conditions of employment, which are different from traditional employment relations with the one and the same employer. The traditional employment relations assume permanent labor contract, full-time employment, protection against layoffs
Payment system	⇒	Low-level and irregular wage payments
Work conditions	⇒	Poor working conditions

Figure 10.1. Risk Factors of the Precarity of Employment
Compiled taking account of Hepp (2012: 96, 342)

Analysis of the precarity of employment can be given from different perspectives, including economic, social, environmental, political and psychological. The variety of approaches is linked to the fact that the precarity of employment, on the one hand, is closely connected with the ongoing activities in all spheres of social life, and on the other hand, the precarity of employment influences all of these activities. This chapter develops the economic approach, based on the objective data, to assess the scope, structure, forms, dynamics, causes and consequences of the precarity of employment in Russia. One of the first international publications of Russian authors on the precarity of employment was the article by Bobkov et al. (2011a).

The economic approach developed in this chapter to identify the precarity of employment in Russia is based on the indicators that objectively characterize the increased level of risk associated with labor relations. In particular, we use such indicators as *volatility* (spread relatively average) of income related to the job (wage) and *discreteness* (irregularity) of income associated with the work. Despite the concept of the precarity of employment being in the stage of formation, the key factors that increase the risk of being in this state can be classified (see Figure 10.1).

Assessing the Scale of Precarity of Formal Employment in Organizations

As the main statistical database to analyze and assess the extent of the precarity of employment in Russia, the Russia Longitudinal Monitoring Survey—Higher School of Economics (RLMS) (hereinafter, Monitoring) is used; it is both an alternative and a supplement to the state statistics agency of ROSSTAT database. The Monitoring is an annual series of nationally representative surveys based on a probabilistic stratified multistage area sampling. The sampling model is a "repeated sample" with "split-panel." The ability to analyze households and individuals is based on a sample of dwellings. The Monitoring meets the standards adopted in the world. It is the only nongovernmental monitoring of socio-economic status and health of the population in Russia and has been carried out since 1992. It was designed to monitor the effects of Russian reforms on the health and economic welfare of households and individuals. These effects are measured by a variety of means: precise measurement of income and consumption structures, material health, structure of employment and migration behavior, among others. Data have been collected nineteen times since 1992 (Russia Longitudinal Monitoring Survey).

Our estimations are based directly on a representative sample of the nineteenth wave of the Monitoring, which was held from October 2010 to March 2011 and contains 16,867 observations. Below are the results assessing the extent of the precarity of employment in Russia. It should be noted that the estimation is given only for formal employment and did not consider informal employment and unemployment. For example, 8 percent of employees among those who, at the time of the Monitoring, were working in an organization (with two or more employees) experienced for the last twelve months wage cuts and forced unpaid holidays. One out of five of these employees experienced these violations simultaneously. It is these workers, according to the approach developed in the article (based on the indicators of volatility and discreteness of income), who are in the precarity of employment. The comparison of the data of the nineteenth and eighteenth waves of the Monitoring revealed that 12.6 percent of workers stayed in the precarity of employment during these years, forming a so-called stable core of the precarity of employment.

We also tried to paint a portrait of those workers in a state of the precarity of employment to be able to assess the risk factors specific to this condition. First, we analyzed workers by the type of labor contract (legally signed or not signed legally). It turned out that 97 percent of workers in the precarity of employment have a legally signed labor contract. From 6 percent of workers who did not have a legally signed labor contract, 69 percent were forced into one by their employers.

Second, it was possible to identify the types of economic activities for which the precarity of employment is a more usual phenomenon. To do this, the proportion of

Table 10.4. Distribution of Workers in Precarity of Employment and the Deviation in Their Average Wage by Kinds of Economic Activity

Kind of economic activity	Proportion of workers in precarity of employment (%)	Share of average wage of precariously employed in average wage by kinds of economic activity (%)
Manufacturing	27	74
Transport and communications	12	84
Wholesale and retail trade	12	81
Construction	12	86
Education	11	92
Agriculture, hunting and forestry	7	100
Health and social service	7	97
Governance and defense; social insurance	5	72
Other community, social and personal services	5	73
Mining	1	74
Financial activities	1	76
Other activities	0.03	74
TOTAL	100	–

Estimations are based on ROSSTAT (2011d: 186).

precariously employed by sectors of economy, calculated on the basis of the Monitoring data has been extended to the total number of legally employed by kinds of economic activity, according to the Federal State Statistics Service. The results are presented in Table 10.4. As can be seen, about 75 percent of workers in precarity of employment are concentrated in the first five kinds of economic activity, which can be classified as clusters of economic activities with higher risks of precarity of employment.

Third, the average wage of workers under the precarity of employment was, as expected, lower than the average wage by kinds of the economic activity in the parent population—on average 20 percent (the maximum deviation was about 30 percent). Fourth, with regard to the list and coverage of workers under the precarity of employment by social benefits (such as paid sick leave, medical care and education at the expense of the employer), 87 percent had paid sick leave, 23 percent had medical care and 19 percent had training. It can be noted that for the total sample of formally employed people, the percentage of those with the social benefits mentioned above are 87, 20 and 21 percent, respectively.

These data show insignificant differences in the social security system for precarity and non-precarity employees in organizations. It follows that, if a legal employment contract is in force (if the employee is not transferred from formal employment to a civil-legal contract), the Russian social security system almost universally protects employees. Nevertheless, this is different for employees in informal precarity of employment, but this aspect of precarity is not a subject of this chapter. However, it should be noted that this huge part of the workforce is completely dropped out of the Russian social security system, which enhances greatly their economic and social deprivation and transfers them into marginalized groups of society.

Precarity Employment Clusters in the Formal Economy and the Role of Trade Unions in the Protection of Employees' Interests

To the greatest extent precarity of employment in forms of income volatility (wage cutting) and irregularity is typical for manufacturing. Russian reforms have led to contraction of this sector compared both to its scale and level of development in the Soviet planned economy and to mining and financial activities sectors in the market economy. Some experts classify this phenomenon as "deindustrialization" and argue a question of "reindustrialization" (new industrialization) of the economy (Gubanov 2012). Modernization of the economy as described in the Forecast of Long-Term Socio-economic Development of the Russian Federation for the period up to 2030 (Ministry of Economic Development of the Russian Federation 2012), adopted by the Russian government, implies accelerated rates of job creation mainly in manufacturing. Of a total of 25 million jobs, 20 percent of modern jobs are expected to be created here (see Table 10.5). This will inevitably lead to the reduction of precarity risks in this cluster of the economy. However, it remains to be seen how successfully the problem will be practically solved.

Table 5 illustrates that measures to improve employment productivity are also planned to be introduced in construction and transport and communications, as well

Table 10.5. The Demand of the Russian Economy on the New Workplaces

Kind of economic activity	Degree of capital funds depreciation (%)	Demand on the new workplaces (million people)
Total in economy	45.3	25
including		
Manufacturing	45.6	4.3
Transport and communications	55.1	2.5
Wholesale and retail trade	33.8	3.4
Construction	45.5	2.1
Education	51.0	2.6
Agriculture	42.2	2.4
Health	50.6	2.0
Other community, social and personal services	40.7	0.9
Mining	50.9	0.4
Other activities	–	4.4

According to Ministry of Economic Development of the Russian Federation (2012)

as in trade, which are all areas characterized by high risks of precarity. However, increasing the employment productivity in these kinds of economic activity is not of the same priority (from the perspective of the share of newly created jobs) as in manufacturing. It follows that negative aspects of precarity of employment are not fully taken into consideration by the legal authorities while making decisions on priorities of jobs development.

Due to objective processes of increasing flexibility on labor markets in combination with the absence of adequate policies of jobs' development and protection of employees from precarity, there is an increasing pressure to transfer certain types of risk, cost and responsibility from companies and society to employees. As a result, one should expect an increase in precarity of employment in the formal economy of Russia. Trade unions are supposed to play an important role in preventing and minimizing the effects of precarity of employment in the formal economy. Russian trade unions are mainly represented by the Federation of Independent Trade Unions. They are called old (official) trade unions, as they were converted from the planned economy of the USSR into the market economy. Newly organized in the 1990s, alternative trade unions do not have as much power as a system in the Russian labor movement.

According to the Russian Labour Code, trade unions' role is associated with social partnership in the labor sphere, which aims to ensure coordination of the interests of employees and employers on the regulation of labor relations. Social partnership is executed in forms of collective bargaining on design and conclusion of collective agreements and contracts, consultation on the regulation of labor relations, employees' participation in the management of the organization and resolution of labor disputes.

So that all of these functions are realized, special social partnership bodies have been created—the commissions for the regulation of social-labor relations. These commissions do work at the federal, regional and sector levels, and in large organizations, involving experts, representing parties' interests. Under Russian law, all questions affecting the interests of employees are preliminarily reviewed by the commissions with the participation of trade unions before decisions are made by the federal, regional and municipal governments.

However, Russian trade unions, according to several prominent labor movement experts, always lag behind in recognition of the real situation, demonstrate a low level of claims and are careful with their requirements. They do not dare to organize any powerful resistance against cuts for workers' and trade unions' rights (Rakitskaya 2007). Organized by the trade unions, and often without their participation, resistance to laws that worsen the situation of employees and create conditions for definite employers' dictate is patchy (local), episodic and non-mass by character. And it is mainly resistance, that is, protest-defensive action, and not offensive action to articulate requirements to improve the situation of employees. Leaders of official trade unions are actually in the political integration of the legal party (parties) in power (Rakitskaya 2007).

The conciliatory position of trade unions in a number of key issues causes a broad perception that unions in their current form are completely exhausted; they are not able to resist the modern capital massive attack on the rights, freedoms and interests of the mass of society. However, we do not advocate such a position. Trade unions are the first among other organizations of civil society to raise questions of protection of the labor rights of workers. More than the other institutions of society, they demand the results of scientific knowledge. As for the problem of precarity, representatives of Russian trade unions were among the first to attract public attention to it (Starostin 2008).

We believe, despite that precarity destroys the former gains of trade unions, their role as an organization that defends the rights of employees should be considered now as insufficient and needs to be radically improved. It, however, depends on the maturity of the labor movement in Russia. The latter has not yet demonstrated its readiness to actively defend socio-economic rights. Another group against precarity is represented by social movements of direct action. According to some experts (Insarov), such social movements are precisely the form of self-organization and struggle that fits the conditions of the present stage of capitalism—the conditions of capitalist globalization. However, in Russia, social movements and employees' organizations are disconnected, which reduces the overall potential of opposition to the oligarchy and plutocracy attack on workers' rights.

Conclusion

For more than twenty years, state-monopoly capitalism of low social quality in Russia has demonstrated the instability of social development. The first stage in the formation of Russian capitalism (1992–2000) led to a sharp economic downturn and hyperprecarity due to the enrichment of a narrow layer of private property owners and the impoverishment of the population in general. In the second stage (2000–2012), as a result of economic growth, the standard of living has increased for all groups of the population. However, economic inequality did not decrease and instead continued to grow.

According to sociological research (Institute of Sociological Research of the Russian Academy of Science 2012), about 40 percent of the population believe that Russia is a dead end or requires replacement of power, about 20 percent dream of a more just society but do not believe that Russia is a dead end or requires replacement of power and about 40 percent believe that all is going well and focus on solving personal problems. In the future, the intermediate 20 percent, depending on the country's further development and realization of their hopes for a more just society, will likely join either the first or the second group and provide them with an advantage in evaluating the results of future social transformations in Russia.

Using the approach developed in the article analyzing the precarity of employment using data from the Russia Longitudinal Monitoring Survey—Higher School of Economics, it was found that precarity of employment in Russia is experienced by about 8 percent of the (officially employed) workforce. Recall that volatility and discreteness of income associated with the work were suggested as the objective economic signs of the precarity of employment.

In addition to the observed volatility and discreteness in income related to work, workers experiencing precarity of employment earned lower wages on average. Precariously employed workers are concentrated mainly in the following kinds of economic activity in Russia: manufacturing, transport and communication, wholesale and retail trade, construction and education. The government does not fully consider such negative effects on the Russian labor market when making decisions regarding the creation of new productive jobs, while trade unions stay on a conciliatory position on many key issues of protection of employees in the labor market and in employment.

Precarity of employment is a characteristic feature of labor relations under capitalism. Currently, one can generally speak about the trend to transfer certain types of risk, costs and responsibility from companies and the society to workers. The presence of such a trend has been already noted (Bollé 2001: 473). As a result, we should expect an expansion of precarity of employment, including in the Russian labor market.

Social and economic impacts of precarity of employment vary. Among the main negative consequences are unstable incomes, job insecurity and the feeling of uncertainty. In many countries, including Russia, workers experiencing precarity of employment lack social benefits and, as a rule, earn lower wages. So, precarity of employment can result in greater income inequality in the population.

Recently, the Russian government introduced to the public a forecast of socio-economic development for the period up to 2030, that is, for another twenty years. The success of targeted strategies and their implementation will basically determine the competitiveness of the economy in the global world and positive changes in the quality of life in Russia.

Vyacheslav N. Bobkov is a doctor of economics, Director General of the All-Russian Centre of Living Standard, Head of the Labour Economics and Staff Management Department of Plekhanov Russian University of Economics and Professor at the

Moscow State University. His main scientific and research areas are level and quality of life, labor economics and social policy. His is the author of several monographs published in Russian and English languages and has also published more than three hundred articles in Russian and international journals. As a scientific expert, Dr. Bobkov has participated in more than one hundred research projects including international projects carried out under the ILO and UNDP.

Olesya V. Veredyuk is a PhD candidate in economics and an associate professor at the Saint Petersburg State University (Russia). Her main scientific and research interests are labor economics, employment and social and labor relations. Some research results are published in journals indexed in Scopus. Prof. Veredyuk has scientific experience at universities in Germany and lecturing experience at universities in Finland.

Ulvi T. Aliyev has a PhD in mathematics from 1990, and is currently working on his dissertation work for a doctor of economics at the All-Russian Centre of Living Standard (Moscow). He heads the Caspian Quality of Life Centre (CQOLC), Baku, Azerbaijan. Mr. Aliyev's main scientific and research areas are problems of quality of life and living standards of population, distribution of income and inequality in oil exporting countries. He is a member of the International Society for Quality of Life Studies and the Social Uncertainty Precarity network.

References

Abbott, P. and C. Wallace. 2010. "Explaining Economic and Social Transformations in Post-Soviet Russia, Ukraine and Belarus." *European Societies* 12(5): 653–674.

Beck, W., M. Keizer, L. van der Maesen and D. Phillips. 2001. "Indicators of Social Quality." Paper presented at the First Plenary Meeting of the European Foundation on Social Quality, 25–27 October in Amsterdam.

Bobylev, S., N. Soloveva, S. Vlasov and S. Ju, eds. 2011. *Устойчивое развитие: методология и методика измерения* [Sustainable Development: Methodology and Methods of Measurement]. Москва: Экономика.

Bobkov, V. 2012. "Удручающие социальные результаты двадцатилетней капиталистической трансформации России" [Disappointing Social Results of Twenty Years of Capitalist Transformation of Russia]. *Российский экономический журнал* 2: 11–28.

Bobkov, V., E. Chernykh and U. Alijev. 2011a. "Precarity in Russia and Labour and Employment Markets Transformation." pp. 160–180 in *Precarity – More than a Challenge of Social Security Or: Cynicism of EU's Concept of Economic Freedom*, ed. P. Herrmann and S. Kalayciogli. Bremen: Europäischer Hochschulverlag.

Bobkov, V., E. Chernykh, U. Alijev and E. Kurilchenko. 2011b. "Неустойчивость занятости: негативные стороны современных социально-трудовых отношений" [Precarity of Employment: The Negative Aspects of Modern Social and Labour Relations]. *Уровень жизни населения регионов России* 5: 13–26.

Bollé, P. 2001. "The Future of Work, Employment and Social Protection." *International Labour Review* 140(4): 453–474.

Federal Law of the Russian Federation. 1997. "On the Cost of Subsistence Level of Living in the Russian Federation."

Gubanov S. 2012. Державный прорыв. Неоиндустриализация России и вертикальная интеграция. [Sovereign Breakthrough: Neoindustrialization of Russia and Vertical Integration]. Москва: Книжный мир.

Haken, G. 1985. *Синергетика: Иерархии неустойчивостей в самоорганизующихся системах и устройствах* [Synergetics: Hierarchy of Instabilities in Self-Organizing Systems and Devices]. Москва: Мир.

Hepp, R.D., ed. 2012. *Prekarisierung und Flexibilisierung* [Precarity and Flexibilization]. Westfalisches Dampfboot: Scheßlitz.

Insarov M. "Каким быть рабочему движению: революционным или профсоюзным?" [What Should the Workers' Movement Be Like: Revolutionary or Union?] http://aitrus.narod.ru/RB.htm (accessed 7 January 2013).

Kapelyushnikov, R. 2004. "Nonstandard Types of Employment and Unemployment: The Case of Russia." Working paper WP4/2004/06. Moscow: Moscow State.

Kislicina, O. 2011. Здоровье детей: тенденции, факторы риска и стратегии сбережения [Children's Health: Trends, Risk Factors and Strategies for Savings]. Москва: Макс –Пресс.

Ministry of Economic Development of the Russian Federation. 2012. *Сценарные условия долгосрочного прогноза социально–экономического развития Российской Федерации до 2030 года* [Forecast of Long-Term Socio-economic Development of the Russian Federation until the Year 2030].

Ministry of Economic Development of the Russian Federation. 2013. *Мониторинг об итогах социально-экономического развития Российской Федерации в 2012 году* [The Results of the Socio-Economic Development of the Russian Federation in 2012].Human Development Report 2011. Published for the UNDP. Москва: Весь Мир.

Rakitskaya G. 2007. Позиция российских профсоюзов: социальное партнерство или социальная капитуляция? [The Position of the Russian Trade Unions: Social Partnership or Social Capitulation?]. Москва: Институт перспектив и проблем страны.

ROSSTAT. 1996. *Уровень жизни населения России* [Standard of Living of the Population in Russia]. Москва: Росстат.

ROSSTAT. 1997. *Социальное положение и уровень жизни населения России* [Social Status and Standard of Living of the Population in Russia]. Москва: Росстат.

ROSSTAT. 2011a. *Доходы, расходы и потребление домашних хозяйств в 2010 году* [Revenues, Expenses and Household Consumption in 2010]. Москва: Росстат.

ROSSTAT. 2011b. *Российский статистический ежегодник* [Russian Statistical Yearbook]. Москва: Росстат.

ROSSTAT. 2011c. *Социальное положение и уровень жизни населения России* [Social Status and Standard of Living of the Population in Russia]. Москва: Росстат.

ROSSTAT. 2011d. *Труд и занятость в России* [Labor and Employment in Russia]. Москва: Росстат.

ROSSTAT. 2012. *Российский статистический ежегодник* [Russian Statistical Yearbook]. Москва: Росстат.

Russian Academy of Sciences. 2012. "О чем мечтают россияне (размышления социологов)" [What Do the Russians Dream (Sociologists Thoughts)]. Москва: РАН.

"Russia Longitudinal Monitoring Survey, RLMS-HSE," conducted by the National Research University Higher School of Economics and ZAO "Demoscope" together with Carolina Population Center, University of North Carolina at Chapel Hill and the Institute of Sociology RAS.

Shestakova, E. 2010. "Концепция 'Социального качества' как новое содержание социальной политики государства" [The Concept of "Social Quality" as the New Content of Social Policy]. *Россия и современный мир* 1(66): 110–125.

Starostin V. 2008. "Размышление о прекаризации в трудовых отношениях" [Thoughts on Precarity in Labor Relations]. http://sibokt.livejournal.com/4011.html (accessed 7 January 2013).

Subetto, A. 2008. Критика "экономического" разума [Criticism of the "Economic" Mind]. СП-Кострома: КГУ им. Н.А. Некрасова.

United Nations. 2007. *Indicators of Sustainable Development: Guidelines and Methodologies*. New York: United Nations. http://sustainabledevelopment.un.org (accessed 23 November 2012).

United Nations. 2012. *Millennium Development Goals Report 2012*. New York: United Nations. http://www.un.org/millenniumgoals/pdf/MDG%20Report%202012.pdf (accessed 15 December 2012).

Walker, A. 2007. "Which Way for the European Social Model: Minimum Standards or Social Quality? The Changing Face of Welfare." Paper presented at the Second Asian Conference on Social Quality and Sustainable Welfare Societies: Towards a New Partnership between Asian Universities of the European Union, 8–9 June in Taipei.

CHAPTER 11

The Rational Actor Reform Paradigm
Delivering the Goods but Destroying Public Trust?

Peter Taylor-Gooby

Pressures on Social Quality

European welfare states face challenges from many directions. It is becoming increasingly clear that the response is not a retreat to minimalist night-watchman systems with non-state services providing the bulk of care. Rather, European welfare states are restructuring and developing new ways of meeting needs. The picture is less gloomy than it might well be. However, there are fresh challenges that merit attention from a social quality perspective.

The story of the pressures on traditional welfare systems has been told a number of times (for a magisterial review, see Pierson 2001 or Huber and Stephens 2001). The pressures can be divided up into economic, political and social challenges. At the economic level, financial globalization, with the capacity to transfer very large sums between economies, rapidly imposes pressures on the capacity of governments to use neo-Keynesian measures to influence their economies. At the same time, economic globalization imposes stricter competitive pressures in large areas of national economies. As Scharpf and Schmidt (2001: chap. 1) point out, most European governments no longer seek to manipulate interest or exchange rates to influence domestic economic activity and employment levels, and of course the Single European Act and institution of the European Central Bank (ECB) has intensified this process.

Political pressures include the shifts in the patterns of class forces associated with postindustrialism, so that the groups traditionally associated with support for substantial welfare states have grown weaker. In addition, the fragmentation of social risks has led to a corresponding greater diversity in the patterns of support for particular initiatives (Bonoli 2005).

Social changes include population aging and the moves toward more flexible and diverse lifestyles and toward smaller households. The net effect of all these changes is to make it more difficult for governments to run traditional welfare states, providing services to meet needs for health care, education, much social care and interruptions of employment income or retirement across the population. Social shifts, in particular aging, increase need. For some of these services, the constituencies of support have weakened, but for others, particularly for the mass services of health care and pensions, they remain strong. It is essential to make sure that services are more cost efficient and that they are delivered in ways that support the economy in an increasingly competitive international market. This has led in two broad directions: activation and the use of targets and markets within services.

These developments have been extensively analyzed. This chapter considers the intellectual framework implicit in the new approaches and uses a particular example (the National Health Service in the United Kingdom) to discuss their implications. There is intense controversy about whether or not the reforms are successful. The minister responsible has claimed that the NHS is the best it has ever been, while one popular newspaper describes it as "a dead duck." Our contention is that they are both right. The reforms are delivering the goods in the short term. However, there are some indications that this may be at the cost of the maintenance of general social trust in the service in the longer term. This matters since if people no longer trust the service (regardless of its quality) they will not be willing to pay the taxes necessary to support it. This point is particularly significant as society grows more unequal and as the postwar levels of social mobility decline. In short, the new policies may be positive in the short term but destructive of the institutional basis of social quality in the longer term.

Rational Choice as an Engine of Social Quality

The root idea of the policy changes exemplified in the current NHS reforms is a simple one: behavior is driven by individual rational choice. The primacy of self-regarding individualism is at the basis of Adam Smith's much-quoted point: "it is not from the benevolence of the butcher, the brewer, or the baker, that we expect our dinner, but from their regard for their own interest" ([1776] 1991). In a similar vein, in arguing for the primacy of market liberalism more than two centuries later, Margaret Thatcher claimed in her 1987 Conservative Party conference speech (and elsewhere) to be "working with the grain of human nature" in rolling back the state. Smith of course balanced the view with a sophisticated discussion of the role of "moral sentiments." In social science, the rational self-regarding approach is usually contrasted with a broader perspective. Weber, for example, draws attention to more traditional, emotional and value-driven rationalities (1947: 130). This leads to a wider range of understandings of social life than is typically available in the dominant stream in economics.

Welfare states, to put it crudely, involve social actors in three roles: as policy makers and providers, as citizen taxpayers and as citizen service users. The dominant themes in policy-making discourse in each area (most notably in the UK but also elsewhere in Europe) have highlighted individualistic self-regarding action in each area.

At the most general level, the economic success of markets dominates global economic activity. Markets are seen as better than state-directed systems at selecting and applying the most useful innovations because they reward entrepreneurs efficiently without requiring public officials to plan the appropriate distribution of resources (von Hayek 1973; Riker 1986). Corresponding arguments are increasingly applied within social policy, for example, to pensions (see Department for Work and Pensions 2006: paras. 41, 42, which describe choice as central to the "first test" for acceptable reform), and to health care (see Department of Health 2006: 1, which describes patient choice as "driving up standards across the NHS"; for a valuable review of the issues, see Barr 1998: 68–83). Again, it is the free play of the incentive and motivational system that is seen as achieving the most socially valuable outcome.

Within national politics, an important stream of literature has highlighted the notion of politicians as essentially constructing policy platforms in competition with entrepreneurs, in order to attract votes (rather than attracting votes to promote the policies to which they are committed).

In relation to policy makers and providers, if self-regarding individualism is seen as playing the leading role in directing people's behavior, it is easy to argue that interventionist and redistributive welfare states may distract effort from production to activities intended to advantage individuals in distribution, so that the pie fails to grow, to everyone's detriment, while social groups fight over the size of the slices (Olsen and March 1995). Interventionism may also be seen as undermining the structure of motivations necessary for success in the labor market and creating a "dependency culture" that damages individual and economic progress, and (possibly) undermines the family ethic (see, e.g., Auletta 1982; Murray 1984). However, it is at the middle level of policy making and at the level of policy delivery that the self-regarding rational actor critique is most relevant to the issues under discussion.

Public administration experts have been strongly influenced by the analysis of the primacy of self-regarding motivations. This leads to the claim that rather than serve the public interest, public officials and professionals will seek to improve their own conditions of work, reward and status by "cherry-picking" easy or prestigious cases (Le Grand and Bartlett 1993; Propper et al. 2006: 553), seeking to maximize the size and scope of their responsibilities and budgets (Niskanen 1971), ensuring that funders do not have adequate information to provide serious critiques of what they do (Pratt and Zeckhauser 1985) or by controlling entry to helping professions (Klein 2000). Correspondingly, individual service users will employ social skills, social and political contacts and capacity to control information about their own need in making claims. It is a common finding in analysis of the distribution of the outcomes of the major welfare services that resources are inefficiently distributed and often provide disproportionately more for those of higher status—health care and education systems being the most striking cases.

These points introduce a further stream, also from the Scottish Enlightenment, into the debate. Adam Smith's insights are used to demonstrate that people's myriad individual motives can be harnessed for the common good through the mechanisms of market competition. David Hume argued a year earlier that government institutions should be designed on the assumption that "every man ought to be supposed to have no other end than private interest." The core idea is simple: people are driven by their own individual motives. Get the incentives right and you can direct their behavior, as managers, professionals, benefit-claimants or service users, to achieve cost-efficient services.

Targets and Markets

These ideas have led in two related directions in welfare services: set stringent targets and link the rewards for managers and professionals to meeting those targets so that the self-regarding motives of these key actors are linked to delivering the services that government wishes to see in place, rather than meeting separate individual interests. Use market systems (either internal markets in which different budget-holder state agencies compete for service users as consumers, or markets which non-state actors, commercial or not-for-profit, may also enter) to ensure that competitive pressures drive standards up and contain costs. These mechanisms are intended to manage the three groups identified earlier successfully. If applied intelligently, they will align the interests of service providers and professionals with the goals set by government, and competitive pressures will ensure cost efficiency and responsiveness to consumers. Service users become consumers. It is now in their interest to gather information on the quality of different schools and clinics and to use those that best meet their needs. The principle that resources follow users ensures that the providers value their customers. Taxpayers of course will benefit from greater cost efficiency in a time of stringent budgetary pressure.

These systems have been extensively discussed in the literature on new public management. Many problems exist. It remains difficult to ensure that information travels effectively. The design of the market systems is crucial; groups where the cost of good provision is relatively high will go to the back of the queue if the price is not adjusted appropriately. Incorporation of the targets into the information system ensures that the services work to the target, and anything that is not covered is not prioritized. One widely publicized example is the impact of the target for a maximum waiting time of four hours in accident and emergency departments. This led to a sharp increase in the numbers seen at three hours and fifty-nine minutes, rather than earlier. In some cases, patients were kept waiting in ambulances until the department was confident that they could be seen within four hours of entering the building (Bevan and Hood 2006a: 531). These issues lead to a continual interplay of target adjustment and gaming response between central government and the administering department.

In the UK, combined target and market systems have been established across public policy. The systems of competition between decentralized separate agencies, subject to government quality control, are not in place. Specialized agencies (the National Institute for Health and Care Excellence [NICE]; the Social Care Institute for Excellence [SCIE]; the Office for Standards in Education, Children's Services and Skills [Ofsted], etc.) are established to advise on standards, carry out inspections and promote best practice. In education, examination results and additional key stage test results, and Ofsted reports on individual schools are published. In health care, systems of star ratings are published as well as detailed reviews of performance against targets and overall assessments of different trusts and clinics. In local government services, generally, the best value system requires state agencies to compete directly for contracts for a range of services, from refuse collection to children's services, leisure to transport. (An interesting insight into the market is provided through the for-profit service provider Serco's web page: www. serco.com/markets/localgov/index.asp.)

Non-state providers are introduced in a number of areas: private provisions are run alongside state ones, private management is introduced in education authorities deemed unsatisfactory and independent treatment and diagnostic centers are being rolled out in health care, treating 250,000 patients in 2005. In social security, direct incentives apply through the workfare New Deal to benefit claimers as part of the "making work pay" strategy, and it is a declared policy object to expand the private provision of pensions from 40 percent to 60 percent of the workforce.

The Example of NHS Reform in the UK

The experience of the UK NHS provides a powerful example of these developments and of their implications. The NHS is a major public service. It is also anomalous— traditionally a tax-funded universal service within a welfare system that is more often seen as leaning toward the liberal market model (Esping-Andersen 1999: 76). Like health care systems throughout the world (see Saltman et al. 1998; Rico et al. 2003), it is under severe pressure from population aging and rising costs, and faces difficulties in staff recruitment. It is widely seen as the flagship of the UK welfare state, and as a service profoundly associated with the Labour Party, in power since 1997.

The previous Conservative government, in accordance with its market ideology, broke up much of NHS provision and introduced a commissioning system, whereby family doctors, GPs, held budgets and purchased services from NHS hospitals and clinics on behalf of patients. However, this system was not pursued with vigor against the vested interests of the high-status professionals located within hospitals. New Labour initially stated that it would reverse the fund-holding GP reform, but in fact replaced it with a similar commissioning system from groups of GPs and associated frontline services. It undertook extensive reviews of the NHS. The major changes have been:

- a substantial injection of resources to take NHS funding closer to the average European level. As Figure 11.1 shows, funding (taking average price movements into account) has risen from about £6.5 to nearly £9 billion annually in four years, a truly exceptional rate of increase;
- the more stringent rolling out of the decentralization system, establishing services and hospitals into quasi-independent trusts;
- the increasingly rigorous use of targets to manage the service;
- much more emphasis on the quality of information available to the public; and
- a fully fledged market system including non-state suppliers and much greater user choice.

The NHS is high profile, highly regarded, receiving extra resources and undergoing very radical change. All these changes make the UK NHS an excellent example to consider the impact of the new public management of the individual self-regarding theories of action that lie behind it.

The Controversy over Quality

Current NHS policies are actually performing well. Deaths from heart disease are down by a third since 1997 and from cancer by 14 percent (the largest fall ever). Universal health services free at the point of demand often rational by waiting lists and waiting times have been a central issues in the NHS. Waiting times in accident and emergency services have fallen, and the percentage of patients waiting less than four hours risen from 74 percent in 2002 to 94 percent at the end of 2005. The numbers waiting for elective admission more than twelve months fell from 60,000 in 1998 to virtually zero by 2004 and the numbers waiting more than nine months from 180,000 also to zero (Bevan and Hood 2006a: 526–527). Waiting times are now below six months and continuing to fall. Spending has gone up by 71 percent in real terms since 1997—the biggest increase ever. Naturally, there remain a number of problem areas, but perhaps the most striking evidence of real improvement is the response of informed critics of government policy. The King's Fund, often a critic of government, concludes in a recent review: "Nevertheless, increased funding has bought more staff and equipment, and together with tough targets in England, this has helped reduce waiting times to an historic low" (2005). An up-to-date study by Bevan and Hood reports that "the star rating system has improved reported performance on key targets" (2006b: 421).

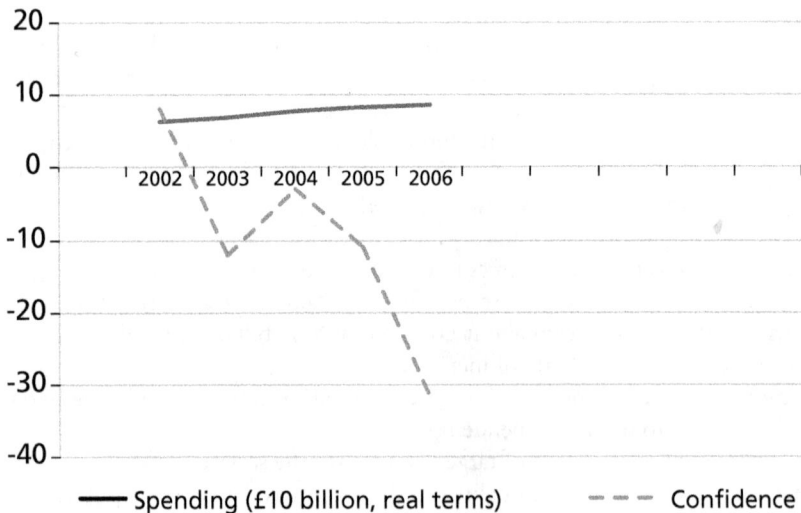

Figure 11.1. NHS: Trends in Public Spending and Public Confidence
Source: MORI: sample 957; HM Treasury 2006

However, public attitudes fail to respond to the evidence of dramatic improvement in the service. The lower line in Figure 11.1 shows that confidence in the NHS fell sharply, despite a short-lived recovery around the election. In more detailed interviews of the Ipsos MORI Public Services Delivery Index, half of those interviewed believe the NHS will get worse during the next few years, while only 18 percent think it will get better, the most negative outcome since the index started in 2002. The most widely read newspaper in the UK, the *Sun*, stated in an editorial (12 October 2006) "the NHS in its present form is a dead duck." Most of its readers seem to agree. It is slightly puzzling why this should be, since a service like the NHS touches large numbers in the population and people ought to notice improvements.

The conflicts in relation to the NHS were well summarized in a highly publicized incident in 2006. In response to evidence of mounting public anxiety, former Prime Minister Tony Blair called a "crisis summit" of ministers and other stakeholders in April. He insisted that most people's experience of the service was positive: "There is very, very strong delivery going on and that is the context in which to put these issues to do with financial deficits" (Politics.co.uk 2006). Two weeks later, the minister then responsible for the NHS, Patricia Hewitt, addressed the main nurses' annual conference and claimed that the NHS was "enjoying its best year ever." The delegates barracked her and she was prevented from finishing her speech, a very unusual event at such a gathering. Perhaps most revealing are the newspaper headlines that covered the incident (see Table 11.1). While the antigovernment *Daily Mail* and the more centrist and measured *Telegraph* take the opportunity to attack Labour politics and the *Sun* seeks sensationalism (it actually gave more coverage in the issue to allegations about unprofessional behavior by gay nurses), it is instructive that the normally pro-welfare *Guardian* also assumes that there is a serious problem associated with management ("paperwork") in the NHS.

This gives rise to a broader issue. It does seem that, despite their failings and limitations, new public management principles can deliver good results, when operating in the relatively benign circumstances of an NHS receiving big funding increases. However, these outcomes are not acknowledged by the public. Why should this be?

In the case of the NHS, there are many controversies involving various interests. Staff like higher pay and do not like central targets that constrain their autonomy. Private interests wish to enter as providers. Drug companies and others are opposed to central standards that limit prescribing more cost-effective medicines. Political interests stir up controversy. However, these issues have always influenced NHS controversies and do not explain why they should be so pressing currently. In fact, pay increases in the most recent settlement have been extremely generous, leading to the highest pay in Europe for UK doctors and relative ease in attracting professionals from overseas.

Table 11.1 Main Newspaper Headlines Following Hewitt's Address to Nurses, May 2006

"Something Rotten at the Heart of the NHS" (*Telegraph*)
"Labour Fantasies and NHS Realities" (*Daily Mail*)
"Life, Death and Paperwork" (*Guardian*)
"Living Proof That our NHS Is Failing"(*Sun*)

Rational Action and Social Values in Understanding Social Trust

One explanation is to be found in the enormous social science literature on trust: Das and Teng identify twenty-eight definitions of trust (2004: 96; see Luhmann 1979: 10, 24; see also Rousseau et al. 1998: 395; Dasgupta 1988: 51; Gambetta 1988: 218; Crasswell 1993: 104; Sztompka 1999: 25). Here we focus on citizen trust in institutions like the NHS, sometimes termed confidence. The NHS reforms develop from the model of the rational self-regarding individual. From the rational deliberative perspective, trust is based on judgments about whether the trusted person or institution is likely to act in the future in the appropriate way, and action is driven by interests. As Hardin puts it, trust implies "reason to expect you to act, for your own reasons, *as my agent* with respect to the relevant matter. Your interest encapsulates my interests" (1999: 26). The question then is whether the expectation is reasonable. Trust in institutions requires evidence of a good track record (and, therefore, confidence in the transparency of the agency and the quality of the information made available) and an indication that past record is likely to be a good guide to the future, for example, a system of regulation. It would seem that the NHS as reformed and in receipt of more finance should command trust. It is doing rather better in many key areas than before, and one should expect it to do so.

Research on trust points to complexity in people's attitudes. It suggests that the reasons for behavior identified by Weber also play a role. This stream of work is more prominent in psychology and sociology. Psychological studies of trust typically operate by asking batteries of questions covering various aspects of a trusted object and of the subject's orientation to it, feelings about it and expectations from it. These are then condensed into a smaller number of underlying themes using factor analysis or similar techniques. These lead to a multidimensional account of trust. Hovland's initial studies distinguished two dimensions: competence, to do with whether one believed the trusted object to be in a position to deliver as trusted, and care, or trustworthiness, to do with whether the object was believed to be likely to value the trustor sufficiently to deliver for them (Hovland et al. 1953). Similar components emerge in work by other researchers (Renn and Levine 1991; Frewer et al. 1996; Metlay 1999; Poortinga and Pidgeon 2003). Almost all distinguish the capacity of the trustee to actually carry out the relevant task from the belief that the object of trust will actually provide for them, because, for example, she shares their values or is committed to them in some way. Rational judgment of a track record and so on may be a reasonable guide to competence, but trustworthiness—confidence that you are trusting someone who actually takes your interests to heart—requires an extra-rational leap of faith supplied by affect or cultural factors. This is particularly important in relation to situations of uncertainty (such as may affect individuals for whom health care is a vital need in a context where the media are producing confusing messages), where past record may not be a helpful guide.

Similar points are made in social science literature, pointing out that the rational action notion of trust is not so much misleading as in need of supplementation from approaches that also take into account the value side of trust and its contribution to human behavior (Barbalet 2002; Pixley 2004). In relation to health care, Page (2004) summarizes MORI attitude studies in the UK to show that "there is a very strong correlation between the extent to which patients feel they are treated with care and respect and their overall perception of the hospital." In a review of the literature on trust studies, Calnan and Rowe describe trust as "primarily consisting of a cognitive element (grounded on rational and instrumental judgments) and an affective dimension (grounded on relationships and affective bonds generated through interaction, empathy and identification with others)" (2005: 1).

The implications for the debate about trust in the reformed UK NHS are that the new policies, driven by a rational actor approach, perform well in relation to the rational side of trust. They provide reasonable grounds for believing that the service will deliver the goods. Where they encounter problems is in relation to the value side. The highly public use of targets and markets (and individuals cannot be expected to act like rational actors unless the market context and the availability of consumer choice is highly publicized) carries with it the implication that the service is run to meet the targets laid down from the Center and by individuals whose concern is their competitive position vis-à-vis alternative providers. The driving force is not commitment to the patients' interests. It may well be this aspect of the reform process that is currently undermining public trust.

We go on to examine some empirical data on trust in the NHS from the British Social Attitudes survey, a major national random sample survey with a sample of approximately 3,600, which provides a high-quality source of data (Park 2002 gives details). A random subsample of 1,800 were asked the relevant questions.

Attitudes to NHS Reform

The survey asked a series of well-validated questions about aspects of the service. In Table 11.2 we report the results of a factor analysis of the responses. Factor analysis is a statistical

Table 11.2. Factor Analysis of Perceptions of the NHS (BSA 2001)—Varimax Rotation

	Quality (factor loadings)	Commitment (factor loadings)
Condition of hospital buildings	**.69**	−.07
Staffing level: nurses	**.84**	−.05
Staffing level: doctors	**.85**	−.07
Quality of medical treatment in hospital	**.74**	−.25
Quality of nursing care in hospital	**.70**	−.26
Doctors tell you all you need to know	−.13	**.71**
Doctors take your views on treatment seriously	−.08	**.76**
Nurses take any complaint seriously	−.12	**.74**
Doctors take any complaint seriously	−.12	**.81**
Particular nurse to deal with problems	−.14	**.52**
Eigenvalue	3.80	1.91
% total variance explained	38.00	19.09
N	1806	

technique that analyzes the relationships between a set of variables in order to identify underlying themes. It is widely used to explore data that contains answers to a series of questions covering different aspects of a topic. In this case, two factors were identified with an Eigenvalue (a measure of the proportion of total variance explained by the factor) greater than one. This is a conventionally used cutoff point to decide when the amount of variance explained by a factor merits further investigation.

Taken together, the two factors explain nearly 60 percent of the total variance in the variables and thus sum up major underlying themes conveniently. The first, labeled "Quality," includes questions concerned with objective aspects: level of staffing, condition of buildings, quality of care and so on. The common theme in responses to these questions is that they are different aspects of quality of provision—this appears to be what the factor measures. It explains nearly 40 percent of total variance and is clearly a substantial factor. The second, labeled "Commitment," concerns more the way the service treated individuals: the questions cover level of information, responsiveness to views and complaints and so on. The common theme is how well the service appears to take the views and interests of the users seriously and to respect them as people. It accounts for nearly 40 percent of total variance and makes a further substantial contribution to explanation. The analysis shows that these two aspects of NHS treatment are separate in the public mind, corresponding to the two dimensions in the work on trust discussed above, and that the commitment factor, which deals with the value aspects of trust, is more prominent in the answers to the questions.

The survey also included a general question on trust in the NHS ("Do you trust NHS managers to spend taxpayers' money wisely in the patients' interest?"). We go on to explore the relation between this and perceptions of commitment and quality, in order to examine how understanding of changes in the way the service treats individuals influences people's general level of trust in it. A variable to represent trust is constructed by scoring those who answered that they trusted the service "a great deal" or "quite a bit" (positive responses) one, and all others zero. Nearly 60 percent of the sample were scored positive. The commitment and quality items can be examined by constructing variables that represent them in statistical analysis. The variables are constructed by adding up the factor loadings so that the variables correspond respectively to the social value of commitment and to judgment of quality.

Trust in a major social service is a complex matter, and many aspects of people's lives will contribute to their thoughts and feelings in this area. Previous work shows that social class, age, gender, level of education, service use, newspaper readership and political support are all relevant to trust, in addition to the issues of commitment and quality. In order to set the contribution of the commitment and quality variables in context, we pursue a multivariate analysis, which includes the commitment and quality aspects of perceptions of the services and also variables representing the socio-demographic characteristics and political views of the sample listed above. A full list of variables is given in the annex. The multivariate modeling technique chosen uses binary logistic regression equations (Table 11.3). The method of model-building is forward conditional so that variables are included in order of greatest significance up to a 5 percent threshold.

Table 11.3. Logistic Regressions on Trust: Odds Ratios

	Trust
Commitment	2.24**
Quality	1.75**
35 or younger	2.89**
Professional/managerial	.77*
Labour Party support	1.51**
Tabloid reader	0.80*
Constant	1.52**
Nagelkerke r square	.11
Chi-squared	133.22** (6df)
N	1526

significant at 5 percent level
**significant at 1 percent level*

Source: British Social Attitudes Survey, Sample 1,55

In Table 11.3, the "chi-squared" statistic measures the significance of the model as a whole, and this is significant at better than the 1 percent level. The "r squared" statistic gives the proportion of variance in the dependent variable (trust in the NHS), explained by all the variables included taken together. It can be seen that this is evident but not large. The variables used contribute to trust, but other factors we have not been able to measure satisfactorily are also important. This focuses attention on the significance of relationships as well as on their strength. As can be seen, the social value and judgment of quality variables, as well as age (below 35) and Labour Party voting are significant at the 1 percent level. Being a member of the professional and managerial class and being a tabloid reader are significant at the 5 percent level. The relationship with the other variables listed in the annex did not attain these levels of significance and are omitted from the final model.

The statistics given are odds ratios: the odds of someone with the characteristic represented by the particular independent variable displaying the characteristic measured in the dependent variable, compared with the reference group. The annex gives the percentage who are not in the reference group, so that 58.7 percent of the sample who trust in the NHS a great deal or quite a bit are contrasted with the 41.3 percent who do not fall into this category, the 46.3 percent who score above the mean on the Commitment Index are contrasted with the 53.7 percent who do not and so on. It is those who do not fall into the category of trust a great deal or quite a bit and are of above the mean who constitute the reference group for the particular variable. Odds ratios below 1 indicate a negative relation, and above 1 a positive relation. Thus, the model shows, taking the other variables into account, that those whose score on the Commitment Index are above the mean are 2.24 times more likely to express trust in the NHS compared with those with scores on the Index below the mean; those with score on the Quality Judgment Index above the mean are 1.74 times more likely to express trust than those with scores below the mean and so on.

The model shows that the commitment measure makes the strongest contribution to trust in the service, followed by age, then perception of objective quality and political and social class and media-use variables. Younger people, Labour Party members, those who are not members of the professional and managerial class and those who do not read tabloids have the stronger trust among the socio-demographic groups, an interesting mix of different groups. However, the importance of the social values measured by the commitment variable plays a leading role.

The modeling is admittedly imperfect. More work needs to be done to disentangle the socio-demographic factors and to improve the proportion of variance explained by the model. However, the factor analysis does show that the social value of commitment is a separate theme in the public mind from objective judgments of quality of provision, despite the emphasis in UK policy making on the latter to the exclusion of the former. This provides prima facie evidence of the importance of the subjective factors measuring commitment, and value issues in relation to how citizens perceive the service. This is something of central importance to the future of a strong public conviction that the NHS is of value, which is central to continuing political support for the service.

Conclusion

This chapter discusses an important trend in current social policy. European welfare states face substantial pressures. They have not retreated and declined as some predicted in the 1980s and early 1990s, but rather restructured. This is to be welcomed. An important trend in the new developments in order to achieve goals of both consumer responsiveness and greater cost efficiency is new public management in the shape of targets and use of market systems. This chapter reviews the impact of such systems in an area where, arguably, the results have been on balance positive.

It considers an aspect that has received relatively little attention and is important for the future of social quality: the implications for public trust. It is puzzling why the reforms are not more highly trusted by the public. A review of the literature indicates that both sociologists and psychologists have tended to understand trust as composed of two components: not only the reasonable expectation of good performance (as the rational actor model implies) but also a value component entailing commitment to the interests of the consumer. This might reflect a broad contrast between a rational utilitarian morality of the greatest good for the greatest number and a Kantian principle of respect for persons.

Empirical evidence shows that both aspects are important in trust for the NHS, but the value component is by far more important. The concern is that the rational actor logic, now dominant in policy making, fails to take account of this. The outcome may be a service that in an objective sense succeeds, but fails to carry public support with it and ultimately loses public trust and the endorsement of the taxpayers.

To survive at a high social quality, welfare states must ensure that they not only deliver the goods but also gain high levels of public support. These are tough standards. Insights both from economics and from psychology and sociology are necessary to achieve this. Welfare reforms that draw on the former but not on the latter risk alienating the public support on which all welfare states depend.

Peter Taylor-Gooby is Professor of Social Policy at the University of Kent. His main interests are comparative social policy and the theory of the welfare state. His recent publications include *The Double Crisis of the Welfare State and What We Can Do About It* (2013) and *Reframing Social Citizenship* (2009).

Annex: Variables Used in the Regression (Recoded for Use in the Dichotomous Logistic Model)

Trust in the NHS (a great deal or quite a bit)	58.7%
Commitment index (above the mean)	46.3%
Quality index (above the mean)	49.4%
Age: >59*	26.7%
Age: <26	10.1%
Salariat: Professional/managerial	33.1%
Routine: Semi/unskilled working class*	31.6%
Gender: woman*	54.2%
Tabloid reader	37.7%
Broadsheet reader*	11.9%
Education to degree level*	15.7%
No educational qualifications*	25.3%
Conservative voter*	23.0%
Labour voter	44.7%
Liberal voter*	12.9%

* eliminated from final forward conditional model

References

Auletta, K. 1982. *The Underclass*. New York: Random House.
Barbalet, J. 2002. *Emotions and Sociology*. Oxford: Blackwell.
Barr, N. 1998. *Economics of the Welfare State*, 3rd ed. Oxford: Oxford University Press.
Bevan, G. and C. Hood. 2006a. "What's Measured Is What Matters: Targets and Gaming in the English Public Health Care System." *Public Administration* 84(3): 517–538.
Bevan, G. and C. Hood. 2006b. "Have Targets Improved Performance in the English NHS?" *British Medical Journal* 332: 419–422.
Bonoli, G. 2005. "The Politics of the New Social Policies: Providing Coverage against New Social Risks in Mature Welfare States." *Policy and Politics* 33(3): 431–449.
Calnan, M. and R. Rowe. 2005. "Trust Relations in the 'New' NHS: Theoretical and Methodological Challenges." Paper presented at the SCARR Network Trust Conference, 12 December in London.

Crasswell, R. 1993. "On the Uses of 'Trust': Comment on Williamson, 'Calculativeness, Trust, and Economic Organization.'" *Journal of Law and Economics* 36(1): 487–500.

Das, T. and B. Teng. 2004. "The Risk-Based View of Trust: A Conceptual Framework." *Journal of Business and Psychology* 19(1): 85–116.

Dasgupta, P. 1988. "Trust as a Commodity." pp. 49–72 in *Trust: Making and Breaking Cooperative Relations*, ed. D. Gambetta. Oxford: Oxford University Press.

Department of Health. 2006. "Patient Choice Becomes a Reality across the NHS." Press release, 3 January.

Department for Work and Pensions. 2006. *Report on Incapacity Benefits and Pathways to Work*. London: The Stationery Office (TSO).

Esping-Andersen, G. 1999. *Social Foundations of Post-Industrial Economies*. Oxford: Oxford University Press.

Frewer, L.J., C. Howard, D. Hedderley and R. Shepherd. 1996. "What Determines Trust in Information about Food-Related Risks?: Underlying Psychology Constructs." *Risk Analysis* 16(4): 473–485.

Gambetta, D., ed. 1988. *Trust: Making and Breaking Cooperative Relations*. Oxford: Oxford University Press.

Hardin, R. 1999. "Do We Want Trust in Government?" pp. 22–41 in *Democracy and Trust*, ed. M. Warren. Cambridge: Cambridge University Press.

HM Treasury. 2006. *Public Expenditure 2005–2006: Provisional Outturn*. White Paper, Cm 6883. London: TSO.

Hovland, C., I. Janis and H. Kelley. 1953. *Communication and Persuasion: Psychological Studies of Opinion Change*. New Haven, CT: Yale University Press.

Huber, E. and J. Stephens. 2001. *Development and Crisis of the Welfare State: Parties and Policies in Global Markets*. Chicago: Chicago University Press.

Hume, D. [1754] 1898. *Essays: Moral, Political, and Literary*. London: Longmans.

The King's Fund. 2005. *NHS Funding*. London: The King's Fund.

Klein, R. 1996. "The NHS Reforms Revisited." *British Medical Journal* 313: 504–505.

Klein, R.. 2000. *The New Politics of the NHS: From Creation to Reinvention*. London: Prentice Hall.

Le Grand, J. and W. Bartlett. 1993. *Quasi-Markets and Social Policy*. Basingstoke: Palgrave Macmillan.

Luhmann, N. 1979. *Trust and Power*. New York: Wiley.

Metlay, D. 1999. "Institutional Trust and Confidence." pp. 9–21 in *Social Trust and the Management of Risk*, eds. G.T. Cvetkovich and R.E. Löfstedt. London: Earthscan.

Market and Opinion Research International (MORI). 2003. "Trust in the Government Low." Press release, 23 January.

Murray, C. 1984. *Losing Ground: American Social Policy, 1950–1980*. New York: Basic Books.

Niskanen, W. 1971. *Bureaucracy and Representative Government*. Chicago: Aldine-Atherton.

Olsen, J. and J. March. 1995. *Democratic Governance*. New York: Free Press.

Ostrom, E. and J. Walker, eds. 2002. *Trust and Reciprocity: Interdisciplinary Lessons from Experimental Research*. New York: Russell Sage Foundation.

Page, B. 2004. *Understanding and Perception of the NHS*. MORI Report, May 2004.

Park, A. 2002. "Technical Details" in *British Social Attitudes: The 19th Report*. eds. A. Park, J. Curtice, K. Thomson, L. Jarvis, C. Bromley. London: Sage.

Pierson, P. 2001. *The New Politics of the Welfare State*. Oxford: Oxford University Press.

Pixley, J. 2004. *Emotions in Finance: Distrust and Uncertainty in Global Markets*. Cambridge: Cambridge University Press.

Politics.co.uk. 2006. "Blair Holds NHS Crisis Summit," 12 April.

Poortinga, W.N. and N. Pidgeon. 2003. "Exploring the Dimensionality of Trust in Risk Regulation." *Risk Analysis* 23(5): 961–973.

Pratt, J. and R. Zeckhauser. 1985. *Principals and Agents: The Structure of Business.* Boston: Harvard Business School Press.

Propper, C., D. Wilson and S. Burgess. 2006. "Extending Choice in English Health Care: The Implications of the Economic Evidence." *Journal of Social Policy* 35(4): 537–58.

Rico, A., R. Saltman and W. Boerma. 2003. "Organisational Restructuring in European Health Care Systems: The Role of Primary Care." *Social Policy and Administration* 37(6): 592–608.

Riker, W. 1986a. *The Art of Political Manipulation.* New Haven, CT: Yale University Press.

Riker, W. 1986b. *Liberalism against Populism: A Confrontation between the Theory of Democracy and the Theory of Social Choice.* San Francisco: Freeman.

Rousseau, D.M., S.B. Sitkin, R.S. Burt and C. Camerer. 1998. "Not So Different After All: A Cross-Discipline View of Trust." *Academy of Management Review* 23(3): 393–404.

Saltman, R., J. Figueras and C. Sakellarides, eds. 1998. *Critical Challenges for Health Care Reform in Europe.* New York: Open University Press.

Scharpf, F. 1999. *Governing in Europe: Effective and Democratic?* Oxford: Oxford University Press.

Scharpf, F. and V. Schmidt, eds. 2000. *Welfare and Work in the Open Economy: Diverse Responses to Common Challenges.* Oxford: Oxford University Press.

Seligman, H. 2000. *The Problem of Trust.* Princeton, NJ: Princeton University Press.

Smith, A. [1776]. 1991. *The Wealth of Nations.* New York: Prometheus Books.

Sztompka, P. 1998. *Trust: A Sociological Theory.* Cambridge: Cambridge University Press.

Von Hayek, F. 1973. *Law, Legislation and Liberty, Vol. 1: Rules and Order.* London: Routledge and Kegan Paul.

Weber, M. [1922] 1978. *Economy and Society.* Berkeley: University of California Press.

Social Quality
An Invitation to Dance

Wolfgang Beck

In a different context, Bernhard Pörksen, professor of media science at the University of Tuebingen, talked about a "situational realism" that overcomes a dogmatic sealing-off, opening space for appropriateness for which the individual accepts responsibility. We are not asking for absolute truth or for vacillating pluralism. Any arbitrariness of argumentation remains suspect.

> Sometimes perhaps the absolute (or the idea of the absolute) is useful, sometimes tradition and sometimes history. And sometimes we need a versatile dance of thinking that may appear to lack respectability but helps to turn large and small certainties, own truth and ideologies of others to such a point that the verge begins to blur. And one begins to see more than in the beginning. (Pörksen 2014)

The attempt to understand "lifeworld," understood as the world of people's everyday life, undertaken for twenty years now, also carries with it a notion of this dance. This attempt to mediate between biography and society, as well as to instrumentalize the gained insights, needs to be approached by confrontation; it lives from unrest of the want for more knowledge and is far from searching for complacent confirmation.

The wide field of topics and experiences that concern us and employ our thinking thus requires reassurance, also in the scientific sense. It begins with the readiness and the ability to acknowledge the foremost openness of the lifeworlds, questioning biography and socio-structural conditions in their historical-societal context and to develop new perspectives. From here, scientific work enters the minefield of reconstruction and intervention, always striving for "collective validation" of its discoveries, first internally—that is, within the scientific community—but then also societally by changing those who are objects of the research to subjects. Any sovereign reading by academics remains problematic, as it suggests close and genuine knowledge of the lifeworld by the academics themselves. This openness characterized already the first approach to define social quality.

From the beginning, five pillars were important for the small boat of social quality, an approach that at its very core is designed as bottom-up, holistically oriented, geared toward practice and, in its origin, focused on Europe. Briefly, the leitmotif was the question, how can science contribute to enabling people being (again) able to control their own life? Though the question may sound mundane, the discounted questions are essential, incredibly complex and far reaching; the contributions to the present volume show this very well. We—Alan Walker, Laurent van der Maesen and I—were inspired and made vitally alert by contributions from critical medicine that did not simply attribute illness to physiopathological issues but rather also included individuals' socio-economic contexts in the case history.

With the Declaration of Alma-Ata of 1978, the member states of the World Health Organization presented the concept of primary health care. This approach sees health not least as a question of human rights and social justice with an orientation on local living conditions and participation. Inspired from personal experiences in local democracy and enthused by various international symposia and expert meetings on the future of the European social and welfare states, we considered "social quality" the most appropriate term to grasp our intention to revisit the genuine connection between social structures and political and societal institutions on the one hand and life courses with all of their subjectivist micro-perspectives on the other. This initially not only led to increasingly complex quadrants with various components and points of gravitation, as well as constitutional and conditional factors, fields, dimensions and so on, but it also resulted in a multidimensional framework with indicators, criteria and profiles as the core of the empirical foundation. After all, who would decide what quality should be?

The search for criteria is even more critical if the assessment of the material and procedural aspects by the people concerned is considered to be of central importance. As result of this concern, the proposition was made to use "criteria" and "profiles" as points of reference for citizens' self-assessment of their actions. Admittedly, this was the least elaborated part of the search for a methodology that could help to explore realities of social quality in a holistic way. Unfortunately, due to various (not in the least political-administrative) reasons, the genuine triad of indicators, criteria and profiles could not be issued within the framework of one single project. The study on social quality indicators shows how fruitful such reflections could have been. The meaning of the study on indicators must be seen on another level.

It may sound strange to admit, but in the history of social quality thinking, personal friendship came first, followed by the concept's development. Particularly, the informal—and, as far as Alan, Laurent and I were concerned, also the personal— played an important role. Laurent especially made sure that on the manifold of meetings, workshops, conferences and symposia, the city of Amsterdam, with its historical and cultural treasures, set the scene. It could easily happen that we went out for a lunch break and were surprised by a cello sextet; or academics from the EU member states could temporarily forget the intense discussions on social quality while setting the sails of a vessel for a trip across the Ijsselmeer. Laurent has a good feeling for the meaning of rituals.

Thus, the proclamation of the Amsterdam Declaration on the Social Quality of Europe on 10 June 1997 opened with the celebratory entry of the participants of the congress into the Beurs van Berlage, a major monument of the city. Six professors read the declaration, in six languages. This way, the participating academics expressed a sense of unity with the approximately 50,000 participants of a rally against unemployment, poverty and social exclusion and in favor of more social policy in Europe, who, after long solidarity marches, had arrived three days earlier from across the continent to Amsterdam.

Social quality does not emerge in a vacuum, without germs and as an organically growing gift. In the best case, it is a result of a political discourse, penetrated by various interests in power, vanities and other emotional aspects. Scientific insights can surely play a role. However, it is decisive that they emerge in the social and physical environment—as had been the case in 1977 in Amsterdam, when the city decided to convert the green space in the middle of the Bredeweg to parking spaces. An action group of residents emerged and successfully prevented the implementation of the decision. To celebrate this success, the residents organized a street party, which became the annual Bredeweg Festival. Still held on Queen's Day in April thirty-eight years later, the festival attracts about 30,000 people in Amsterdam, and the street belongs to jugglers, acrobats, tightrope artists and clowns—the tradition of the commedia dell'arte is incredibly lively.

On the eve of the festival in 2014, the street opera *Drama Queens*, an adaptation of Gaetano Donizetti's *Anna Bolena,* was performed. Six women and one king—it was not going to work out. The weather matched the scene: black clouds darkened the sky, appropriate for a drama full of strives for a murderer. And there he stood on the small stage in the spotlight, with a white wavy shirt barely covering his chest. He declaimed the prologue with the weight that causes tragedies of obsession, allowing the audience to see the abyss of the human's soul. The festival opened, accompanied by snappish comments from Catharina of Aragon on her small balcony opposite the stage, with an eagerness for power, love, jealousy and revenge.

The Dutch historian Johan Huizinga explored the world of games and recognized the game—the play element of culture—as a form of life, with a meaningful social function, allowing for the development of a social structure and constituting communities that define a new, a different order:

> It decorates life and completes it and as such it is indispensable … because of its inherent meaning, because of the spiritual and social connections that emerge from its own dynamic; in short, it has a cultural function. (Huizinga 1956)

Wolfgang Beck worked as lecturer (*wetenschappelijk hoofddocent*) at the University of Amsterdam between 1974 and 2002. After obtaining his doctorate from the Rijksuniversiteit Utrecht, he was especially interested in issues of social movements, local government and processes of democratization. His elaboration of the social quality approach, working together with Laurent van der Maesen and Alan Walker, aimed at confronting the economization of everyday life and the global agenda with a normative theory of the social. This theory proposed understanding the complex interdependencies of structural and social matters to allow for new perspectives of humane ways of living together.

References

Huizinga, J. [1938] 1956. *Homo Ludens: Vom Ursprung der Kultur im Spiel* [Homo Ludens: A Study of the Play-Element in Culture]. Hamburg: Rowohlt.

Pörksen, B. 2014. "Es Braucht den Tanz des Denkens" [It Takes the Dance of Thinking]." *Die Zeit* 21, 15 May.

Index